HOW TO HEAR
FROM GOD

HOW TO HEAR FROM GOD

*Learn to Know His Voice and
Make Right Decisions*

Joyce Meyer

NEW YORK   NASHVILLE

FaithWords
Hachette Book Group
1290 Avenue of the Americas, New York, NY 10104
faithwords.com
twitter.com/faithwords
First published in October 2016
This edition: May 2017

FaithWords is a division of Hachette Book Group, Inc. The FaithWords name and logo are trademarks of Hachette Book Group, Inc.
The publisher is not responsible for websites (or their content) that are not owned by the publisher.

The Hachette Speakers Bureau provides a wide range of authors for speaking events. To find out more, go to www.hachettespeakersbureau.com or call (866) 376-6591.

ISBN: 978-1-4555-4249-9

Printed in the United States of America

LSC-C

10 9 8 7 6 5 4 3 2 1

HOW TO HEAR FROM GOD

CONTENTS

CONTENTS

INTRODUCTION

Learning to hear from God and be led by the Holy Spirit is very exciting. God wants to speak to us about the plan He has for our lives. His plan is a good plan, but we are in danger of missing it if we don't learn how to listen to and obey God's voice.

We talk to our children all the time—why wouldn't our heavenly Father talk to His children? We would not expect our children to know what we wanted them to do if we did not talk to them, so why would God feel any different?

God wants to speak to us about the good plan He has for our lives. He sent His Holy Spirit to dwell in us and be our Counselor and Helper in life as well as other things. John 14:26 says that He will teach us all things and will bring to our remembrance things God has taught us. The Holy Spirit is the Spirit of Truth; therefore, He will lead us into truth, not error.

God speaks to us in many ways; they include but are not limited to: His Word, nature, people, circumstances, peace, wisdom, supernatural intervention, dreams, visions, and what we call the inner witness. The inner witness is best described as a "knowing" deep inside. He also speaks in what the Bible calls a still, small voice, which I believe refers to this inner witness.

God also speaks through our conscience, our desires, and

an audible voice. Hearing the audible voice of God is rare for most people and nonexistent for many. I have heard the audible voice of God three or four times in my life. Two of those times were at night when I was awakened by His voice simply calling my name. All I heard was, "Joyce," but I knew it was God calling me. He did not say what He wanted, but I knew instinctively it had something to do with a ministry call on my life, although clarity did not come in that area for several more years.

I heard the audible voice of God the day I was filled with the Holy Spirit in February 1976. That morning I cried out to God about how awful my life was, telling Him something was missing in my relationship with Him. I felt I was at the end of my rope, so to speak.

His voice seemed to fill my entire car, and He simply said, "Joyce, I have been teaching you patience." Since that was my first time to hear anything of that magnitude, it both thrilled and shocked me. I instinctively knew what He meant. Several months prior to that time I had asked God to teach me patience, not realizing the lesson would include a lengthy period of feeling my life was on hold. The frustration of that feeling peaked that morning in February when I cried out to God in desperation, asking Him to do something and give me whatever it was I was missing.

When I heard God's voice, I was suddenly filled with faith that He was going to do something wonderful in my life. Although I did not know what it would be, I spent the day in expectation and thanksgiving. That evening in my car, while returning home from my job, God's Spirit touched me in a special way and filled me with His presence. That event was the beginning of a new level in my relationship with God. I think it is safe to say that every new level in God is preceded by His speaking to us in some way.

Ask God to open your ears and sanctify them so you can

be sensitive to His voice. He wants to talk to you, to develop a closer relationship with you. It is your privilege and right as a born-again believer in Jesus Christ to fellowship daily with God the Father, Jesus Christ His Son, and the Holy Spirit.

We should ask God to circumcise our ears so that we are not distracted by fleshly desires that keep us from hearing His still, small voice. We must learn to listen, for it is impossible to hear without listening. We should learn to love solitude and be sure we enjoy it regularly. We don't hear God very well when our lives are noisy and overly busy. This book will help you learn to create an atmosphere in your life that is conducive to hearing from God.

The Bible tells us that our steps are ordered by the Lord (see Psalm 37:23), and we can trust Him not to let us lose our way. In this book I will share with you how to overcome some of the hindrances to hearing God speak and how to develop a tender conscience that is tuned to the sound of God's voice.

This book will help you enjoy the pleasure of living a Spirit-led life. It will show you how to hear from God and not let Satan, the deceiver, lead you astray.

PART ONE

◦────◦

Learning to Listen

Be careful therefore how you listen. For to him who has [spiritual knowledge] will more be given; and from him who does not have [spiritual knowledge], even what he thinks and guesses and supposes that he has will be taken away.

———JESUS IN LUKE 8:18

1

God Talks to People Every Day

~~⟋

 T he world makes it easy for us to fill our ears with all kinds of things that drown out the voice of God and push Him far, far into the background of our lives. However, the day comes for every person when only God remains. Everything else in life eventually passes away; when it does, God will still be there.

The Word of God teaches that what is known about God is evident to all because He has made Himself known in the inner consciousness of mankind (see Romans 1:19-21). Each person will someday stand before Him and give an account of his or her life (see Romans 14:12). When people don't want to serve God with their lives, when they want to go their own way, they find ways to hide from and ignore this instinctive inner knowledge of their Creator who wants to talk to them and guide them in the way they should go.

Nothing can satisfy our longing for God, except communion and fellowship with Him. Isaiah expressed well our own hunger for God when he wrote, "My soul yearns for You [O Lord] in the night, yes, my spirit within me seeks You earnestly" (Isaiah 26:9). The apostle John wrote, "And the world passes away and disappears, and with it the forbidden cravings (the passionate desires, the lust) of it; but he who does the will of God and carries out His purposes in his life abides (remains) forever" (1 John 2:17).

3

Hearing from God is vital to enjoying God's eternal plan for our lives. Listening to God is our decision; no one else can make it for us. God won't *force* us to choose His will, but He will do everything He can to *encourage* us to say yes to His ways.

God wants to be involved in even the smallest details of our lives. His Word tells us to acknowledge Him in *all our ways,* and He will direct our paths (see Proverbs 3:6). To acknowledge God is to care what He thinks and to ask for His opinion. Verse 7 of Proverbs 3 says, "Be not wise in your own eyes." In other words, don't even think that you can run your life and do a good job without God's help and direction. It takes most of us far too long to learn this important lesson.

Even though I sincerely loved Jesus, I went to church for years without knowing that God talks to people. I observed all the religious rules and holidays and went to church every Sunday. I was really doing all that I knew to do at that time, but it wasn't enough to satisfy my longing for God.

I could have spent every moment in church or in Bible study, but it wouldn't have quenched the thirst I had for a deeper fellowship with the Lord. I needed to talk to Him about my past and hear Him talk to me about my future. But nobody taught me that God wanted to talk directly to me. No one offered a solution for the dissatisfied feelings I endured.

Through reading the Word, I learned that God does want to talk to us and that He has a plan for our lives that will lead us to a place of peace and contentment. It is God's will for us to attain knowledge of His plan through His divine guidance. It sounds like a pretty foundational point, but I believe there are many people who still question whether God really talks to people. And if He does, they wonder:

- Is God really involved on a day-to-day basis in running our lives?
- Does He really want to be involved in all the little tiny details of our lives?
- Should we only bother God and expect to hear from Him concerning major issues that we can't handle ourselves?

The Bible teaches that God has a good plan for all those who will put their faith in Jesus Christ as Lord of their lives. His plan is complete in great detail, and it will lead all who follow Him to an abundant life.

> He has a plan for our lives that will lead us to a place of peace.

But I am convinced that only a few ever enjoy the fulfillment of God's perfect plan for their lives because most people don't know how to listen to God's leading and follow Him. Instead, they choose (either willfully or ignorantly) to go their own way. More people could walk in the perfect will of God if they would learn how to hear from Him and follow His instructions.

Never hesitate to take what you think are small things to God; after all, *everything* is small to God. Sometimes we act as if we think we will tax God's ability if we ask Him for too much help. I remember a woman who came to me for prayer. She wanted to know if it would be all right if she asked God for two things; if not, she assured me that she would only ask for one.

It is vital to know what God's Word says about His role in your life, because it confirms His divine plan to be intimately involved with all that concerns you. "'For I know the plans I have for you," declares the LORD, "plans to prosper you and not to harm you, plans to give you hope and a future. Then you will call upon me and come and pray to me, and I will listen to you. You will seek me and find me when you seek me with all your heart. I will be found by you,' declares the LORD" (Jeremiah 29:11-14 NIV).

EXPECT HIM TO SPEAK TO YOU

Jesus told His disciples, "I have still many things to say to you, but you are not able to bear them or to take them upon you or to grasp them now. But when He, the Spirit of Truth (the Truth-giving Spirit) comes, He will guide you into all the Truth (the whole, full Truth)" (John 16:12-13). He also said that the Holy Spirit would continue to teach us all things and bring to our remembrance all that God has said through His Word (see John 14:26).

When Jesus spoke these words, He was talking to men with whom He had spent the previous three years. They had been with Him day and night, yet He indicated that He had more to teach them. We would think that if Jesus was with us personally for three years, day and night, we would have learned all there is to know. I think that if I had one uninterrupted month with people, I could tell them everything I know. But Jesus said to expect more because He will always have something to say to us about new situations we are facing.

Jesus always knew what was the right thing to do because He only did what He saw His Father do. As our Lord, we can trust Him to lead us to the right path every day. He is the only begotten Son of God, but we are also adopted sons and daughters of God, and we are to imitate Him in all we do. He became flesh and experienced all of the things we experience, so He understands our needs. He was baptized in the Holy Ghost, just as we are to be baptized in the Holy Ghost (see John 1:32-33). And He was led by the Spirit, just as we can be led by the Spirit, because He ascended to heaven and sent the Holy Spirit to lead and guide us.

In John 16:13 Jesus continued to explain the work of the Holy Spirit in our lives, saying, "For He will not speak His own message [on His own authority]; but He will tell whatever He hears [from the Father; He will give the message that has been given to Him], and He will announce and declare to you the things that are

> He is our Guide,
> our Teacher
> of truth,
> our Counselor,
> and our Helper.

to come [that will happen in the future]."

The book of John offers an extensive study of God's promise to intimately guide us. In chapter 6, Jesus said, "It is written in [the book of] the Prophets, And they shall all be taught of God [have Him in person for their Teacher]. Everyone who has listened to and learned from the Father comes to Me" (v. 45).

God knew we would need help in understanding His plan for us, so He sent the Holy Spirit to dwell on the inside of every Christian. He is our Guide, our Teacher of truth, our Counselor, and our Helper. He is also our Comforter, or the *parakletos* (par-ak'-lay-tos), which is explained in *Vine's Expository Dictionary* as one who is "called to one's

7

side."[1] The term "was used in a court of justice to denote a legal assistant, counsel for the defense, an advocate . . . who pleads another's cause, an intercessor."[2] The Holy Spirt promises never to leave us or forsake us. We can live the abundant life if we learn to *listen* to him. Jesus said it was better for us that He went away, because if He didn't go, the Counselor (the Holy Spirit) would not come to us (see John 16:7). Jesus was confined to a body just as we are and could be only at one place at a time. But the Holy Spirit can be in every single one of us everywhere we go, all the time, individually leading and guiding each one of us. In John 14:15-20 Jesus explained:

> If you [really] love Me, you will keep (obey) My commands. And I will ask the Father, and He will give you another Comforter (Counselor, Helper, Intercessor, Advocate, Strengthener, and Standby), that He may remain with you forever—The Spirit of Truth, Whom the world cannot receive (welcome, take to its heart), because it does not see Him or know and recognize Him. But you know and recognize Him, for He lives with you [constantly] and will be in you. I will not leave you as orphans [comfortless, desolate, bereaved, forlorn, helpless]; I will come [back] to you. Just a little while now, and the world will not see Me any more, but you will see Me; because I live, you will live also. At that time [when that day comes] you will know [for yourselves] that I am in My Father, and you [are] in Me, and I [am] in you.

Jesus said that He Himself would come to us and that we would realize He is *in* us.

EXPECT TO HEAR HIM

Through Christ, and the power of His Holy Spirit, God wants to speak to you on a One-to-one basis, every day. He wants to lead you step by step to the good things He has in store for you. He cares about the tiniest details of your life. He even keeps track of how many hairs you have on your head (see Matthew 10:30). He cares about the desires of your heart. And He wants to reveal truth to you that will set you free from worry and fear.

His plan to share an intimate relationship with you existed before you were even born. The psalmist said of God, "Your eyes saw my unformed substance, and in Your book *all the days [of my life] were written before they took shape, when as yet there was none of them*" (Psalm 139:16 emphasis mine).

In the book of Acts the apostle Paul said of God, "From one man he made every nation of men, that they should inhabit the whole earth; and *he determined the times set for them and the exact places where they should live.* God did this so that men would seek him and perhaps reach out for him and find him, though he is not far from any one of us" (Acts 17:26-27 NIV emphasis mine).

Doesn't it stand to reason that, if God knows all of our days and where we are going to live before we are even born, it is important to learn how to hear from Him? Hearing God's voice is not only exciting, it also keeps us on the right track.

In Matthew 7:13-14 Jesus spoke of a narrow path that leads to life and a broad path that leads to destruction, and

He told us to stay on the narrow one. If we can discern God's voice, we can know if we are veering off onto the wrong track, and we can make an adjustment before we reap bad results from a bad decision.

Hearing God's voice throughout the day has become a natural way of life for me since I received the fullness of the Holy Spirit whom Jesus promised to send us. The Father will give the gift of His Spirit to all who ask for Him (see Luke 11:13), and the Holy Spirit will help us understand the Bible so we will know how to apply its wisdom to our lives (see John 14:26). I want to say again emphatically that each of us *can* hear from God and be led by the Holy Spirit *daily.*

It seems incomprehensible that God could have a plan for every person on earth, but it also brings great peace to know that He can take our chaos and turn it into something meaningful and worthwhile. God's plan is unveiled through an intimate relationship with Him.

If you desire to know God in a deeper way, I recommend that you read my book titled *Knowing God Intimately.* In that book, I share in great detail how you can be as close to God as you want to be.

GOD OFFERS A LIFETIME PARTNERSHIP

Psalm 48:14 cheered my heart one day. It says that God will be our guide even unto death! How wonderful to know that we have a guide to get us from one destination in life to the next. Sometimes when my husband, Dave, and I travel, we hire a guide to show us the best and most important sites to see.

Once, we decided to explore by ourselves; that way we could do what we wanted to and when we wanted to. However, we quickly found that our independent trips were nearly wasted. We often spent a large part of the day getting lost and then trying to find our way again. We have found it to be the best use of our time to follow a guide rather than wandering aimlessly to find places ourselves.

I believe this example relates to how we are in life. We want to go our own way so we can do what we want to do, when we want to do it, but we end up getting lost and wasting our life. We need the Holy Spirit guiding us through every day of our time on this earth. God is committed to guide us even until we leave this life, so it seems important to learn how to hear what He is telling us.

One of the many benefits of hearing from God is that He helps us prepare for the future. The Holy Spirit gives the message to us that has been given to Him from the Father. He announces and declares to us things that will happen in the future (see again John 16:13).

> We need the Holy Spirit guiding us through every day of our time on this earth.

We see many instances in the Bible when God gave people information about the future. Noah was told to prepare for a flood that would come to destroy the people of the earth (see Genesis 6:13-17). Moses was told to go to Pharaoh and ask for the release of the Israelites, but he was also told that

Pharaoh would not let them go (see Exodus 7). Obviously, God does not tell us everything that will happen in the future, but the Bible says He will tell us of things to come.

There are times when I can sense inside my spirit that something good or something challenging is going to happen. Of course, when I sense something challenging is about to happen, I always hope I am wrong and that it is just my imagination. But if I am right then having the knowledge ahead of time acts as a shock absorber in my life. If an automobile with good shock absorbers hits a hole in the road, the absorbers cushion the impact for the passengers so no one gets hurt. God's giving us information ahead of time works the same way.

I remember many times when God informed me of things coming in the future. One time in particular was when I felt strongly inside my heart that one of my children was really struggling with something major. When I asked my child about it, I was told that everything was just fine, but by the Spirit I knew something was wrong. Several days later I received some news that was painful and discouraging—but it would have been a lot more difficult had I not had a previous warning.

First Corinthians 2:5 teaches us not to put our faith in the wisdom of men (human philosophy), but in the power of God. Verse 11 says that no one discerns the thoughts of God except the Spirit of God. Since the Holy Spirit knows the secret counsels of God, it is a vital necessity for us to know how to hear what He wants to say to us. The Holy Spirit will help us realize and comprehend and appreciate the gifts of divine favor and blessing that God has bestowed on us. Human wisdom doesn't teach us this truth; it comes from the Holy Spirit who gives us the mind of Christ (see vv. 12-13).

The Holy Spirit knows both the mind of God and God's individual plan for you. His road map for you is not necessarily like anybody else's, so it doesn't work to try to pattern your life after someone else or what he or she has heard from God. God has a unique plan for you, and the Holy Spirit knows what it is and will reveal it to you.

The Spirit of God will lead us, and God Himself will be our Shepherd (see Ezekiel 34:1-16). First John 2:27 teaches that as believers in Jesus Christ we have received an anointing from the Lord that remains in us to teach us about all things, so we don't need anyone else to teach us.

> God will tell us the way to go, but then we have to do the walking.

I am not saying that we shouldn't assemble and study God's Word together. I will discuss in a later chapter how to know when God *is* speaking to us through someone else, but it is important to know that we can find out what God is saying to us personally and be led by His Spirit without running to someone else all the time.

I had been a believer for many years before I learned that God wanted to talk directly to me on a daily basis so I could confidently walk in the fullness of His plan for my life. In those early days of faith, I never knew that I could hear God's voice and not be deceived. But now I know my Father's voice, and the voice of a stranger I will not follow (see John 10:4-5).

The Bible is full of great promises for our individual walk with God. It says, "The steps of a [good] man are directed and established by the Lord when He delights in his way [and He busies Himself with his every step]. Though he falls, he shall not be utterly cast down, for the Lord grasps his hand in support and upholds him" (Psalm 37:23, 24).

God will tell us the way to go, but then we have to do the

walking. A walk with God takes place through one step of obedience at a time. Some people want the entire blueprint for their life before they will make one decision. God does not usually operate that way; He leads us one step at a time.

By faith, we take the step God has shown us, and then He gives us the next one. At times we may fall down and must get back up; we may stumble, but He always helps us. We continue on by His strength and His grace, knowing that every time we face a fork in the road, God will guide us.

DON'T MISS OUT

Recently God told me that when we are *unwilling* to hear in one area, it may render us *unable* to hear in other areas. Sometimes we choose to turn a deaf ear to what we know the Lord is clearly saying to us. We only hear what we want to hear; it's called "selective hearing." After a while, people think they can't hear from God anymore but in reality there are lots of things they already know He wants them to respond to, and they haven't done so. I have learned that the more quickly I do whatever it is the Lord tells me to do, the more quickly He reveals the next step I am to take.

A woman once shared with me that she asked God to give her direction concerning what He wanted her to do. He clearly put in her heart that He wanted her to forgive her sister for an offense that had happened between them months earlier. Because this woman wasn't willing to do so, she pulled away from her prayer time. When she did seek the Lord again for something, He always responded, "Forgive your sister first."

Over a period of *two years*, every time she asked the Lord

for guidance about something new, He gently reminded her, "I want you to forgive your sister." Finally, she realized that she would never grow spiritually if she didn't do the last thing God had told her to do.

She got on her knees and prayed, "Lord, give me the power to forgive my sister." Instantly she understood many things from her sibling's perspective that she hadn't considered before, and within a short time their relationship was healed and made stronger than it had ever been before.

If we really want to hear from God, we can't approach Him with selective hearing, hoping to narrow the topics down to only what we want to hear. People take time to listen for God's voice when they have issues *they* want solved. If they have a problem or concerns about their job or need wisdom on how to have more prosperity or how to deal with a child, then they are all ears to hear what God has to say.

Don't just go to God and talk to Him when you want or need something; also spend time with Him just listening. He will open up many issues if you will be still before Him and simply listen.

For many people, listening is an ability that must be developed by practice. I have always been a talker; I never had to try to talk. But I have had to learn to listen on purpose. The Lord says, "Be still, and know that I am God" (Psalm 46:10). Our flesh is full of energy and usually wants to be active doing something, so it can be difficult for us to be still.

As I said, talking has always been easy for me. I told my husband one day that we needed to talk more. It seemed to me that he never wanted to just spend time sitting and talking. He responded by saying, "Joyce, we don't talk; you talk and I listen." He was right, and I needed to change if I expected him to want to fellowship with me. I also discovered I was doing the same thing with God; I talked and expected God to listen. I complained that I never heard from God, but the truth is I never listened.

When you do ask God something, take some time and listen. Even if He does not respond right at that moment, He will in due time. You may be doing some ordinary task when God decides to speak to you, but if you have honored Him by listening as part of your fellowship with Him, He will speak at the right time.

In the next few chapters, I will share many ways that God chooses to speak to us and guide us. I will share with you important truths I have learned that will keep your "receiver" deceiver free. First and foremost, God speaks to us through His written Word, and every other way that He communicates to us will always agree with the Bible. I will also share ways that we can create an atmosphere to hear from God and thus increase our expectancy to hear His voice.

Once we begin listening to and hearing from God, it is important to obey whatever we hear Him say to us. Obedience sharpens our fellowship with Him. We might say that practice makes perfect. In other words, we become more and more confident as we gain experience. It takes a lot of practice to get to the point of complete submission to God's leading. Even knowing that God's ways are perfect and that if we will submit to His plan, it will always work, we can still feign ignorance when it sounds like a personal sacrifice may be required of us. But there is no error in God's ways.

When face to face with God's truth, we should let it set us free to enjoy His best for our lives. I assure you that if you fight with God every time He tells you to do something, it will make you just plain miserable.

Jesus said, "Follow Me." He did not say, "You take the

lead, and I will follow you." I have learned that we may as well just do quickly whatever God says, the way He wants it done, because in the long run, if we want to enjoy God's perfect plan for our lives, we are going to have to follow Him.

I recently told one of my children, "I will never tell you anything that I don't believe is for your benefit." As I thought about it, I realized that God is the same way with us. He will never tell you or me anything that is not for our benefit. As I searched Scripture, I found many references that simply said in different ways, "Do all that I command you, for your good."

> Jesus said,
> "Follow Me."
> He did not say,
> "You take the lead,
> and I will follow
> you."

Perhaps you are like I was and have wasted many years walking your own way without seeking God's guidance. The good news is that it's not too late to turn and go in a new direction—toward God's plan and purpose for your life. It is not too late to learn how to hear from God. You are interested, or you would not be reading this book. If you are sincerely willing to obey God, He will guide you on an exciting journey of learning to hear from Him every day of your life.

As I said earlier, God has a good plan for our lives. We must follow Him in order to have it manifest. A great exercise to practice listening to God is to ask Him if there is anyone He wants you to encourage or bless—then be still and listen. You will be surprised at how quickly He responds. He will fill your heart with godly thoughts and goals. He will name people who will be blessed by your attention to them, and He may tell you specific things to do to encourage them. He has ideas to present to you that you haven't even considered. Listen carefully to Him. Then follow the advice given in John 2:5; *"Whatever He says to you, do it."*

Questions for Discussion

1. Have you experienced a time when "only God remain[ed]"? If so, describe it. What were your emotions? What truths did you hold on to? How and what did God speak to you during this time? Was it worth losing everything to experience God in this way?

2. How has God encouraged you to say yes to His ways?

3. Do you believe that God has a good plan to prosper you, a plan to give you hope and a future? If so, how does your life reflect this belief? If not, pray and ask God to help you accept and believe His Word.

4. Why do you think God tells us some things that will come to pass but not all things? How does this develop hope, patience, and trust?

5. Describe an instance when you realized you were putting faith in the wisdom of men. How did this differ from the truth of God?

6. How have you tried to pattern your life after someone else or what someone else has heard from God? Is this an experience from the past or a current situation?

7. What are the dangers in turning primarily to others to tell us what God is saying? What checks and balances do you have in place for discerning God's voice?

8. Is there anything God has spoken to you that you have not yet obeyed? Why are you hesitating? Is there a promise in Scripture you are having difficulty believing?

9. Who is someone God wants you to encourage? Have you done this?

2

Create an Atmosphere to Hear from God

⁓

If we want to be led into victory by the Spirit of God, then we have to be willing to change our lifestyle as God speaks to us. The first change we may encounter is the need to create an atmosphere that is conducive to hearing from God. By atmosphere I mean the climate, environment, or predominant mood that surrounds us. Atmosphere is created by attitudes, and certain attitudes enhance or hinder our relationship with God.

For example, if we live in a constant state of strife, which is a spiritual problem, we can feel that strife in the atmosphere. If we enter a room where several people are angry and upset, we can feel that dissension even if nobody is saying anything right then. We should work to create and maintain a peaceful atmosphere: "If possible, as far as it depends on you, live at peace with everyone" (Romans 12:18).

We can flippantly think that we want to hear from God, but seeking Him with our *whole* heart is a full-time job. To enjoy the fullness of God's presence, we must consistently maintain an atmosphere conducive to seeking Him, honoring Him, and being faithful and obedient to Him. If we want to hear from God, we must yield our attitudes to the lordship of Jesus Christ and learn to be led of the Spirit in *all* of our ways.

21

Keep a Listening Attitude

Listening is an important key to hearing! Have you ever met someone who asks questions, but doesn't listen to the answers? It is hard to talk to people who aren't listening. I am confident that God doesn't bother to speak to closed ears. If we are not going to listen to Him, God will find someone with a ready ear, someone who is listening for the sound of His voice.

Hebrews 5:11 warns us that we will miss learning rich life principles if we don't have a *listening* attitude: "Concerning this we have much to say which is hard to explain, since you have become dull in your [spiritual] hearing and sluggish [even slothful in achieving spiritual insight]."

A listening attitude will keep us from becoming dull in hearing. We shouldn't have the mentality of only listening for God's instruction when we desperately need help. Of course we're ready to hear from Him if we're in trouble. But God wants to speak to us on a regular basis. We need to have a listening ear all the time.

I sat down at my computer today and was ready to begin working on this book project when I sensed the Lord saying, "Take a few minutes and just wait on Me." I waited very briefly, then started to make a phone call. The Lord gently said, "I didn't tell you to make phone calls; I told you to wait on Me." Our flesh is so full of energy it is difficult for us to just be still. We need to develop new habits in this all-important area.

So I waited quietly for a period of time, and the Lord began to talk to me about angels—something I certainly was not expecting. He led me to look up several Scriptures, and I ended up receiving a mini Bible lesson on the power and presence of angels. God has reasons for everything He does, and I believe He wanted me to be more aware of His angels working on my behalf—something I honestly had not thought about for a long, long time.

You might ask, "Joyce, how do you know for sure God was talking to you, that your mind was not just making it up?" The answer is that I had peace about what I was receiving. It felt right inside me. My spirit confirmed it as being truly from the Lord. We know things about God by the spirit, not necessarily by the head. We take information into our minds, but revelation comes to our spirits through the Holy Spirit.

There have been other times when I have waited on God and heard a similar voice but intuitively knew it was not God's. We must know God's character in order to know what is from Him and what isn't. As we will see, He is gentle, not harsh, hard, sharp, or pressing (see Matthew 11:28-30). For example, when I began

> Our flesh is so full of energy it is difficult for us to just be still.

to pick up the phone to make a call, God didn't become angry and yell at me. His voice was gentle and kind. God understands our nature. He knew I was not purposely being disobedient but that my flesh just wanted to be busy "doing something."

There are many facets of God's character, and each one of them seems to be more wonderful than the next. He is faithful, true, loving, kind, long-suffering, just, and honest—among many other wonderful attributes. If I thought I heard God tell me to give up on something just because it was difficult for me, I would question whether that message was from Him, because I know His character is to be faithful. His Word says that even when we are faithless, He remains faithful (see 2 Timothy 2:13); therefore, it is unlikely He would tell me to give up quickly.

If I went shopping and came home with an extra item in my package that I didn't pay for and thought God was telling me that it was His way of blessing me, I would know the voice was not God's because He is always honest. He would not keep something He did not pay for, and we should not do so either. I recently purchased two pairs of shoes and the purse that matched one pair. When I returned home I found that the clerk had given me two pairs of shoes and purses to match both pairs, but had only charged me for one purse. It was an effort to return the purse—it actually cost me time and gas money to be honest—but I knew honesty was God's way.

The clerk was so impressed that as I was leaving I saw him telling others he could not believe I had returned the purse. People need to see God in action and He wants to work through His children. Don't let Satan deceive you in this area of hearing from God. Know God, know His character, and you will be able to discern the voices that come to you, whether they are His, yours, or the enemy's.

Jesus said that people have ears to hear, but they hear not; and eyes to see, but they see not (see Matthew 13:9-16). He wasn't talking about our physical ears; He was talking about the spiritual ears we are given when we are born into the kingdom of God. Our spiritual ears are tuned in to God's voice. We need to have a quiet, expectant attitude to be able to hear Him.

An example of a listening attitude is what happens in natural circumstance when Dave and I make tentative plans for the weekend. If what we want to do requires good weather, we start listening for the weekend forecast. When we don't have a desire to go anywhere, we don't really care about the weather forecast. When we need information, we keep a listening ear tuned for the answers we need. We may not know exactly what time the weather report will be given, so we turn on our radio, hoping to catch the weather broadcast.

We can get busy doing things around our house, but because we are determined to keep one ear listening for the weather report, we are quick to separate ourselves from what we are doing as soon we hear anything said about the weather. We need to listen for God with this same kind of anticipation, as if we know He is about to give us important information that will influence the plans we are making.

When people come to the altar for prayer, I have learned not only to listen to them with my physical ears, but also with my spiritual ears. I listen to hear if God is telling me something to

> Maintaining a listening ear takes practice.

pray for them. Many times what people tell me is not the whole story, and they don't even know it.

God knows the whole story, and that's why He wants us to train ourselves to have an attitude of listening to Him. Maintaining a listening ear takes practice because it is not something that comes naturally. We need to create an atmosphere of expectancy that says, "I am listening, God. If You don't like what I am doing, please let me know. I am listening."

During our conferences, it is obvious that our worship leaders and musicians are listening to the Lord, because they frequently choose songs that perfectly complement the message God tells me to share. Many times it is impossible to coordinate song selections ahead of time, so I am grateful to work with people who listen to God and are led of His Spirit. When God confirms His message in many people at the same time, it builds faith in us to know that we really do recognize and discern His voice.

KEEP AN ATTITUDE THAT HONORS GOD

Another attitude that invites the presence of God into our atmosphere is one that honors Him above all others. We need to have an attitude that says, "God, no matter what anybody else is telling me, no matter what I think myself, no matter what my own plan is, if I clearly hear You say something to me, and I know it's You, I am going to honor You and what You say above anything else."

Sometimes we give more consideration to what people tell us than to what God has said to us. If we pray diligently, hear from God, but then start asking everybody else what they think, we are honoring people's opinions above the Word of God. This attitude will prevent us from developing a relationship in which we consistently hear from God.

The Word confirms that we can trust God to instruct us without needing constant reassurance from others: "But as for you, the anointing (the sacred appointment, the unction) which you received from Him abides [permanently] in you; [so] then you have no need that anyone should instruct you. But just as His anointing teaches you concerning everything and is true and is no falsehood, so you must abide in (live in, never depart from) Him [being rooted in Him, knit to Him], just as [His anointing] has taught you [to do]" (1 John 2:27).

This verse isn't saying that we don't need anybody to teach us the Word. Otherwise, God wouldn't appoint some to teach in the body of Christ. But it does say that if we are in Christ, we have an anointing that abides on the inside of us to guide and direct our lives. We might occasionally ask somebody for their wisdom, but we need not go constantly to other people to ask them about decisions we need to make for our lives.

When our staff members ask me, "What do you think I ought to do?" I tell them, "You have to hear from God."

> God is the only One who can minister life to us.

If we are ever going to develop an ability to hear from God and be led by His Spirit, we have to start making our own decisions and trust the wisdom God has deposited in our own heart.

The devil wants us to think we are not capable of hearing from God, but the Word says that's not true. The Holy Spirit dwells inside of us because God wants us to be individually led by His Spirit. We are not living under the old covenant in which we have to run to the priest to find out what we ought to be doing all the time.

In Jeremiah 17:5-7 the prophet tells us:

> Thus says the Lord: Cursed [with great evil] is the strong man who trusts in and relies on frail man, making weak [human] flesh his arm, and whose mind and heart turn aside from the Lord. For he shall be like a shrub or a person naked and destitute in the desert; and he shall not see any good come, but shall dwell in the parched places in the wilderness, in an uninhabited salt land. [Most] blessed is the man who believes in, trusts in, and relies on the Lord, and whose hope and confidence the Lord is.

The Lord is clearly saying not to make human flesh our strength. Severe consequences happen to those who trust in the frailty of people. Blessed are those who trust and honor the anointing from God that abides within them. Good things happen if we listen to God. He wants to be our right arm and our strength. God is the only One who can minister life to us.

Jesus heard clearly from His Father that He needed to go to the cross. In Mark 8:31 Jesus told the disciples that it was necessary for Him to suffer many things, be tested, approved, rejected by the elders and the chief priests and scribes, and be put to death; but, after three days, He would rise again from the dead. Verse 32 says that Peter "took Him by the hand and led Him aside and then [facing Him] began to rebuke Him."

But Jesus didn't consider the direction of frail men, like Peter, and "turning around [His back to Peter] and seeing His disciples, He rebuked Peter, saying, Get behind Me, Satan! For you do not have a mind intent on promoting what God wills, but what pleases men [you are not on God's side, but that of men]" (v. 33).

Jesus honored whatever His Father said, no matter what the personal cost to Himself. Sometimes we only listen to God if what He says isn't going to cost us anything, or if He tells us what we want to hear. Most of the time, if we receive a discomforting word, we act like Peter and say, "Oh no, this can't be God!" But if we want to have ears that hear God's voice, we must honor His words above all others.

KEEP AN ATTITUDE OF FAITH

When I was called to the ministry, I wanted to tell every-body. When I did so, I was met with a lot of unbelief. But when God speaks a word to us, there is no doubt in our heart what we are supposed to do. We must maintain faith in what God tells us, even when no one else believes it with us.

Paul had been persecuting Christians and was not a likely

person to be called to preach. If I had been one of Paul's peers, I would have had a hard time believing that he was called. He knew what the reaction to his ministry would be, so he wrote:

> But when He, Who had chosen and set me apart [even] before I was born and had called me by His grace (His undeserved favor and blessing), saw fit and was pleased to reveal (unveil, disclose) His Son within me so that I might proclaim Him among the Gentiles (the non-Jewish world) as the glad tidings (Gospel), immediately I did not confer with flesh and blood [did not consult or counsel with any frail human being or communicate with anyone]. Nor did I [even] go up to Jerusalem to those who were apostles. (Galatians 1:15-17)

Paul said that he kept the news of his calling to himself; he didn't check it out with "the big guys" who were supposed to always be hearing from God. He knew what God had done with him on that road to Damascus. He knew that he had been changed forever (see Acts 9:3-8). He knew that the Son of God had been unveiled and disclosed on the inside of him. He knew that he could never go back to the life he had lived. He knew that for the rest of his life he would have to preach the gospel and remain faithful to what he had heard Jesus say to him.

But he also had wisdom to know people would find his calling unbelievable. So he waited on God. He didn't go running around checking with the other disciples, saying, "Hey guys, I saw a light on the road and fell off my horse and this happened and that happened. What do you all think?" Instead, he went away and retired into Arabia. Afterward he came back to Damascus. Three years later, he did "go up to Jerusalem to become [personally] acquainted with Cephas (Peter), and remained with him for fifteen days" (Galatians 1:18).

Paul kept God's Word in his heart and let it grow and manifest on its own. Then he started doing what he was called to do. Soon others recognized that the calling on him must have been from God. Paul finished by saying, "And they glorified God [as the Author and Source of what had taken place] in me" (Galatians 1:24).

People often say they want confirmation when God speaks to them, citing the biblical rule that we should expect every word to be confirmed by two or three witnesses (see 2 Corinthains 13:1). But that Scripture about two or three witnesses has nothing to do with hearing from God. It was intended for the purpose of correction when an accusation was being brought against a Christian. If a believer was being accused of doing something wrong, accusation was not to be believed unless it was confirmed by two or three other believers.

Finding two or three witnesses was never used in reference to seeking counsel for God's direction in the life of an individual Christian. When we hear from God, we do not need to wait for three people to tell us the same thing; we simply need to have an attitude of faith, like Paul, and wait for God to show us the next step.

Sometimes people want God to confirm their calling with a sign, as Gideon did when he laid out a fleece on the threshing floor (Judges 6:36-40). God honored Gideon's request, but it wasn't God's best. When Thomas was full of doubt, saying he had to see before he believed, Jesus said to him, "'Blessed are those who have not seen and yet have believed'" (John 20:29 NIV).

God will do some special things for us when we are young Christians, but as we mature in our knowledge of God's leading, He is pleased when we learn to operate in faith.

Sometimes people open their Bible at random, hoping it opens to a Scripture that is relevant to their situation. They are afraid to proceed in faith with what God has told them to do. There were times in the past when God would honor such requests for signs, but that "well" of reassurance will dry up real quickly when it's time to simply act in faith.

I had to learn how to be led by my inner man. As the apostle Paul said, "My conscience bears me witness in the Holy Spirit" (see Romans 9:1). That is the only confirmation that we are required to have when God calls us to do something.

> "'Blessed are those who have not seen and yet have believed.'"

I like the way my pastor, Rick Shelton, said he operated. When he thought he heard from God, he would say, "I am not going to move on this until I know for sure that it *fits inside*." Everything that is right for our lives has a place on the inside of us, where it is going to settle comfortably.

God may call us to do something we don't always like in the flesh, but deep inside it will give us pleasure if it is truly a calling from God. For example, I am not eager to stay in hotel rooms every weekend, because to me they all look alike, but I know what I am called to do. I am excited about preaching, so I don't think about the parts of my ministry that are less pleasant.

There is a deep desire on the inside of me that is settled with any inconvenience associated with my calling. I know I have to stay in hotels in order to do what I love to do.

God may call you into things that you are not be used to doing. You may be scared in the natural, but you will feel that what you are doing fits inside with everything else that

God has developed in you. An attitude of faith will keep you moving toward the fulfillment of your calling.

KEEP AN ATTITUDE OF PATIENCE

I need to hear from God every day, and I want to hear from Him about everything. To hear God, we must be willing to wait on wisdom out of a passion for wanting God's will more than anything else. We will hear from God much more clearly if we are determined not to move in the heat of our fleshly desires or emotions. We will be blessed if we wait and make sure that we have heard from God before we take any steps at all. Then we should do what God is saying to do, even if it hurts, and even if it costs us something.

Several years ago I started collecting classic movies on video because there wasn't anything decent to watch on television. As a result of my buying them and people giving them to me over the years, I have a pretty nice video collection. As a matter of fact, my kids tease me sometimes and call my collection the "Joyce-Buster" movies (instead of Blockbuster).

A magazine arrived at our house listing many good, clean movies. Everything listed was Christian-based, moral entertainment, and it seemed that God had just dropped the opportunity in my lap. I got excited and probably checked fifteen different videos I wanted to order. I then decided to just lay the list aside for a few days. I finally came back to it after I was able to patiently overcome my emotions and use godly wisdom. I ordered only two new movies.

If I had acted the night my emotions were stirred, I would have ordered too many videos, and it wouldn't have been God leading me to do it. We need to wait for sound wisdom before we act on an impulse that we think is from God.

Learn to wait. Emotions that rise and energize us will fall, and emotional energy won't carry us where we really need to go. We need God's energy, which is Holy Ghost determination to follow through and do what God has said.

God has a will and a plan for everyone. Each person needs to find out what it is that God wants him or her to do, then wait on His timing to do it. All of us need to follow Wisdom:

> Blessed (happy, fortunate, to be envied) is the man who listens to me, watching daily at my gates, waiting at the posts of my doors. For whoever finds me [Wisdom] finds life and draws forth and obtains favor from the Lord. But he who misses me or sins against me wrongs and injures himself; all who hate me love and court death. (Proverbs 8:34-36)

We can miss God by being in a hurry to get what we want. If we don't wait, especially in important areas, we will bring trouble into our lives. Patience is becoming more finely tuned in my life all the time.

I am a natural-born confronter. In the past, if I wanted something solved, I confronted the issue and forced a solution. It took me years to learn that sometimes it wasn't good for me to deal with issues that directly. I learned that I could make matters worse, or get in God's way and end up having to go through the same situation again because I didn't wait for God's timing. Because I was impatient, I didn't give God a chance to solve things for me.

I have learned that when I feel anxiety rise in me to handle something, I should let it rest for at least twenty-four hours. It is amazing how we can change our mind if we will just let things settle for a few hours. We can save ourselves so much trouble if we will learn to wait on God.

KEEP AN ATTITUDE OF OBEDIENCE

The psalmist David said of God, "Sacrifice and offering You do not desire, nor have You delight in them; You have given me the capacity to hear and obey [Your law, a more valuable service than] burnt offerings and sin offerings [which] You do not require" (Psalm 40:6).

God delights in the atmosphere of our obedience. Naturally, it doesn't do God any good to talk to us if we aren't going to listen and obey.

For many years, I wanted God to talk to me, but I wanted to pick and choose what to obey. I wanted to do what He said if I thought it was a good idea. If I didn't like what I was hearing, then I would act like it wasn't from God. God has given us the capacity both to hear Him and to obey Him. He does not require a higher sacrifice than obedience.

Some of what God says to you will be exciting. Some things God tells you might not be so thrilling to hear. But that doesn't mean that what He tells you won't work out for good if you will just do it His way.

If God tells you that you were rude to a person, and He wants you to apologize, it won't work to answer back, "Well, that person

> It is amazing how we can change our mind if we will just let things settle for a few hours.

was rude to me too!" If you talk back with excuses, you may have prayed, and even heard, but you haven't obeyed.

Instead, go apologize if God tells you to do so. Take yourself through the walk of obedience and say to that person, "I was rude to you, and I'm sorry." *Now* you have obeyed. Now God's anointing can flow through your life, because you are obedient.

I was moved by a story about a message from a pastor of a very large church who spoke at a pastors conference in Tulsa, Oklahoma. Hundreds of pastors came from all over the nation to hear this man tell what he did to build his church. He told them simply, "I pray, and I obey. I pray, and I obey."

One of the ministers who attended this meeting expressed to me his disappointment in the pastor's message. He said, "I spent all that money and went all that distance to hear this world-renowned leader tell me how his ministry grew to the point it is. For three hours, in various ways, he said the same thing, 'I pray. I obey. I pray. I obey. I pray. I obey. I pray. I obey.' I kept thinking, Surely there's something else."

Looking back over nearly three decades of walking with God, I would have to agree that if I put into words the simplest explanation for all the success we have enjoyed, we too have learned to pray, hear from God, and then do what God tells us to do. Over the years I have been seeking God about the call on my life and pressing forward in what I feel He has told me to do. The essence of it all is that I have prayed, and I have obeyed. It has not always been popular with everyone else, but I have prayed, I have obeyed—and it has worked. God's plan is not hard; *we* make it hard.

If you want God's will for your life, I can tell you the recipe in its simplest form: *Pray and obey.* God has given you the capacity to do both.

Pray.

And obey.

Pray.

And obey.

Pray.

And obey.

Pray.

And obey.

If you do that, before you know it, you will have stepped right into God's perfect plan for your life.

Questions for Discussion

1. What atmosphere (climate, environment, or predominant mood) is surrounding you? What personal attitudes created this atmosphere? *To pray + obey*

   Knowing God loves me *yes*

2. Describe a time when you heard God's voice. How did you know it was God's voice? What confirmed this?

   It was His word that spoke to me

3. Describe a time when you heard a voice other than God's. How did you know this was not God's voice? What confirmed this? *B/c it wasn't God's word*

4. How do you consistently distinguish between God's voice and other voices? *Does it line up w/ Gods word*

5. Are you wavering in remaining steadfast to something God has told you? Why have you lost hope? Are you listening more to other people? What are you to do with what God has spoken to you? Something specific or are you to continue prayerfully seeking God and waiting on Him?

   Stand firm

6. Is there someone in your life God has told you to forgive or ask forgiveness from? If so, have you acted accordingly? If you have not acted obediently, what is keeping you from doing what God has spoken? *My children yes & willingly forgive them.*

7. Note the aspects important in creating an atmosphere to hear God—listening, honoring, faith, patience, and obedience. What are the areas in which you are strongest? What are the more challenging areas? *Spending time w/ Him waiting / Praying / be honest w/ God - pour out my heart to Him*

8. In what ways are you currently walking in obedience? Are there any ways you are currently walking in disobedience? *too muc* If so, what or how? Be specific in your answer. *Isolation*

9. What do you believe God is leading you to in response to this chapter? *Wait for God to act on your behalf; He knows our deepest needs.*

3

God Speaks through Supernatural Revelation

⌒

Sometimes God transcends the laws of nature and speaks to us through supernatural revelation. There is nothing more supernatural than the Word of God, which is given to us by divine inspiration of the Holy Spirit speaking through His prophets and disciples. The Bible has an answer for every question we might ever have. The Word of God is full of life principles, true stories of God's mercy toward human behavior, and rich parables filled with important truths for every individual on earth.

Anyone who wants to hear God's voice must be a student of the Word. Of all the other ways that God may speak to us, He will never contradict the written Word, which was originally referred to by the Greek word *logos*. His spoken Word is called the *rhema*. God specifically brings to our remembrance His *logos* for every situation. His *rhema* may not be word for word in the Bible, but the principle will always be supported in the written Word. The Bible confirms whether or not what we are sensing is of God.

For example, the written Word of God, the *logos* Word, doesn't tell us when to buy a new car or what type of car to buy; we may need a spoken or revealed word (a *rhema*) from God concerning that. Even though the written Word gives no specific instruction on the buying of an automobile, it does say a lot about wisdom. Therefore, if I need a car, and if I believe I am hearing God tell me to buy a certain car, yet the car costs more than I can afford and would mean years of deep debt that would place my family in bondage, I should have enough common sense (wisdom) to know the voice I think I am hearing is not God's.

There are many voices that speak to our thoughts, and our own is one of them. I have discovered when I desire something in a strong way, it is easy for me to think God is telling me to get it. For this reason we must always check to see if we have peace and if what we are doing is wise.

The Bible is written as a personal letter to each of us. God speaks to us, ministers to our needs, and directs us in the way we should go in His written Word. He tells us what we should do and how we should live. Sometimes a Scripture will seem illuminated or made alive in a particular way, and that is when a portion of the *logos* becomes a specific *rhema* to us. The Word is made alive as though God just spoke it into our ears.

There may be times when God speaks something to us that is outside a specific chapter and verse of the Bible, but it will always be in agreement with His Word. For example, the Bible doesn't tell us where to work, but God will speak to us if we seek Him.

If we think we can hear clearly from God without spending time in the Word, we are mistaken. Listening for God's voice without being dedicated to spending time in the Word on a regular basis opens us up to hearing voices that are not from God. Knowing the written Word protects us from deception.

Trying to hear from God without reading His Word is irresponsible and even dangerous. People who want to be led by the Spirit, but who are too lazy to spend time in the Word or time in prayer, set themselves up for easy decep-

40

tion. There are many evil spirits ready to whisper lies to a listening ear.

Some people only come to God when they are in trouble and need help. But if they are not used to hearing from God, they will find it difficult to recognize His voice when they really need Him. Even Jesus resisted Satan's lies by answering, "It is written" (see Luke 4).

Any idea, or prompting, or thought that comes to us needs to be compared to the Word of God. All vain imaginations are to be cast down and ignored (see 2 Corinthians 10:5), but knowledge of the Word is of vital importance in discerning the voice of God.

Many people feel they are too busy to read the Word, but if that is true, they are just plain *too* busy. A surprising number of people who work in ministry use their full-time service as an excuse for not devoting personal time to reading the Word and fellowshipping with God. They feel their service *for* Him is spending time *with* Him. We are all to work as

> Knowing the written Word protects us from deception.

unto the Lord, regardless of whether or not our job is classified as ministry. If we are going to be fit to work for God, we must *always* spend time with God, reading His Word, and praying to Him. Anyone working in ministry is a sure target of the enemy and needs the protection of the written Word even more than others. The apostle Paul tells us:

> For though we walk (live) in the flesh, we are not carrying on our warfare according to the flesh and using mere human weapons. For the weapons of our warfare are not physical [weapons of flesh and blood], but they are mighty before God for the overthrow and destruc-

tion of strongholds, [inasmuch as we] refute arguments and theories and reasonings and every proud and lofty thing that sets itself up against the [true] knowledge of God; and we lead every thought and purpose away captive into the obedience of Christ (the Messiah, the Anointed One). (2 Corinthians 10:3-5)

If we don't know the Word, we won't have anything with which to compare the theories and arguments that make war against God's perfect will for us. The devil can present wild ideas that make sense to us, but just because something seems logical to us doesn't necessarily mean it is from God. We may hear what we want to hear, but it doesn't necessarily mean we have heard from God. An idea can *feel* good to our emotions but fail to give us peace when it isn't in line with God's Word.

Commit time each day just to read the Word. You may enjoy a certain reading plan. I enjoy The Amplified Bible because it explains the meaning of important words. It is also good to read various versions of the Bible for new insight. There are wonderful reference books available to provide background history of the Word and the cultural implications from the time period in which the Scriptures were written. The important thing is just to read. God can bring to life the answers that are hidden in the pages of His written Word for any trial you may face.

GOD SPEAKS THROUGH WISDOM AND COMMON SENSE

One of my favorite ways to hear from God is through conventional wisdom and common sense. Wisdom discerns truth in a situation, while common sense provides good judgment in what to do about the truth. I consider wisdom supernatural because it isn't taught by men, but is a gift from God.

Many sophisticated and intelligent people still lack wisdom and common sense. The Word says, "If any of you is deficient in wisdom, let him ask of the giving God [Who gives] to everyone liberally and ungrudgingly, without reproaching or faultfinding, and it will be given him" (James 1:5).

Actually it amazes me how many people seem to think that all their common sense must vanish in order for them to be "spiritual." Spiritual people don't float around all day on clouds of glory while seeing angels and hearing disembodied voices. We live in a real world with real issues and need real answers. The answers are found in God's Word and are revealed to us by His Spirit.

We do the seeking, and He does the speaking, but He is the Spirit of Wisdom and will not tell us to do things that are unwise. Wisdom and common sense are closely linked. I like to say that wisdom is choosing to do today what we will be satisfied with tomorrow or later on in life.

When I am shopping, I often seek God for wisdom about my purchases. I don't pray about everything I buy, but I do try to acknowledge God in all my ways. If I am going to spend any sizable amount of money, I wait on the Lord for a minute to see if I feel peace about it or not.

Many times we ask God to speak to us and lead us, but if He doesn't respond with a specific word, we still have to live our daily lives. We make decisions all day long, and He is not going to dictate every little choice we make, but He does give us wisdom to carry us through our day. When we don't get a *rhema* from God, we need to use conventional wisdom in the choices we make.

If God does speak to me, I have learned to do specifically what He says to do. But if God doesn't speak to me specifically, it doesn't mean He isn't leading me. There are some issues about which God already trusts me enough to know what is right or wrong. I don't have to have a "big word" from God. But I have learned to wait on Him to see if there is a need for Him to intervene in the way I am planning to go.

For example, if I am pondering, *Lord, is it okay for me to buy this?* and I don't hear anything from God, then one of the things I ask myself is, *Can I afford it?* Obviously, if I can't afford it, then wisdom says, "Don't buy it." The audible voice of God is not needed when wisdom is already shouting the truth.

If people would listen to wisdom, they would keep themselves out of a lot of trouble. The book of Proverbs is a great source for wisdom. I recommend that you read at least a few verses of Proverbs or Psalms daily. I am not trying to establish rules or regulations, but I simply share what has profited me. Most days, I read something from these two books. Psalms always encourages me and builds me up, and Proverbs tells me how to stay out of trouble.

God speaks wisdom to us through what I call "sanctified common sense." A lot of people, even Christians, ignore their common sense and make foolish decisions. An example of *not* using common sense is when people get a sense that something bad is going to happen to someone

> If people would listen to wisdom, they would keep themselves out of a lot of trouble.

else, so they call that person and say, "I have been praying for you, and I sense that something really bad is going to happen to you." The bottom line is, I don't believe there is wisdom in telling anyone such things. That kind of news can only bring fear, and God's Word says to fear not. Common sense tells us that if what we are hearing about someone else is from God, then He has given us that warning so that we will pray for that person's protection. What good would it do to scare the person with such news?

I won't discount that God may lead us to tell someone a specific word for a specific event, but He would not tell us to impress someone with a generalized fear. There is a great difference between the two. Only common sense will help us reason out the possible fruit of our decisions and help us know which way we ought to go. Ask God for sanctified common sense to lead you.

I greatly appreciate people who use common sense. Sometimes I would rather be around a person who is known for good common sense than someone who is considered to be a spiritual giant.

GOD SPEAKS THROUGH DREAMS AND VISIONS

In the Bible there are many accounts of God speaking to people through dreams and visions, but this is one of the least common ways that God speaks to us. We can't assume that every dream is a godly dream. If we do, we may misinterpret images that will lead us astray.

I dream a lot, but most of my dreams are not prophetic. I haven't had many dreams that I feel were spiritual messages, but I have had a few that I know were from God, because either I received an interpretation immediately upon waking up, or it simply would not fade from my memory until God revealed its meaning.

Here is an example of a spiritual dream I once had. I had left my job at a church in St. Louis to go out on my own. I was *really* scared to step out into full-time ministry. One night I dreamed this dream:

I was driving down a road, and I was in a line of traffic. All the other drivers were suddenly pulling off the road and parking on the side of it, or they were slowing down to find a place where they could turn around and go back in the other direction.

I wondered what was going on ahead of me that was causing all those people to park their cars or turn around and go back the way they had come. I strained to look ahead, and I saw that the highway led to a bridge that was totally submerged in water. Of course, I realized why all the people were afraid to keep going forward.

I looked at the bridge, then I turned to look back from where I came. Then I looked at the bridge again and turned to look back from where I came.

The minute I woke up, God spoke to me saying, "Joyce, you're on a new journey. You're on a road that will sometimes look a little bit dangerous or unsafe. You are going to be a little unsure." But He said, "There are always going to be plenty of places in the road where you can park, plenty of places where you can turn around and go back where you came from, but I'm looking for someone who will go all the way through and do what I tell them to do."

I knew right then what God was telling me, and I've trusted that word many times when I've been in struggles or when things have seemed hard. I remembered how God warned me in the beginning that I would be tempted to park myself right where I was or turn myself around because I didn't know what was ahead for me. Knowing that difficult times would be part of His plan kept me moving ahead through uncertain paths.

During a certain period of time, God was dealing severely with me about my attitude. He chastised me concerning my actions over a couple of rough, rebellious days. It was obvious God was not going to relent until I humbled myself to His instruction.

In this time of discouragement, I dreamed of a row of five or six fine-looking model homes on display in a new subdivision. The houses were varied in size, and the particular house I noticed was one of the bigger ones. I watched people enter the house. As they toured the rooms, they saw all kinds of trash left from the construction crew. Bits and pieces of unattractive scraps were everywhere, all over the house, and especially in the one room that everyone entered. As I woke up, I understood immediately the interpretation of that dream.

The Lord said to me, "We are getting ready to go on television in just a few weeks, and I am getting ready to put you on display; but when the people look into your life, I don't want them to find trash."

That dream comforted me, because it was a positive word from the Lord. Even though it was hard to endure His correction, I understood that He really could not put me on display as He wanted to until I conformed more to His plan.

On the other hand, I have had literally thousands of dreams that didn't make any sense at all. Actually, if I tried to make them say something specific, I could get very confused and possibly cause lots of trouble. Dreams are interesting but usually very unstable in giving us direction. As you may have heard, many dreams are "pizza dreams" or "taco dreams"; in other words, they are the result of eating some spicy food before going to bed that prevents us from falling into a deep, restful sleep, so we dream rather unusual things most of the night.

My daughter recently dreamed that I was the president of the United States and that everyone was angry with me because I was letting people get sick. I was put into prison, but the court agreed to let my daughter go with me so she could take care of me. She loaded up the car with all the things I like so I would be comfortable in prison; she even had the sparkling water of which I drink many bottles each day.

> Dreams are interesting but usually very unstable in giving us direction.

She saw the guard suddenly go off to do something else, and so she told me to get in the car and make my getaway. I jumped in the car and drove off at high speed while she stood calling after me trying to let me know that I had forgotten my cell phone.

I actually know people who would try to "interpret" this dream and make something spiritual out of it. The fact is my family teases me about becoming the first woman president; that my daughter is in charge of many of the details of my life, including packing me for trips; and that our entire family are on our cell phones far too much. I really don't know why we dream so many unique and seemingly mixed-up things. But one thing is for sure, in my opinion, people who try to make too much out of their dreams are asking to be deceived.

We realize God does speak through dreams. He spoke to Joseph in a dream, and Joseph interpreted dreams for Pharaoh, as well as for Pharaoh's servants, with whom he was in prison (see Genesis 40 and 41). There are numerous others recorded in the Bible to whom God spoke through dreams. Joel 2:28 states that in the last days the old men shall dream dreams, and the young men shall see visions.

I have a friend who has many spiritual dreams. I have known her since 1983, and during those years she has shared four dreams she has had about me. Each of them has been amazingly accurate.

Dreams are certainly one of the valid ways God speaks, but this is also an area in which people can easily get out of balance, simply because so many people worldwide dream almost nightly and they are not all spiritual dreams. Use discernment, wisdom, and balance, and I believe you will have confirmation in your heart if a dream you have is God trying to speak to you or show you something.

God also speaks to us through visions, which differ from dreams that occur while we are asleep. I have experienced two kinds of visions. One I refer to as an open vision, which happens when my eyes are open, but I see only the spirit realm instead of the room around me.

God gave me a brief vision that showed me I was to take our ministry north, south, east, and west. I had entered a special time of prayer and fasting. It was the first time I had ever tried to fast with water. I was desperate to hear from God, because I thought He was telling me to leave my job at a church and begin my own ministry. It was a serious decision, so I wanted to be sure I was hearing clearly from Him.

God doesn't give us visions just for fun; I believe that God speaks to us in these more spectacular ways during times in our life when we need definite direction. Visions also seem to come to people when they are specifically seeking God.

Another kind of vision I have experienced more frequently is when I see things in the spirit. There have been occasions when I was looking at someone, but in my spirit I was seeing something concerning that person that my natural eyes did not perceive. Usually when I see something in the spirit realm for someone, I am also given prophetic words to give specific encouragement to him or her.

Visions are much like dreams; they are definitely used by God, but we must be cautious and test the spirits as the Bible instructs us to do (see 1 John 4:1-3). I do believe there are people who are gifted in visions and dreams more than others.

I have known a few people who seem to always be seeing something in the spirit realm. They talk about seeing angels the way I see people. I don't want to assume they don't see angels simply because my gifts don't function in that way; neither do I try to make something happen myself just because some people have told me it happens to them. I have learned to leave these things to God. In this book, I choose to speak more about what *normally* happens to *most* people, not what *may* happen to a *few*.

I think if we exalt what happens to a few, it makes all of those who don't have similar experiences think they are lacking in some way—that they are spiritually dwarfed or that they simply don't know how to hear from God. I know people to whom Jesus has appeared several times, even sitting on the side of their bed and carrying on a conversation for a lengthy time; but that has never happened to me.

When I was less secure in my own spiritual gifting, I compared myself with those people, wondering, *What is wrong with me?* I have since learned that I am a unique individual, with a unique, individual calling. I have received gifts from God accordingly, and they are all for His purpose and in His plan.

I am content and satisfied, and I strongly encourage you to adopt the same attitude. After all, "A man can receive nothing [he can claim nothing, he can take unto himself nothing] except as it has been granted to him from heaven. [A man must be content to receive the gift which is given him from heaven; there is no other source]" (John 3:27).

GOD SPEAKS THROUGH PROPHECY

Sometimes the Lord speaks prophetically through other people to reveal His will for our lives. A prophecy inspired by God will strengthen, encourage, and comfort the one who receives it (see 1 Corinthians 14:3).

> I am a unique individual, with a unique, individual calling.

There is a difference between a person who has a gift of prophecy and someone who is appointed to the office of prophet in the body of Christ. A prophet has a stronger word for the church at large than someone who is operating in the gift of prophecy to simply strengthen and encourage individual believers. The Word encourages us to welcome divinely inspired prophecy:

Earnestly desire and cultivate the spiritual endowments (gifts), especially that you may prophesy (interpret the divine will and purpose in inspired preaching and teaching) . . . the one who prophesies [who interprets the divine will and purpose in inspired preaching and teaching] speaks to men for their upbuilding and constructive spiritual progress and encouragement and consolation . . . he who prophesies [interpreting the divine will and purpose and teaching with inspiration] edifies and improves the church and promotes growth [in Christian wisdom, piety, holiness, and happiness]. (1 Corinthians 14:1,3,4)

Prophecy must be in line with the Word of God, and a personal word of prophecy should confirm something that's already in your heart. It's nice when that happens, because you know that person didn't know anything about what God was saying to you. But if somebody tells you to go to the mission field, or to Bible college, don't quit your job and go unless *you know* that God has spoken to your heart this same word. I've seen people get into horrendous messes by trying to run their lives based on what other people have told them was a "prophetic message from God."

If the prophecy doesn't bear agreement in your heart, don't worry about it. There are a lot of well-meaning people who think they are hearing from God for others, but they're not. If someone prophesies something to you that is not already in your heart, then I suggest you write down the words that are spoken over you and just wait for the Lord to reveal to you whether or not the words are from Him.

Many times, people come to me and share their disturbing concern that they are trying to do something because somebody has prophesied to them that they should do it. Many times they aren't getting a breakthrough, so they are confused. It grieves me when I see people working to make a prophecy come to pass, because we are not to run our lives by those kinds of things.

> Opposition is one of the greatest signs that their message was truly from God.

If a word is truly from God, *He will make it happen* in His own time. Lay aside the prophecy and just wait to see if God brings it to pass. He will speak to you in other ways to confirm it, if it is really from Him.

I know of situations in which five to ten years have passed before something happened to prove that a prophecy was truly from God. So even when we have clear direction from God, we need to let Him fulfill His promises without trying to manipulate their manifestation. When a promise does come to pass, the Holy Ghost will call our remembrance back to that word we received years before to let us know we are indeed walking in God's perfect plan.

If a good word has been spoken over you from other prayerful and godly believers, then opposition is one of the greatest signs that their message was truly from God. Refer back to the spoken or written message when the devil tells you that you are not called or that you are never going to do what is in your heart to do or that you are never going to prosper or that you are never going to get a breakthrough in your situation. Your weapon against his attacks will be the words that have been prophesied to you.

Remember, what has been said through the gift of prophecy will help you remain steadfast in faith when the devil wages war against your calling. If the prophecy is truly from God, the devil will eventually show up to discourage you from believing the truth, and you will be able to stand firm in faith because you know what the Lord has said about you.

While waiting for God to move, you should follow the instruction given to Timothy by the apostle Paul:

> Until I come, devote yourself to the public reading of Scripture, to preaching and to teaching. Do not neglect your gift, which was given you through a prophetic message when the body of elders laid their hands on you. Be diligent in these matters; give yourself wholly to them, so that everyone may see your progress. Watch your life and doctrine closely. Persevere in them, because if you do, you will save both yourself and your hearers. (1 Timothy 4:13-16 NIV)

We are not to specifically seek a certain way for God to speak to us. There are times when I tell the Lord that I would like for Him to give me a word, but I don't ask Him to send it in a certain way. I am not devastated or disappointed when someone who is anointed with a prophetic gift doesn't have a word for me. I trust that if God wants to speak to me a certain way, He will do it.

Of all the prayer requests that we get in our office, the largest percentage is from people who have problems and don't know what to do. They want to hear from God. They need to make a decision, so they ask for prayer to know what to do. Indecision makes us feel uncomfortable, but our confusion is magnified when we start running to other people asking them what we ought to do.

I find it interesting that I can preach the Word for an entire weekend, and yet invariably somebody will come to me after the meeting and say, "I believe that God said you've got a word for me."

I am perplexed, thinking, *Well what do you think I've had for you the last three days?* Now, I will show them the courtesy of praying to see if God speaks to me on their behalf, but most of the time people just want to be led around by what somebody else has to say. It's sad that there are so many insecure people in the world who believe they can't hear from God themselves. They spend all of their life trying to hear from God through other people.

If you get out of balance by always asking others what you should do, it will hinder your ability to hear from God yourself. Besides, most people don't even know what *they* are doing, so they are not qualified to tell you what you ought to do. I don't mean that statement to be insulting, but most people have enough issues in their own lives that they are trying to sort out without taking responsibility for your life too.

There are times when people ask me what I think God would have them do in a situation. If I know what the Word says about their particular situation, I share it with them. Or if I have some discernment about their situation, I share it. But many times I feel pressured when people want me to make their decisions for them. It helps me know that it is not my job to hear from God for other people. My job is to *teach* people how to hear from God themselves, not to hear for them! The Holy Spirit can lead us all individually.

Some time ago we had a couple who had worked for us for more than twelve years, had become dissatisfied with their positions, and were feeling God wanted them to do something else; however, they had no idea what it was. They felt their season with our ministry was at an end and that they had lost their grace to do their jobs. They did not want to work for us any longer, but they did not want to be without jobs either. They came to Dave and me and said,

"We believe God will show you what we are supposed to do."

Some people delight in telling other people what to do with their lives, but I am not one of them. I don't particularly like taking that kind of responsibility. I feel I have enough to do trying to run my own life and ministry and hear from God for myself. In addition, people need to have assurance and confidence that they have heard from God, not other people. If they don't, they will become unsure and even confused during testing seasons, which almost always come sooner or later.

We shared with that couple what we felt were several points of just plain wisdom, but we could not tell them definitely either to stay or to go. It was an important decision, one that needed to be made by them, especially since it would affect their income and destiny.

> We have to let God initiate prophecy into our lives.

God is a jealous God, and He doesn't approve if we are always putting people ahead of Him by running to them to ask what we ought to do. I believe that we should find out what God says about our situation in His Word, explore His wisdom, and let our decision establish itself through peace in our heart. Then, if we feel we need to, we can go occasionally to someone we trust to prayerfully seek God's will on our behalf just to double check that what we want to do is right. I will share in a later chapter how God sometimes uses the counsel of others, but even then we must seek balance in this area. The advice of people should be in line with God's Word and tested against our inner witness of God's truth.

We have to let God initiate prophecy into our lives, or else we will never know if it's something we provoked on our own. If we ask people if they have a word from the Lord for us, they may speak something out of their flesh just because they don't know what else to do.

We need to trust God to speak to our heart. In the many years I have walked with God, I have never yet asked anyone if they had a prophecy for me. If somebody has a word for us, God will work that out supernaturally without us seeking it. We don't have to search or ask, "Do you have a word for me?" I prophesy occasionally, but I tell people not to run their lives by personal prophecy.

A man named Fred attended one of our marriage seminars. Fred shared with us that he was being mistreated at his job and was underpaid. He was demeaned and made fun of even though he had given years of faithful service to his employer. It was obvious he was not being treated right.

The Spirit of the Lord came upon me, and I prophesied to Fred that he was going to have a job where he would have respect, where people would come to him for advice, and where he would make good money. Then his situation got a whole lot worse before God's word to him proved to be true. But *it did get better.* It didn't happen quickly, but a true word from God will always happen. Prophecy is meant to encourage us with God's promise to us while we wait for Him to work it out in our lives.

I admit I'm no different from anybody else in that I like to get a refreshing word that is truly from the Lord. It is wonderful to hear God speak to us specifically through someone who couldn't possibly know our needs. Prophecy is a tremendous gift from God, but we must not become dependent on a word of prophecy. It's more important to get direction from the Word of God.

The more mature we are in the Lord, the more we will hear from God on our own without the supernatural intervention of a prophetic message from someone else. As you learn how to hear from God yourself, you may find that you will receive fewer words from others than you did in the beginning of your walk with the Lord.

When God called me into the ministry, I received many prophetic utterances from people. But there have been times in my ministry that I have gone for years without a single prophetic word spoken to me. It is a great gift when it is given to us, but we must not wait for a word or let our lives be run by something someone has spoken to us. We are to diligently read and study the Word, preach, and teach the good news. As we do that, God will work His plan through us and for us.

QUESTIONS FOR DISCUSSION

1. Have you felt the Lord speak something to you? Are you allowing Him to fulfill His word, or are you yourself attempting to make it come to pass?

2. Why is being in the Word so important? How does it protect us from deception? What are you doing now to ensure you are drinking deeply of the Word? Do you have a plan?

3. How can you determine if what someone spoke over you is true or not?

4. Do you hold a prejudice against prophetic words? If so, try to explain or analyze why you feel this way.

5. Do you find yourself given to seeking out others' prophetic words for your own situation? If so, are you intimidated about seeking an answer from the Lord yourself? Why?

6. What are the ways—outlined in this chapter—that the Lord speaks to us? Have you experienced God speaking to you in these ways? Describe.

7. What do you believe God is leading you to in response to this chapter?

4

God Speaks through Natural Things

In God's compassion for mankind, He did not hide the truth of His existence from anyone. The Word says that God reveals Himself to *all* people:

> For that which is known about God is evident to them and made plain in their inner consciousness, because God [Himself] has shown it to them. For ever since the creation of the world His invisible nature and attributes, that is, His eternal power and divinity, have been made intelligible and clearly discernible in and through the things that have been made (His handiworks). So [men] are without excuse [altogether without any defense or justification]. (Romans 1:19-20)

People who now claim to be atheists will one day stand defenseless before the Lord, because God speaks to everyone through His handiworks. Even people living outside the will of God perceive right from wrong and the reality of God, because nature itself testifies of God's power and divine plan. Psalm 19:1-4 says:

> The heavens declare the glory of God; and the firmament shows and proclaims His handiwork. Day after day pours forth speech, night after night shows forth knowledge.

There is no speech nor spoken word [from the stars]; their voice is not heard. Yet their voice [in evidence] goes out through all the earth, their sayings to the end of the world. Of the heavens has God made a tent for the sun.

I encourage you to take time to look at what God has created. The main thing God says to us through nature is that *He is*. Period. It is an important revelation because the Bible says that before we can get anywhere with God, we must first believe He is: "Without faith it is impossible to please and be satisfactory to Him. For whoever would come near to God must [necessarily] believe that God exists and that He is the rewarder of those who earnestly and diligently seek Him [out]" (Hebrews 11:6).

God has given every person a measure of faith to believe in Him (see Romans 12:3). The very first words of the Bible are our first lesson of faith, "In the beginning God . . ." Many people acknowledge that God exists, but they have not learned to relate to Him on a day-to-day level when they face struggles or difficulties. By grace, God tries to reach us every day, and He places reminders of Himself everywhere. He leaves clues of Himself all around us, clues that bellow out clearly, "I am here. You don't have to live in fear, you don't have to worry, I am here."

Jesus said to consider the lilies of the field (see Matthew 6:28) and the ravens of the air (see Luke 12:24). Meditating on how God adorns the fields and provides for the birds can remind us that He cares even more for us. A nice walk outdoors is a great opportunity to take a short vacation from the pressures of daily living and look at the trees, the birds, the flowers, and the children playing. How can anyone look at a baby and doubt the existence of God?

When we consider how some trees look totally dead in the winter and yet come back to life each spring, it reminds us that God will bring our lives back into full bloom even if we feel our circumstances are hopeless. We can look at a tree and think, *Last winter it looked barren, but now it flourishes.*

When I need a break from my work, I enjoy just looking at a tree and watching it blow in the wind. I have noticed dead pine needles clinging to the branches, but then a strong wind blows away the dried needles and makes room for the new buds ready to grow and thrive. It reminds me of how the wind of the Spirit is faithful to blow away things that aren't needed in our lives anymore, and how we can trust God to protect all that needs to remain.

Every morning the sun comes up, and every evening it goes down. The stars come out in the sky, and the universe remains in order as a

> By grace, God tries to reach us every day.

reminder that God is watching over us. He keeps the planets in orbit, and He can keep our lives in order too.

The ocean is so amazingly massive, and yet the mighty roaring waves stop at a certain place because God has commanded them to go no farther (see Proverbs 8:29). Think of all the different animals and how God has given each one of them a way to protect themselves. There are some that change color to match their environment when danger is near, and others that spew forth poison against their attacker.

In the book of Job God asked Job, "Where is the way where light dwells? And as for darkness, where is its abode?" (see Job 38:19). The point is that we do not know everything there is to know about God; we have not seen where the wind, rain, or lightning is stored (v. 22). It seems that any reasoning person could be assured of God's existence by simply being in and seeing nature, and yet there are those who persist in unbelief.

GOD SPEAKS THROUGH OUR NATURAL ABILITIES

We wonder, *What am I to do with my life? What is my purpose here? Does God have a calling on my life?* God answers these questions through our natural gifts and abilities. He leads us to our purpose through the natural skills and unique talents He bestows upon us.

God-given gifts are the skills a person easily performs without formal training. Many great artists know just how to put shapes and colors together, and so they enjoy designing buildings or sculpting beautiful and useful items. Many songwriters just write down the music they hear in their head. Some people are great at organizing, while others are natural counselors, helping people sort out their lives and their relationships. We derive great pleasure from doing what we are naturally good at doing.

If you aren't sure of your purpose, just do what you are good at doing, and then watch God confirm you by blessing your endeavors. Don't spend your life trying to do what you are not gifted to do. I tried to grow a garden and can tomatoes and sew my husband's clothes. I wasn't at all good at any of these things, and I even despised trying! It was obvious that God wasn't calling me to grow and preserve vegetables or to sew. But what if no one enjoyed gardening or canning or making clothes? God keeps our world in balance by giving each of us natural talent and pleasure in doing what needs to be done for the good of everyone around us.

God speaks of this division of gifts several places in His Word. Genesis 4:20-22 mentions that Jabal was the father of those who raised cattle and purchased possessions. His brother Jubal was the father of all the musicians who played the lyre and pipe. His half-brother Tubal-cain forged instruments made of bronze and iron. When Solomon built the temple, God empowered skilled craftsmen to do the work (see 2 Chronicles 2).

Then again, in the New Testament church, God makes it clear that He calls us to work together as one body in Christ. He appoints some to be apostles, some prophets, and some teachers. Some people are given the faith to be workers of miracles, some have gifts of healing, some are gifted to help others, some have gifts of administration, and the Word says that some are speakers in different tongues (see 1 Corinthians 12:28).

I tried to be like other women I admired, but I didn't understand at the time that they were gifted to do what they did. If we work at doing what we hate to do, we won't be good at it, and we won't glorify God with our lives. God came to give us an abundant life, not a miserable one (see John 10:10).

God wants us to enjoy life. How can we enjoy spending time doing something that we hate to do? There are wonderful tests available to help us discover which jobs we might enjoy. There are tests to help us understand how we process information and make decisions unique to our personalities. And there are tests that measure our spiritual gifts.

When people work at jobs they aren't gifted to do, they quickly become unhappy, and they make everyone around them unhappy too. Even in raising our children, we need to see what they are good at and give them household chores in line with their gifts. It is senseless to make everyone conform, because we are not alike. God needs each of us in our place. He needs every one of us to function to our fullness, without wasting time competing with someone with different gifts and talents.

When teams of employees are in their right places with everyone in his or her niche, operations run like a finely tuned machine. If we do what we are good at doing, we will enjoy it, because we will sense God's anointing on our efforts and achievements.

God speaks to us through this inner anointing. We know we are operating in our gifts and calling when what we do ministers life to others. If what we do makes us miserable and fills us with a sense of dread, it's possible we are not in God's perfect will. God gives us peace and joy to let us know we are fulfilling His perfect plan.

You can be called to do something that feels difficult to your flesh, but if you can get beyond your initial doubts and find that you have peace once you are doing it, then you will know that God is confirming your natural talents.

> It is senseless to make everyone conform, because we are not alike.

A woman I will refer to as Sharon (though that's not her real name) worked as our housekeeper a long time ago, but she didn't feel that her work was important. She wanted to do something else, so she begged God to lead her elsewhere. When Sharon left us, she tried several other jobs, but nothing ever gave her a sense of fulfillment. She finally started keeping house for somebody else and discovered that it was easy for her to do the work and to find people who needed her. She came full circle and worked for us again doing exactly what she had done years earlier. The difference was that this time she was happy—and peaceful.

People who are anointed to the "helps" ministries often struggle with the feeling that their work is not important. Satan deceives them to keep them from fulfilling their purpose. God's ideas are never achieved without help from the entire body working together toward His common goal. The devil hates our anointing and our unity when we use our gifts to supplement one another's calling.

It is important to hear from God and find out where you are called to bloom. Then get where you are supposed to be—get planted, rooted, and grounded—so you can bear fruit. We don't have enough years left on this earth to be miserable working at the wrong assignments. Sometimes we become tired of doing what we are anointed to do. But we find that we become miserable when we try to do something we are not called to do.

God will speak to you through your own gifts and talents. Make sure that what you are doing ministers life to you and not death. Watch for the evidence of grace on your life. If grace is not present, you will struggle through works of the flesh that are not ordained of God. I know I'm into works if I'm pushing and pushing to get something done and becoming resentful of the process. When there is no desire or energy from the Holy Spirit, and I dread the task, I know that God is telling me there is something wrong with my plan.

When we were working hard to get on television, I became so tired I cried, but I still loved the process. Sometimes I am so tired after our seminars that I just weep before the Lord. But then I get built up again and feel a burning desire to get to the next conference. I have to have grace on me to do that. God won't give us the grace to do something He hasn't called us to do.

I encourage you to look at what you enjoy, what you're good at, what God is giving you grace to do—and then let

God be God in your life. He wants to flow through you in many different ways, but it may not be the same way He flows through others. Trust His ability in and through you, and don't be afraid to be unique.

GOD SPEAKS THROUGH PEOPLE

As I have mentioned, we should be maturing in our faith to the point that we don't run to somebody else every time we need to know what to do in a certain situation. I am not implying that it's wrong to go to people whom we feel are wiser than we are to ask them for a word of counsel or advice. But I do believe it is wrong, and insulting to God, to go to people too often. Having someone give us advice is not necessarily a problem; the problem comes when we seek man rather than God. God is a jealous God (see James 4:5 and Deuteronomy 4:24), and He wants us to ask for His advice.

King David asked, "Where does my help come from? My help comes from the LORD, the Maker of heaven and earth" (Psalm 121:1-2 NIV). It is important to clearly establish in our hearts that we will seek God first, as David did. God wants to guide each one of us—not just full-time preachers, but every individual who puts their trust in Him.

I encourage you to seek balance in this area and to wean yourself from seeking other people's opinions, if you have a consistent habit of doing so. Discipline yourself to go to God first, but understand that He may use the counsel of other believers to clarify things for you or to give you assurance that you are truly hearing from Him.

People who will never ask for or take advice usually have

a big problem with pride. People can give us a word of advice that confirms what we already feel in our own spirit. The best policy is to seek God and let Him choose how and through whom He wants to speak to us. In Numbers 22:20-28 we see that God chose to speak to the prophet Balaam through his donkey. If we won't, or for some reason cannot, hear God ourselves, He uses many natural sources to reach us—including man.

There certainly are times when God uses people to speak "a word in due season" to one of His children (see Proverbs 15:23). If He chooses to speak through someone else, which He frequently does, we should humbly receive from anyone God chooses to use.

> Where there is no counsel, purposes are frustrated, but with many counselors they are accomplished. A man has joy in making an apt answer, and a word spoken at the right moment—how good it is! (Proverbs 15:22-23)

These Scriptures tell us that a right word spoken at the right time is a good thing.

Our ministry founded and provides oversight to a church in the inner city of St. Louis. I hired a new secretary, and she began attending that church. After about two years, I sensed that she might want to go to church somewhere else but felt it might offend me if she did so since the church she would be leaving was an outreach of Joyce Meyer Ministries.

> Seek God and let Him choose how and through whom He wants to speak.

I waited for a few weeks before saying anything to her because I wanted to be sure I was hearing from God. I have discovered that if what I am sensing *is* from God, it stays with me over a period of time. Sure enough, the feeling did not go away, so I approached her one day and said, "I don't know if you're happy at the city church or not, but I realize it might not be meeting your needs as a single woman. I just wanted to say that if you ever want to go somewhere else it will not offend me."

She looked at me in amazement and said, "Joyce, this is so good. I have been feeling like God wanted me to go somewhere else, but I really wanted to be sure I was hearing from God. This is great confirmation that what I have been feeling is correct."

As I have said, it is not wrong to go to other people. It can even be very beneficial. But mainly we should lean on God; if He chooses to speak to us through someone else, that is His choice. As in the case of my secretary, she was

> God was offering an answer, but I didn't like receiving it through a messenger.

seeking God, not me. God chose to speak to her through me.

Here is another example from my own life. When everything is right in my life, I sense a liberty when I preach. I also sense when there is great opposition against my message, because I feel a loss of freedom. At those times I know to pray and depend on God to move on my behalf.

There was a time that I knew something wasn't right, but I couldn't discern what was bothering me. It went on long enough that it affected my preaching more than once. Every week that I went to hold a certain meeting in St. Louis, I felt like it was the biggest mess I ever had. Each time we left the meeting I would comment to Dave, "Oh, that was terrible."

He'd ask, "What do you mean? That was a great message."

Something was bothering me, and God was gracious enough to keep it from showing through my preaching, but I was uncomfortable. After more than three weeks of concern, I thought, *That's it. I'm staying up tonight until I find out what's going on in my life. I can't go on like this anymore.* It seemed to bother me particularly when I was preaching. I stayed up late that night to seek God, but I couldn't get any direction from Him.

Then I learned that God sometimes speaks to us through other people. When I got up the next morning, Dave said, "I think I know what your problem is."

I thought, *Oh great! God won't tell me what my problem is, but He's going to tell Dave what my problem is.* So right away I had a poor attitude, thinking, *Oh sure, Dave is going to tell me what my problem is when he has problems himself. He doesn't need to tell me what my problems are.*

Perhaps you can relate to the apprehension I felt knowing that Dave was going to tell me what was wrong with me. I had cried out to God, "Lord, show me what's wrong!" God was offering an answer, but I didn't like receiving it through a messenger. All I could think was, *Well, who do you think you are, trying to tell me what's wrong?* We beg to hear from God, and yet it can make us mad if someone hears on our behalf. But sometimes that is the way God speaks.

So I said, "What do you think is wrong with me?"

He answered, "The other night when we were talking about so and so . . ." We had listened to a preacher, and I had commented that I felt he took too many directions in his message without bringing his main points to a close. I like to organize my thoughts and finish up loose ends when I preach. I really didn't say that much about him, but in my heart I was comparing his style with my own. I had simply said that he was kind of scattered in his preaching, and that it was hard to follow and understand.

Dave had agreed with me. Now he was saying, "I feel God told me you're having problems because of what you said about that preacher."

I resented being told by Dave that God had told him I had done something wrong, when Dave had fully agreed with me. Of course my first response was, "Yeah, well you said the same thing!"

Dave said, "Look, I'm not trying to start anything with you. All I'm telling you is what I believe God showed me. I wasn't asking God to show me what's wrong with you. God just showed me."

Dave is a matter-of-fact sort of person. You can take what he says or leave it, and it won't make any difference to him. He's kind of like God when it comes to truth, saying, "Here it is; do what you want to with it."

It took me a few hours, but I finally laid it before God and I asked, "Is that really why I am having these problems?"

Once my heart was opened to the truth, God showed me James 3:1, which says that those who are called to be teachers of the Word will be judged with greater severity than others. The chapter deals with the fact that teachers will be judged for sins of the mouth. As a teacher, I can't have a mixture of blessing and cursing coming out of my mouth (see v. 10). I can't preach the gospel and expect the anointing to be upon it if I gossip about somebody between services. If I judge the style of another preacher, I am judging God's anointing on him, and that will always affect my own preaching.

God taught me this lesson in a way I would never forget. If we take our God-given talent for granted by criticizing someone who is doing the same thing, our critical, judgmental eye will turn back upon ourselves until we remember that what we do well is only by the grace of God.

Judging others brings condemnation and judgment on ourselves, because in judging that person we are saying, "I'm great at this, but you have a problem." God lifted what I call the "holy ease" from what I did until I learned this lesson. God worked me over until I finally fasted and submitted to a state of repentance.

When I understood what I had done, I wept and cried out to God, because I knew He had worked greatly in my life. God spoke to me through Dave. He was also speaking to me through inner discomfort, which I will discuss in a later chapter. But the point I am making here is that we need to be open to messages God may send through people who love us and are praying for us. God wants us to keep humble hearts and be ready to hear from Him whichever way He chooses to speak.

GOD SPEAKS TO US OUT OF OUR OWN MOUTHS

Proverbs 16:1 says, "The plans of the mind and orderly thinking belong to man, but from the Lord comes the [wise] answer of the tongue." Many times God speaks to me out of my own mouth. I learned this when I was in a situation where I didn't know what to do. My own thoughts left me confused. God gave us rationalization to sort things out, but we can get weary from meditating on something if we're not on track with His wisdom. I wasn't getting anywhere with my circumstance until I took a walk with a friend.

I was facing a major decision that needed a godly answer, but I couldn't seem to find God's leading. My friend and I discussed a certain issue for about an hour as we walked together, enjoying the fresh air and each other's company. That's when I learned that sometimes wisdom comes out of our own mouth as we begin to talk to someone about a situation.

We talked about the situation and discussed several different possible solutions and their potential outcome. We talked about how good it might be if we handled the situation one way and how bad it might be if we handled it another way. Suddenly one particular answer settled in my heart.

What I decided I needed to do wasn't something I naturally wanted to do. A stubborn mindset is a great enemy of peace. Some of my struggle was because I wanted to convince God my situation should be dealt with differently from the way He was leading me. His voice was difficult to discern because my mind was already set against His plan.

We have to be willing to lay aside our own desires or we may miss a clear word from God. Our natural inclination is to manipulate things to work the way we want them to work. Some of our best childhood toys taught us that square pegs won't fit into round holes, and we must remember our plans don't always fit God's ways—no matter how violent we may become trying to make the two work together.

While my friend and I reasoned together, a wise answer came out of my mouth that I knew was from the Lord. It didn't come from my mind, but it rose from my inner being. God promises that if we seek Him, He will fill our mouth (see Psalm 81:10). Jesus promises to give us words and wisdom that none of our adversaries will be able to resist or contradict (see Luke 21:15).

I have learned not to discount anything, because God can and does speak through a variety of ways—and not all of them are something we would consider to be particularly spiritual. I have heard God speak to me through children and adults who had no idea that what they were saying was a direct word from the Lord for me.

> We have to be willing to lay aside our own desires.

GOD SPEAKS TO US THROUGH CORRECTION

When we need correction—and there are times when we all need it—I believe it is the Lord's first desire to correct us Himself. Whom the Lord loves, He chastens (see Hebrews 12:6). God's correction or chastisement is not a bad thing; it is always and ultimately only for our good. The fact that it works toward our good does not mean it always feels good or that it is something we enjoy immediately:

> For the time being no discipline brings joy, but seems grievous and painful; but afterwards it yields a peaceable fruit of righteousness to those who have been trained by it [a harvest of fruit which consists in righteousness—in conformity to God's will in purpose, thought, and action, resulting in right living and right standing with God]. (Hebrews 12:11)

In the example about the preacher whom I had judged, God used Dave to bring a word of correction to me as well as a word of revelation. I needed revelation to know why I felt so miserable, but to be honest, I was not expecting a correction about my behavior.

Correction is probably one of the most difficult things for most of us to receive, especially when it comes through another person. Even if we have problems, we don't want others to know we have them. I believe God prefers to correct us privately, but if we won't accept His correction, or if we don't know how to allow Him to correct us privately, He will correct us publicly, using whatever source He needs to use. In Balaam's case, God used his donkey.

Recently we were ministering in a foreign country, and the food was very unpleasant to us. We were not accustomed to the type of food served or the spices used in its preparation. I was in a restaurant where I was trying to convey to the waiter what I would like to have. He did not speak English very well, and I did not speak his language at all. Several people got involved, each of them trying to help me; but as it turned out, four different people ordered food for me.

I became frustrated, and my frustration was evident in my attitude and voice tone. I was behaving poorly in front of people who knew I had come to minister, and of course, my example to them was important. I already knew that my behavior was not very good, but the Lord wanted me to "really know." So when we got back to our room, Dave said, "You really must be careful about how you talk to people in situations like the one at lunch; your example wasn't very good."

Although I knew he was right, and I also knew God was using him to drive the point home and make sure I fully realized how important it was, my inclination was to say to Dave, "Well, I've seen you do the same thing." Had I done that, I would not have received the word, and God would have just tried to reach me another way—possibly one that would have been even more embarrassing or painful.

Often our first impulse upon being corrected by someone is to find fault with him or her. Satan tempts us to do this so we will divert the conversation away from the real issue. Being corrected by God through people in authority, such as the government, employers, parents, and teachers, is something each of us will encounter throughout life. We may not always like the source God chooses to use, but it is wisdom to accept correction in order to avoid "going around the mountain one more time" (see Deuteronomy 2:3).

Many think that hearing from God will always be supremely spiritual, but we can see from these examples that God uses natural things to reveal Himself to us as well as spiritual ones. Begin listening and watching for God to speak or show Himself strongly everywhere (see 2 Chronicles 16:9). You just never know when—or how—He may show up!

Questions for Discussion

1. How does nature testify to the reality of God? Give some personal examples.

2. What parts of creation do you most enjoy? What parts of creation most speak to you of the wonder and existence of God?

3. Do you know your calling in life? If not, what do you enjoying doing? What are your natural abilities and desires? Do you find that you derive pleasure from these things? Could this be your calling?

4. If you know your calling, has it been confirmed? How so?

5. Do you find yourself seeking man's opinion over God's opinion? How will you go about disciplining yourself to seek God first and foremost?

6. Have you ever experienced a situation where you felt the Lord speak something to you, and then it was confirmed by someone else? If so, describe. How did this help you?

7. What do you believe God is leading you to in response to this chapter?

5

God Speaks through Internal Peace

When God speaks, He gives us a deep sense of internal peace to confirm that the message is truly from Him. Even if He speaks to chastise us, the companion of truth leaves a calming sense of comfort in our soul. Jesus said, "Peace I leave with you; My [own] peace I now give and bequeath to you. Not as the world gives do I give to you. Do not let your hearts be troubled, neither let them be afraid" (John 14:27).

When the deceiver speaks to us, he cannot give peace. When we try to solve things with our own reasoning, we cannot get peace, because "the mind of the flesh [which is sense and reason without the Holy Spirit] is death [death that comprises all the miseries arising from sin, both here and hereafter]. But the mind of the [Holy] Spirit is life and [soul] peace [both now and forever]" (Romans 8:6).

Lay your decision on the scale with peace; don't proceed if peace cannot hold its weight against the guidance you have heard. You don't have to explain to others why you don't have peace about it; sometimes you won't know why yourself. You can say simply, "It's not wisdom for me to do this, because I don't have peace about it."

Even when you believe God has spoken to you, you should wait until peace fills your soul to do what He has instructed you to do. In this way you are assured your timing is right—plus peace is true confirmation that you are hearing from God. If you wait for peace, you will be able to be obedient with faith. Seek peace; there's power in having peace. Once you know that God has instructed you, You must do what you can to keep your peace and not become fearful.

I run my life by finding peace. If I am shopping, I don't buy something if I don't have peace about it. If I get into a conversation and start losing my peace, I become quiet. I have learned that it's important to keep peace in order to maintain power.

We should never act without peace. One might say that peace is an "internal confirmation" that action being taken is approved of by God: "And let the peace (soul harmony which comes) from Christ rule (act as umpire continually) in your hearts [deciding and settling with finality all questions that arise in your minds, in that peaceful state] to which as [members of Christ's] one body you were also called [to live]. And be thankful (appreciative), [giving praise to God always]" (Colossians 3:15).

God leads us by peace. The Bible says that peace is like an umpire that decides what is "safe" or what is "out." No peace? It's "out"! We are to *let* the inner harmony in our minds and souls rule and act as an umpire continually in our hearts, deciding and settling with finality all questions that arise in our minds. We are called to live in a peaceful state as members of one body in Christ.

We must learn to obey our own sense of right and wrong and resist doing things our inner conscience is uncomfortable doing. God gives or takes peace from our conscience to let us know whether we are on track.

We shouldn't look for unrealistic methods of communication from God. The majority of Christians never have a face-to-face encounter with Jesus as Paul did on his way to

Damascus. Even Paul didn't always experience the heavens opening up, angels appearing, or trumpets blasting every time God spoke to him. We can be led of the Spirit through internal peace every day of our lives.

> We shouldn't look for unrealistic methods of communication from God.

Beware of false peace. When we have a strong desire to do something, it can produce a false peace that actually comes only from our excitement. As time passes, this false peace disappears, and God's true will emerges for our lives. For this reason we should never move too quickly on important decisions. A little time of waiting is always wise and prudent. The Bible tells us not to be rash in what we say or hasty in the commitments we make (see Ecclesiastes 5:2-5). Here is an example that may help you better understand this point.

Someone Dave and I love very much was in need, and we wanted to meet that need. Doing so would have provided great joy for the individual with the need. It actually would have provided something this person had desired for a long time. I got excited about meeting this person's need and went to Dave, who agreed we should help. We proceeded with our plan, but the longer we went on with it, the more I lost my peace. This created a problem because I felt we had made a commitment—we had given our word, and I didn't want to go to the person and say I had changed my mind. I didn't mind saying I had made a mistake, but I didn't want to disappoint the person who by now was very excited.

A couple more weeks went by, and I just kept praying, "God, if what we are doing is not right, please make the entire thing fall through. Cause something to happen to let us know for sure what we are supposed to do."

I became more and more troubled inside and finally went to the individual and said, "Something is wrong with our plan; I have absolutely no peace about it." To my great relief the person felt the same way. Both of us had lost our peace, and neither one of us wanted to tell the other.

I highly respect the principle of "following peace." It has kept me out of trouble many times. Had I waited awhile after getting the "bright idea" to help this person, I am sure I would have sensed the lack of peace; but in my zeal and excitement to be a blessing, I had interpreted what I felt as peace, when in reality it was not. False peace can be dangerous, so be wise in these areas. Don't make serious decisions and commitments without doing an "inner check" to see if true peace abides within you.

God Speaks through Persistent Promptings

The Apostle Paul said his inner conscience was enlightened and prompted by the Holy Spirit bearing witness with him (see Romans 9:1). We can know if we are doing right, because our conscience will sense the evidence of truth. My conscience becomes more sensitive the more I grow in the Lord and the more responsibility He gives to me.

If I drop a piece of paper in the street and keep walking, my conscience convicts me, so I have learned to quickly turn myself around and pick up whatever I have dropped. It may sound extreme, but God is very involved with my conscience. Being faithful in little things is important to God.

According to Song of Solomon 2:15, it is the "little foxes" that spoil the vineyard. When we are willing to be faithful and obedient in little things, then God can trust us to be faithful over much greater things (see Matthew 25:14-23). I also believe being faithful to the small things God requires gives us faith for the greater things because our conscience is entirely clear. Obedience to our inner conscience brings the power of God into our life.

If we don't feel right about something like littering, we shouldn't just go ahead and do it anyway. It doesn't work to use the excuse that everyone else does what we're convicted not to do. Many of God's people are powerless because they continually do things their conscience tells them not to do. When we don't pay heed to our conscience, we lose our peace. The Word teaches us to be true to our convictions; if we do something we feel uneasy about, we stand condemned because we are not acting from faith (see Romans 14:23).

Sometimes God even prompts me to pick up somebody else's trash. I don't hear the audible voice of the Holy Spirit, but I feel an inner nudge to leave a place better than I found it. The Lord uses my obedience to teach me more about His character. He says to me, "When you make messes, would you like somebody else to clean after you? Everything you do in life is an act of sowing seeds that will return to you. You will reap *whatever* you sow. If you leave a mess for somebody else, someday someone will leave messes for you."

Quite often, Dave and I are led of the Lord to do something for someone who has demonstrated a valid need and a right heart before the Lord. We knew a man who needed a financial blessing. He had worked hard, and we had noticed his faithfulness over a long period of time. But, God had not led us to contribute to him in any specific way.

Then one day, I suddenly felt a prompting to do something for him. I let it rest and didn't act on it, but a few days later, I felt an inner prompting to give him a gift of money. Over a period of days, that prompting became stronger and stronger until I finally mentioned it to Dave. We were in agreement that the Lord was leading us to do something extra to help this man with his debt so he could move on in God.

If God is leading us by an inner prompting, that nudge will become stronger until it is obeyed. The fruit of our obedience will prove the prompting was truly from God. If we wait too long to respond to that prompting, God may have to move on to someone else in order to get His will accomplished. Therefore, we see that even in waiting we need balance. Don't move so fast that you don't even know if you have peace, and don't wait so long that God must choose someone else to use.

God Speaks through Our Heart's Desires

God speaks to us through the *sanctified* desires of our heart. I'm not saying that everything on our "want list" is from God, but when we long in our heart for the works of the Spirit to operate in our lives, we know God is leading us in His plan for us. Psalm 37:4 says, "Delight yourself also in the Lord, and He will give you the desires and secret petitions of your heart." This works two ways: yes, He gives us what we long for, but He also puts a longing in our heart for things He wants us to have.

We need to ask God to give us sanctified, or holy, desires. The Word says we are to eagerly pursue and seek to acquire love, and earnestly desire and cultivate spiritual endowments (see 1 Corinthians 14:1). We are to yearn for sanctified desires—not carnal desires!

The desires of the flesh are opposed to the desires of the Spirit, and the desires of the Spirit are opposed to the godless human nature (see Galatians 5:17). God puts a desire in us for something that will bring His righteousness, peace, and joy to situations in our lives (see Romans 14:17).

When God leads us to do something, there is growing zeal in us to see it achieved. Thinking about doing it motivates us. It is extremely different from desires of the flesh, because lusting for selfish pleasures leaves us tormented. But the inner drive for God's desires exhilarates us with enthusiasm.

> Therefore, we see that even in waiting we need balance.

We also sense a deep peace if the desire we have is truly from God and not merely a fleshly desire. I know God often leads us by desire, and yet I was hesitant to add this section about desires in the book because I do not want people to think that everything they desire is something they should have.

There are desires of the Spirit, and there are fleshly, carnal desires—right and wrong desires. We can desire something that isn't necessarily wrong in and of itself, and yet, it may be wrong for us.

I have asked God on several occasions what He wanted me to do about a specific thing, and He has responded in my heart, "Do what you want to do." The first time I heard Him say that, I almost rebuked it as being from Satan. I was afraid to believe God would give me that kind of liberty, but I know now that He gives more and more liberty as people grow spiritually into a state of maturity.

All I needed to do was think of my own children. When they were young and inexperienced, I made all their decisions for them. As they got older and more mature, I let them do more of what they wanted to do. They had been around Dave and me for a long time and were beginning to know our heart. Now all four of our children are grown, and most of the time they do what they want to do and rarely ever offend us because they know our heart and act accordingly.

After we walk with God for a number of years, we get to know His heart, His character, and His ways. If we are committed to following them, He can give us a greater liberty because we start acting as though we are "one with Him." Our spirit becomes filled with His Spirit, and our desires begin to merge with His. In John 10:30 Jesus said, "I and the Father are One." In John 8:28, He said, "I do nothing of Myself (of My own accord or on My own authority), but I say [exactly] what My Father has taught me."

In 1 Chronicles 17:2 we see that Nathan the prophet told King David to do all that was in his heart, for God was with him. At the time he said this, David was making preparations to build a tabernacle for God to dwell in. In verse 4 the prophet delivered a direct word from God saying that David was *not* to build the tabernacle, because God had assigned that task to another.

The thing that has always interested me about this particular situation is that it appears that the "normal" method of operation between David and God was for David to do what was in his heart, and God would be with him. Then obviously in this situation we see that God had another plan, and so He interrupted David's plan to build a house for Him. He even told David later that it was good that he had it in his heart, but that it was not His will for him to build it. He had chosen David's son Solomon to do it.

When I was learning how to hear from God and desiring with all my heart to be led by the Spirit, these verses really helped me to realize that we can move about with some degree of freedom following our *sanctified* desires, as long as we are ready to immediately go in another direction if God shows us we need to do so. It is not wrong to have a plan and follow it . . . if we are willing to give up our plan when God does not approve of it.

> The goal of every true believer is to be one with God.

In John 15:7 Jesus said, "If you live in Me [abide vitally united to Me] and My words remain in you and continue to live in your hearts, ask whatever you will, and it shall be done for you." How can this be possible unless there really is a merging of our desires with God's as we mature in Him?

The goal of every true believer is to be one with God. It happens spiritually when we are born again, and it occurs in mind, will, and emotion as we grow and mature spiritually. In Ephesians 4:15 the apostle Paul urges us, "Let us grow up in every way and in all things into Him Who is the Head." As we do so, our desires become His desires, and we are safe in following them.

The call that Dave and I have to our ministry is a good example of how God has led us by the desires of our heart. We couldn't travel every weekend, stay in hotels, and be gone from our family if our desire was not God given. God has put such a strong desire in us that we are motivated to make any sacrifice necessary or overcome any opposition that may come against us in order to accomplish God's will for us.

Sometimes simple desires come to us from God, because He likes to bless us. He sometimes puts desires in us for the things He wants to give us. His Word says, "What things soever ye desire, when ye pray, believe that ye receive them, and ye shall have them" (Mark 11:24 KJV).

Several years ago God was dealing with me about being sweet and kind. I had been going through a rough time, and the Lord said to me, "Now just be a sweetheart; just be a sweetheart."

Later, in a meeting, a lady came up to me and gave me a bangle bracelet, saying, "This is my favorite bracelet, but I believe God told me to give it to you." It had a word written on it in what looked like a foreign language. I asked, "What does this word mean?"

She said "Well, I got this bracelet in Hawaii, and this is the Hawaiian word for 'sweetheart.'" I knew then that God was giving me the bracelet as confirmation that He was dealing with my attitude.

I wore the bracelet for many years. It was a little bit small for me, and once I got it on, it was difficult, even inconvenient, to get it off. I really had no release from God to stop wearing it. Sometimes I wanted other bracelets, but there was just no peace in me to buy something else when I knew God had specifically given me that bracelet as a reminder of His direction in my life.

When the carnal part of us wants something, but our spiritual side is opposed, we need to wait for peace. When God is moving us to do something, there is agreement in both our carnal and spiritual desires. We should never override our spiritual desires for something that only our flesh demands.

After a few years I mentioned occasionally to Dave, "I would like to get another bracelet."

He would always say something like, "No, I like that bracelet; it's beautiful on you." Or, "You don't need another one; you couldn't find a prettier one than that."

Then one day I was shopping, and a desire stirred within me for a new bracelet. I hadn't been thinking about jewelry, and this desire was so sudden I felt it was from the Lord. I said, "Well, Lord, if this desire is really from You, I am just going to pray about it." Spiritual desires will motivate us to pray. I said, "God, I don't want anything except what You want for me. I don't need a new bracelet to be happy, but if You want me to have other bracelets, then I pray that You will give them to me, in Jesus' name." Then I went about my business.

I came home from that trip, and a couple of days later my close friend Roxane and I were spending some time together. She said to me, "I've got a present for you; it's something that I felt God told me to give you."

I opened her gift to find a new bracelet.

She continued, "It probably doesn't make sense to you why I would buy a bracelet. I know how you feel about the bracelet that you always wear. But I really believe that God spoke to me to get this for you. So I ordered it some time ago, and it just arrived."

It is interesting that God spoke to Roxane, telling her to get the bracelet, and while it was on its way, He put a desire in my heart to receive it. We wouldn't enjoy receiving something if we didn't desire it. Many times, God has put a desire in my heart for something that He wanted to give me.

The Bible says that God puts in us the desire both to will and to work for His good pleasure (see Philippians 2:13). We should pray for sanctified, holy desires. God puts desires in us to lead us in the way He wants us to go. If we desire to read the Word, then God is *inviting* us to read the Word. If we desire to pray when we are watching television, then God is speaking to us about the *need* to pray.

As we read in John 15, we know that if we abide in

Christ, if we continue our relationship with the Lord and dwell with Him over a period of time, His Word will abide in us. Then we can ask whatever we desire, and He has promised to give it to us.

To abide with Him is to "hang out" with Him, to live with Him, to become like Him, and to nurture the desires He puts in our heart, because that is His will for us. He puts desires in our heart so we will pray and ask for those things He wants us to have. Without prayer, God has no vehicle through which to work.

If you sense that God has put certain desires in your heart, then it's important to pray and ask for those things you desire. If you're not sure whether your desires are from Him, then say, "Lord, I believe You have put this desire in my heart, and so I am asking You for it. But I can be happy without it, because I am happy with You. Now it is up to You to do whatever You want to do."

Above all, remember that we are to be led by peace. No matter how much we may desire something, if we don't have peace deep in our heart about it, then it is not right for us.

GOD SPEAKS THROUGH A VOICE WE KNOW AND TRUST

In the Old Testament, when God started calling to Samuel, Samuel thought that his master, Eli, was calling him. Twice God called, and twice Samuel went to Eli asking what he wanted.

Both times Eli said to Samuel, "I am not calling you." So both times Samuel returned to his room. Then he heard the voice again. "Here I am, Eli, what do you want?" he asked.

Finally Eli said, "It must be God calling you" (see 1 Samuel 3:1-10).

God spoke to Samuel in a voice that was familiar to him so that he wouldn't be frightened. God wants us to listen, so He speaks to us through a voice that we will recognize. Sometimes it may sound like our own voice, sometimes it may sound like the voice of someone we know. But the point is that the voice will always bring peace when God speaks to us.

People who listen to my teaching tapes a lot tell me that frequently when they are about to make a decision or do something they are not sure about, they will hear me say something that gives them direction or correction. What they are really hearing is God speaking through His Word, but they have heard my voice speaking it to them for so long, it sounds like me when it comes to them. Samuel was accustomed to hearing Eli; therefore, when God called him, it sounded to him like Eli.

> Above all, remember that we are to be led by peace.

A woman told me at a meeting, "I was in this situation with my husband that was getting intense. God spoke to me, telling me what to do by reminding me of something you said on one of your tapes. All of a sudden I heard your voice from one of the tapes saying just what it was I needed to remember. God reminded me of it as a 'word in due season.'" Even though it was my voice she heard that was recorded in her memory bank, it was the Holy Spirit who called forth that memory when she needed it.

When God speaks to us, it doesn't sound like a loud voice booming out of heaven. Often He speaks to us through our own inner voice. We may think that we are talking to ourselves, but God's words in our spirit are always filled with a wisdom that we could never have on our own.

People have said to me, "You're always saying 'God said.' You sound like you have a conversation with God all the time." God is trying to talk to them all the time, too. They would hear Him if they would simply ask Him to speak to them, then listen to their inner man or conscience, and wait for Him to speak.

There are many different ways that God speaks to us. Many people think they don't hear from God because they are looking for some supernatural manifestation that simply won't happen. Most of the time, God speaks through a still, small voice within that sounds quite natural. God says that we are His sheep and that He is our Shepherd, and that His sheep know His voice (see John 10:1-5).

He may speak to us through nature, as He did with me a few days after I had received the baptism of the Holy Spirit. I drove past a field full of weeds, and in the middle of those weeds there were two or three patches of pretty flowers. I received an entire message from God about how flowers can grow in the middle of the weeds, and how good things are in our lives even in the midst of struggles and trials.

In all the years I have been listening for God's voice, I have had one open vision, and maybe four or five prophetic dreams. I am not making light of the fact that God speaks to some people through many dreams and visions, but most of the time He just fills my thoughts with His thoughts and confirms them with His written Word. He gives me peace, and I try to follow wisdom.

We need to discern the Lord's voice carefully, but we needn't over-spiritualize hearing from God. It is not as difficult as some may think. If God has something to say, He knows how to get His point across. It is our responsibility just to listen with expectancy and test what we hear against internal peace.

God has something to say about most everything that happens to us each day. It is such a shame for people to be lonely when God is eagerly waiting to talk to them and fellowship with them anytime they are willing to listen.

Questions for Discussion

1. Have you ever experienced peace accompanying direction from God? Describe it.

2. Do you use peace as a compass for internal confirmation regarding both the everyday details of your life and the larger decisions you face? How? And if not, why?

3. Is there something God is prompting you to do by an inner nudging? What is it? Have you noticed the inner prompt growing stronger as time passed?

4. Have you ever experienced God putting a desire in your heart for something? If so, did you pray about it? Did you then receive it? How was this edifying?

5. How do you determine if a desire you possess is from the Spirit or from your flesh? Do you act upon a desire before clearly knowing where it came from?

6. What are some of the ways you or others you know have heard from God?

7. What do you believe God is leading you to in response to this chapter?

6

God Speaks through Conviction

⌒

The Holy Spirit speaks to our conscience to convict us of sin and convince us of righteousness (see John 16:7-11). His conviction is intended to convince us to repent, which means to turn and go in the right direction rather than the wrong one in which we are currently going.

Conviction is entirely different from condemnation. It took me a long time to learn that fact, and as a result I erringly became condemned each time the Holy Spirit convicted me of something in my life that was not God's will. Conviction is meant to lift us out of something, to help us move up higher in God's will and plan for our lives. Condemnation on the other hand presses us down and puts us under a burden of guilt.

It is healthy and normal to feel guilty when we are initially convicted of sin; but to keep the guilty feeling after we have repented of the sin is not healthy, nor is it God's will. Conviction from the Lord never fills us with condemning shame. Shame fills us with a painful sense of disgrace and humiliating regret, often for something that we couldn't help. Frequently, the victims of abuse feel shame even when they did nothing to invite the cruelty. Shame is a vice the devil uses to repress and condemn us:

For God did not send the Son into the world in order to judge (to reject, to condemn, to pass sentence on) the world, but that the world might find salvation and be made safe and sound through Him. He who believes in Him [who clings to, trusts in, relies on Him] is not judged [he who trusts in Him never comes up for judgment; for him there is no rejection, no condemnation—he incurs no damnation]; but he who does not believe (cleave to, rely on, trust in Him) is judged already [he has already been convicted and has already received his sentence] because he has not believed in and trusted in the name of the only begotten Son of God. [He is condemned for refusing to let his trust rest in Christ's name.] (John 3:17-18)

The woman caught in adultery was given the opportunity to rest in the safety of Christ's name. By law she was guilty of breaking a commandment from God, and the Pharisees wanted to stone her. Jesus demonstrated to the crowd that He didn't come into this world to send sinners to their death, but to deliver them from sin so that they could live the abundant life. Jesus showed the crowd that they were all guilty of breaking the law in some way. He invited the woman's accusers to proceed with the stoning, but only if they themselves were guiltless of breaking the law. The Word says:

They listened to Him, and then they began going out, conscience-stricken, one by one, from the oldest down to the last one of them, till Jesus was left alone, with the woman standing there before Him in the center of the court. When Jesus raised Himself up, He said to her, Woman, where are your accusers? Has no man condemned you? She answered, No one, Lord! And Jesus said, I do not condemn you either. Go on your way and from now on sin no more. (John 8:9-11)

Jesus proved that condemnation only leads to death, but conviction delivers us to a new life free from sin. The accusers were convicted of their own sins in their consciences until one by one they learned not to judge the woman caught breaking the law.

Since God doesn't condemn us, we can fearlessly pray:

Lord,
Show me my sin. Convict me of what I am doing that breaks Your law of loving others. Convict me when I speak harshly to others. Keep my conscience tender to hear Your voice. Give me power to be free from sin. Amen.

Our conscience is given to us by God to keep us out of trouble. The Holy Ghost works to enlighten our awareness of what we are doing that leads to death, and what we need to do to enjoy the abundant life. If we ignore our conscience long enough, we will no longer sense God's conviction when we are guilty of sin. But if we tenderize our conscience so that our heart is sensitive to His correction, the Holy Spirit will lovingly judge our actions and convict us of the ungodly acts we do.

> Conviction delivers us to a new life free from sin.

He will nudge us when we speak harsh words against others that do not demonstrate His truth. God wants to work in each of our lives until we are motivated by a kind heart that reflects His presence.

People become hardened when they ignore their natural sense of right and wrong. Even saved people can have hard hearts. The more hard-hearted people are, the more difficult it is for them to quickly and promptly obey God. They have repressed their feelings so often that they are insensitive when their conscience is convicting them about something.

When people hurt us, we justify our own ungodly thoughts toward them, and in defense of not wanting to be hurt again, we treat others harshly. People who are hurting hurt other people. But all ungodly actions are still sin in the eyes of God. The cycle of pain has to be broken, and that's what Jesus came to do for us.

I was a hard-hearted, born-again, baptized-in-the-Holy Ghost woman for a long time. I loved God, but my heart was hard because of abuse that had happened to me. This in turn dulled my conscience. I had to let the Holy Spirit work *with* me and *in* me to break that hardness *off* of me. To do that, I had to pray for God to renew a right spirit *within* me (see Psalm 51:10).

The conscience is a function of our spirit that works like an inward monitor over our behavior. It functions to let us know when something is right and when something is wrong; consequently, it is greatly affected by knowledge of the standards and guidelines that God has established for us in His Word.

Growing in the knowledge of what God has said to His people awakens our conscience from its comalike state. Unsaved people may know when they are doing wrong, but they don't feel conviction like those of us who are born again, filled with the Holy Spirit, and fellowshipping with God on a daily basis.

The more time we spend in the presence of God, the more sensitive we become to our own actions that do not reflect God's heart. When we behave in an ungodly way, we quickly sense that we have stepped out of line with the way Jesus would have handled the situation.

We can have wonderful lives if we fill our minds with

God's Word and then simply obey our conscience. God said of the house of Israel:

> And I will give them one heart [a new heart] and I will put a new spirit within them; and I will take the stony [unnaturally hardened] heart out of their flesh, and will give them a heart of flesh [sensitive and responsive to the touch of their God] that they may walk in My statutes and keep My ordinances, and do them. And they shall be My people, and I will be their God. (Ezekiel 11:19-20)

I was so excited the first time I read that promise. This passage says that God will give us the power to have a tender conscience capable of being sensitive to Him. When God speaks through conviction, we should have a strong *desire* to do what is right.

The devil's condemnation fills people with hopelessness and futility. It's important for believers to discern the difference between conviction and condemnation. Many Christians still have the two mixed up. They think they are being condemned when they are being convicted.

I carried the sense of condemnation from being abused into my spiritual life and into my relationship with God. I felt there must be something wrong with me or else bad things wouldn't have happened to me. When I first learned what the Word said I should be doing, I felt as if every message condemned me, and I was even more ashamed of myself.

I loved God, but going to Bible conferences made me miserable. I would go home feeling worse than I had felt before the meetings. Hearing the Word should convict us, not condemn us. I'm not saying that God's Word should always make us feel comfortable—it should prod us to a higher level. But it should also give us the motivating power to make the climb.

When God works in people's lives, He condemns the sin, but He never condemns the sinner. His Word demonstrates love for the individual and nurtures and encourages him or her to come up out of that sin and to press on. God condemns the sin, but He gives mercy to the sinner, so we never need to be afraid to let God show us what we are doing wrong.

The Holy Ghost lives in us, and He can't get much closer to us than that. He doesn't come just to take up space, or because He has nowhere else to go. The Holy Spirit lives in us because He has a job to do, which is to teach, comfort, and lead us to God's plan for our lives.

The Holy Spirit knows exactly what we need. He is an expert at renewing our conscience so it is tuned to the heart of God. He is like the mechanic who quickly repaired a piece of machinery that no one else knew how to fix and then sent the owners a ten thousand dollar bill.

> The Holy Spirit lives in us because He has a job to do.

"Ten thousand dollars?" the owners argued. "All you did was tinker around a little bit!"

The mechanic answered, "One dollar is for my time. The rest is for knowing where to tinker."

Jesus has already paid the price for our repair, and the Holy Ghost knows exactly where to tinker. He knows what needs to be fixed and when. He doesn't spring everything on us at once, but there's no point in telling God we're not ready to change. He only convicts us to change when He knows we are ready. If it weren't the right time in our lives for that issue to be dealt with, then God would not convict us of it.

CONVICTION CONVINCES US TO ASK FOR GOD'S HELP

When God reveals to you an issue that needs to be dealt with in your life, you can trust that the anointing is also present to break the yoke of its bondage over you. If you put off confronting the behavior until you want to deal with it, you may have to face change without the anointing. When God convicts, He also anoints, so that is the best time to yield to His help in changing. We often want to do things in our own timing, and we struggle and struggle because we're not asking for God's help.

I have learned to deal with issues when God wants to deal with them. Even in the meetings I lead, I used to come with a plan and program. Sometimes I felt that God wanted me to stop the service and pray for somebody; but if it didn't fit into my program, I would put it off. Then later I would try to do what I thought God had wanted me to do earlier, and it would just fall flat. I had missed the flow of what was going on in God's timing. We need to act when God says to act.

At one meeting I took a break and went into the women's restroom where a lady said, "Well, I wish you would have an altar call for smoking; I'm having a terrible time with smoking."

As soon as she spoke, the Holy Ghost filled me with faith for her. I laid hands on her and said, "Be healed in the name of Jesus." She probably thought I was a little bit wild, but I have learned to act when I feel faith move in me. When God's anointing comes to set people free, it is a *now* moment; it isn't something we set aside and pick up later. I knew to pray right then.

I often pray for people who want to be free from smoking. I don't condemn those who smoke, but many people are worn out from the bondage of their addiction and need a miracle from God to be set free of it. Some may believe smoking is no worse than gossip or judgment or overeating or anything else but it is hard on our bodies, and it is expensive.

I started smoking when I was nine years old and smoked for years. I was so grateful when God finally delivered me from the habit. God's conviction led me to believe Him for deliverance from many habits, including the habit of a bad attitude and from speaking negative words, overeating, and smoking.

When conviction comes on us, it is God speaking to us because He wants to help us in some area. He is not condemning us, but He's trying to let us know that He wants us to live a long and healthy life. When the Holy Spirit speaks to your conscience about changes that are needed, pray right then. Ask God to deliver you and bring about those changes through your faith in Jesus. You can pray for deliverance from addictions and ungodly behavior with this prayer:

Father,
In the Name of Jesus, I release my faith to receive Your deliverance right now. I take authority over the habit of _____ (name the habit, e.g., nicotine, alcohol, drugs). I command this thing to be loosed from me, and I pray that You will strengthen me to turn away from this behavior and sin no more.

I pray that You will do one of two things: either deliver me right now, so I will never want to do this again, or give me the strength to say no to this habit until I am no longer in bondage to it. This I pray in the name of Jesus. Amen.

The anointing is present when we call on the name of Jesus. I believe that you can be miraculously delivered of painful addictions while reading this book. Always move in faith when you sense God convicting your conscience. It serves as a trustworthy compass to true godly living.

THE HOLY SPIRIT WILL NEVER CONDEMN US

As I said earlier, Jesus said, "You're going to be better off if I go away, because when I go away, I'm going to send the Holy Spirit to you" (see John 16). It is so wonderful to have close fellowship with the Holy Spirit—it is so wonderful to have Someone in our lives to let us know when we are going the wrong way.

My mouth got me into trouble for years. I ruined relationships and embarrassed myself through the things I said. Now I can sense the Holy Spirit convicting me, and most of the time I choose to turn in another direction before I get into trouble. God no longer has to preach a four-part series to me to convince me to obey Him. He simply sounds an alarm in my spiritual heart and stirs me to act the way Jesus would act. When our conscience is sensitive to the voice of conviction, God can keep us *out* of trouble instead of having to rescue us *from* trouble all the time.

Jesus was speaking of the Holy Spirit when He said, "And when He comes, He will convict and convince the world and bring demonstration to it about sin and about righteousness" (John 16:8). He didn't say anything about the Holy Spirit bringing condemnation. He said He "brings demonstration . . . about sin and about righteousness." The

> God can keep us *out* of trouble instead of having to rescue us *from* trouble.

Holy Ghost reveals the results of sin and the results of righteousness so that people can see life and death set before them and call on God to help them choose life.

People who live in sin have wretched, miserable lives. I have met individuals my age whom I knew years ago and who have not been living for God. The rough, rugged lifestyle they have chosen has taken a toll on them. The sour, sad, miserable choices they have made are visible because sin has left them looking old and ugly.

The power of God can make us look better and keep us feeling younger, because we are not living the hard life of sin. This is the power of God at work in the world today demonstrating the results of sin and the results of righteousness. The line between the two is becoming vividly distinct. It is no longer difficult to tell who belongs to God and who doesn't. The world that we live in is full of gross darkness (see Isaiah 9:2). But God gave Jesus "for a light to the nations" (see Isaiah 42:6). His light is visible in the faces of true believers.

ABIDE IN GOD'S PRESENCE

I often wonder how any human being can get through one day without God. If I feel that I am missing God's intimate presence for a day, I can hardly stand it. I'm like a little kid who has lost his mother in a store; all I can do is spend my time trying to get back to my parent. I don't want to be out of fellowship with the Lord. I must have Him to get through every single day of my life.

Through my conscience the Holy Spirit lets me know if I'm doing something wrong that grieves Him or that interferes with our fellowship. He shows me if I've done something wrong and helps me get back to the place I need to be. He convicts and convinces me, but He never, never condemns me.

God loves us even more than we love our own children, and in His love He disciplines us. I remember how I hated to take privileges away from my children. But I knew they were bound for trouble if they didn't learn to listen to me. God has the same concern for us, but He is patient. He tells us and tells us, again and again, what we ought to do. He may tell us fifteen different ways, trying to get our attention.

His message of convicting love is everywhere. He wants us to listen to Him because He loves us. If we persist in our ways, He withholds privileges and blessings from us. But He only does so because He wants us to mature to a place where He can pour out His full blessings upon us. If God freely gave us His Son Jesus, surely He won't hold back anything else we need. He wants to bless us radically and outrageously:

He who did not withhold or spare [even] His own Son but gave Him up for us all, will He not also with Him freely and graciously give us all [other] things? Who shall bring any charge against God's elect [when it is] God Who justifies [that is, Who puts us in right relation to Himself? Who shall come forward and accuse or impeach those whom God has chosen? Will God, Who acquits us?] Who is there to condemn [us]? Will Christ Jesus (the Messiah), Who died, or rather Who was raised from the dead, Who is at the right hand of God actually pleading as He intercedes for us? (Romans 8:32-34)

If condemnation is filling our conscience it is not from God. He sent Jesus to die for us, to pay the price for our sins. Jesus bore our sin and condemnation (see Isaiah 53). We should get rid of the sin, but not keep the guilt. Once God breaks the yoke of sin from us, He removes the guilt too. He is faithful and just to forgive all of our sins and to continuously cleanse us from all unrighteousness (see 1 John 1:9).

Every single day of our lives we need forgiveness. The Holy Spirit sets off the alarm in our conscience to recognize sin, and He gives us the power of the blood of Jesus to continuously cleanse us from sin and keep us right before Him.

COME BOLDLY TO GOD'S THRONE

Often when we are convicted of sin, we become grouchy while God is dealing with us. Until we admit our sin, become ready to turn from it, and ask for forgiveness, we feel a pressure that squeezes out the worst we have in us. As soon as we come into agreement with God, our peace returns, and our behavior improves.

The devil knows that condemnation and shame keep us from approaching God in prayer so our needs can be met and we can once again enjoy fellowship with God. Feeling bad about ourselves, or thinking that God is angry with us, separates us from His presence. He doesn't leave us, but in fear we withdraw from Him.

That's why it is so important to discern the truth and know the difference between conviction and condemnation. Remember, if you heed conviction, it lifts you up and out of sin; condemnation only makes you feel bad about yourself.

When you pray for people, the Holy Spirit convicts them of their sin, and they often start acting worse than they did before. But don't let that make you believe your prayers are having no effect. It is actually a good sign that God is indeed working, convicting them

> Condemnation and shame keep us from approaching God in prayer.

of sin, and trying to convince them of their need to change. So keep praying!

When praying, ask regularly for God to convict you of your own sin, realizing that conviction is a blessing, not a problem. If only perfect people could pray and receive answers, nobody would be praying. We don't need to be perfect, but we do need to be cleansed of sin. As I begin my prayer time I almost always ask my heavenly Father to cleanse me of all sin and unrighteousness. When we pray in Jesus' name, we are presenting to our Father all that Jesus is, not all that we are.

Conviction is vitally necessary in order to walk with God properly. This gift of conviction is one way to hear from God. Don't make the mistake of letting it condemn you as I did for years. Let conviction lift you to a new level in God. Don't resist it; receive it.

Questions for Discussion

1. Is your heart hardened? Why? Has sin caused you to turn away from God?

2. How can God always be with us and yet our sin separate us from Him?

3. In your life, do you distinguish between condemnation and conviction of the Holy Spirit? If not, what do you need to do to be able to make this distinction?

4. Describe a time when you felt condemned by your sin. What did you do? What was the end result?

5. Describe a time when the Holy Spirit convicted you of sin. What did you do? What was the end result?

6. Is there an addiction in your life that the Spirit is urging you to overcome? If so, what is it? What is your plan of attack?

7. In your own words, what is the difference between conviction by the Holy Spirit and condemnation?

8. What do you believe God is leading you to in response to this chapter?

7

Develop a "Reining Ear"

❧

I was fascinated to learn that some horses have what their trainers call a "reining ear." While most horses are guided and led by a strap fastened to the bit in their mouth, some horses keep one ear turned to their master's voice. One ear is open for natural warnings; the other is sensitive to the trusted trainer.

Elijah needed to hear from God, and fortunately he had a reining ear toward God even though in the natural world he was quite frightened by what he had heard. He had just defeated 450 false prophets in a duel of power between their silent Baal and the God of Abraham, Isaac, and Jacob. Now Queen Jezebel, who had been killing off the Lord's prophets, threatened to kill Elijah within the day. Elijah ran for his life, hid in a cave, and prayed to God to die before Jezebel found him. Then the Lord sent His word to Elijah, asking, "What are you doing here?"

Elijah recounted the events and the threats and said, "They seek my life, to take it away."

So the Lord demonstrated His presence to Elijah once again, telling him to stand on the mountain before Him. A strong wind tore through the mountains, and broke rocks into pieces; but the LORD was not in the wind. After the wind, there was a terrible earthquake; but the LORD was not in the earthquake. After the earthquake, a fire broke out;

but the LORD was not in the fire. After the fire there came "a still, small voice." Then the Lord told Elijah to leave his hiding place and go anoint the next kings to serve over Syria and Israel and the prophet who was to take his place (see 1 Kings 16-19). And Elijah obeyed the still, small voice of the Lord.

Elijah's story helps us understand how to hear God when we need direction. God didn't reassure Elijah with a showy, flashy manifestation of power, although He had already proven that He was capable of doing so. God spoke to His prophet through a still, small voice. God still chooses to communicate directly to His children through a whisper deep within their spirits.

"God is a Spirit (a spiritual Being) and those who worship Him must worship Him in spirit and in truth (reality)" (John 4:24). Jesus explained why some people don't hear the voice of God:

Not one of you has ever given ear to His voice or seen His form (His face—what He is like). [You have always been deaf to His voice and blind to the vision of Him]. And you have not His word (His thought) living in your hearts, because you do not believe and adhere to and trust in and rely on Him Whom He has sent. [That is why you do not keep His message living in you, because you do not believe in the Messenger Whom He has sent.] You search and investigate and pore over the Scriptures diligently, because you suppose and trust that you have eternal life through them. And these [very Scriptures] testify about Me! And still you are not willing [but refuse] to come to Me, so that you might have life. (John 5:37-40)

Jesus also taught:

I assure you, most solemnly I tell you, unless a man is born of water and [even] the Spirit, he cannot [ever] enter the kingdom of God. What is born of [from] the flesh is flesh [of the physical is physical]; and what is born of the Spirit is spirit. Marvel not [do not be surprised, astonished] at My telling you, You must all be born anew (from above). The wind blows (breathes) where it wills; and though you hear its sound, yet you neither know where it comes from nor where it is going. So it is with everyone who is born of the Spirit. (John 3:5-8)

When we are born again, we are made alive in our spirit to be sensitive to the voice of God. We hear His whisper even though we cannot tell where it comes from. He whispers to convict, correct, and direct us by a still, small voice deep within our heart. I can communicate with my husband through my flesh, my visible body, my mouth, my facial expressions, and gestures but if I'm going to talk to God I have to communicate with Him in my spirit.

God speaks to our inner being through direct communion, through our intuition (a sense of unexplainable discernment), and through our conscience (our base convictions of right and wrong). Our spirit can sense knowledge that we may not have evident rational facts to prove.

> If I'm going to talk to God I have to communicate with Him in my spirit.

For example, when we are sensitive to hearing from God, we can look at situations that appear to be in order and just intuitively "know" that something is wrong. That check in our spirit keeps us from jumping into agreement with someone or becoming involved in some situation that is not right for us.

It's wonderful to be led by the Spirit of God. I remember the time we completed a music and Scripture tape, which several people worked on to make sure everything was done correctly. It's tedious work and quite expensive to change a recording once the master copy is completed. I had listened to the tape with our producer, and Dave and I had said, "Yes, it's good."

But one morning during the following week, as I was praying, I kept feeling that I needed to listen to that tape again. To be honest, I didn't want to take time to listen to a tape for another hour when I had other messages I wanted to study. But God sometimes leads me to do things that I don't want to do, and a persistent prompting made me feel that I needed to check the tape one more time. When the feeling didn't go away, I finally said, "Okay, I'll listen to the tape."

As I listened to the first Scriptures on the tape, I realized I had misquoted a Bible reference. The tape was being sent the next day for the final mastering. If I had not listened to it *that* day, the mistake would have been duplicated on ten thousand copies of that tape before we would have been able to correct it. I thank God for the leading of the Holy Spirit.

God's voice has kept us out of trouble many times. In this case, God saved us a lot of money and a lot of embarrassment and phone calls from our audience, members who would have called in to say, "Does Joyce know that she's quoting the wrong Scripture on this tape?"

Thankfully, I was sensitive enough to God's voice that I listened to the tape; by His grace, God kept after me until I did. Thank goodness for grace! If we consistently disobey God's leading, we will eventually sear our conscience and allow it to harden against the voice of God (see 1 Timothy 4:1-2). It's difficult for God to lead us away from trouble if we're not softhearted enough to pick up those gentle little leadings of the Holy Spirit.

It's well worth it to do what God wants us to do. Every single time we do the right thing, it causes us to be more confident in His leading, and our conscience becomes a little more sensitive to His voice. Keep this point in mind: It pays to obey!

The unsaved man is spiritually dead, which means that communion with God and His intuitive promptings are dead. He doesn't get things by revelation; he only knows what he learns in his head. But if we are spiritually alive, God can show us things that we couldn't know any other way except by divine revelation.

I have had jobs in which I did not have the natural knowledge to do the assignments I was given, yet God led me and enabled me to do things that I was not trained to do. I have a high school education, and I never studied how to lead a ministry or use mass communications effectively. But God has equipped me and my team with all we need to minister on television and radio broadcasts worldwide. God leads us step by step, by His Spirit. He teaches us as we take steps of faith.

A believer can be led by the Spirit, but the unregenerate man (the man who is not born again) doesn't have that privilege. All he can do is reason with his mind, walk according to his will, and follow his emotions, because his spirit is not alive to the voice of God. He is limited to his natural abilities. That's why so many people in the world just keep searching for more information and more education. They know nothing of being taught and guided by God's Spirit.

I'm not against education, because I think education is great. But some people think it is the most important thing in life. They believe a person who is not highly educated can do very little.

God's Word says in 1 Corinthians, chapter 1, that He uses the weak and foolish things of the world to confound the wise. He uses what the world would discard as having little or no value so that no mortal flesh can glory in His presence. In other words, God can use anybody who is committed and submitted to Him and His leadership.

Many of the people who have high positions in our ministry have no professional training to do what they are doing. For example, I was a bookkeeper and an office manager, Dave was in the engineering field, our general manager was a welder, one of our division managers was a dockworker, and another was a teachers' aid.

Education certainly can be valuable, and we do have people on our staff with training in their field, but educated people still need to lean on God and not on their education alone.

GOD LEADS US BY OUR CONSCIENCE

A person who is not saved doesn't hear the voice of God, and his intuition is not completely operative. But God makes Himself known to everyone in his conscience, because if a person's conscience is totally dead, God would never be able to convict him of sin and get him saved. So the Holy Ghost works in sinners' lives to wake up their conscience enough to realize their need to repent and receive Christ as their Lord and Savior. But people's conscience can become dull, as if in a coma, if their inner sense of right and wrong is ignored for too long.

I have dedicated my life to the mission of waking up

people's conscience so they will learn to listen for the voice of God calling them to a higher level and a better life. Yes, they can know the love of the Father, the grace of Jesus Christ, and the communion and fellowship of the Holy Spirit (see 2 Corinthians 13:14).

The cleansing blood of Jesus has amazing power on the conscience. I was born again at age nine, and I distinctly remember feeling terribly guilty before I prayed and asked Jesus into my heart, and feeling very clean and fresh after repenting and accepting Him as my Savior. We can maintain that fresh, clean feeling through the power of regular repentance. First John 1:9 teaches us that He is faithful and just to *continuously* cleanse us from all unrighteousness if we freely admit that we have sinned and confess our sins.

> God makes Himself known to everyone.

I spent many years of my life with no knowledge of God's Word and therefore was deceived by Satan and felt guilty all the time. I went to church, yet knew nothing of being truly submitted to God. I was religiously performing my duty, but had no idea I could learn how to be daily led by God's Spirit. I was following church rules, not the Holy Spirit. In some cases the church rules and the leadership of God are the same, but that is not always the case.

I did what I wanted to do; I didn't care how I acted most of the time, nor was I sensitive to how I treated people. Actually I gave very little thought to my behavior in any area. In February 1976 I made a full commitment of my life to the Lord. I accepted Him as my Lord and not just my Savior. I always say that prior to that time I had enough of Jesus to stay out of hell, but not enough to walk in victory. I truly did believe that Jesus was my Savior, and that He died for me and paid for my sins. I believed He was my only way to heaven, but I was not being taught the need to mature and grow up spiritually. I heard a lot of doctrine when I went to church, but very little that was applicable to everyday life.

My ear was not tuned to the Holy Spirit; I certainly did not have a "reining ear." It was time for me to start learning how to follow God's leading, not my own or my friend's or the world's.

Many people live under continual guilt and condemnation because they don't know how to heed the voice of conscience. Their conscience bothers them, but instead of finding out why and trusting God's grace to help them change or correct what is wrong, they ignore God's leading and remain miserable.

Whenever your conscience bothers you, it's important to find out why and do something about it as quickly as possible. If you don't have peace, get alone with God and talk to Him to find out why you are uncomfortable and let Him work a change in your life.

If we want to be led by the Spirit of God, we must be willing to grow up and become mature sons and daughters of God. We are not to be led around by the appetites of our flesh. We are not to be led around by the devil, our friends, our emotions, our mind, or our own will. We are to be led by the Spirit of God.

The more you know His Word, the more you understand that He will not lead you astray or direct you into anything that is bad for you. Even things that may seem uncomfortable in the beginning will ultimately turn into glorious blessings for your life if you will just follow the leading of the Holy Spirit. Spiritual maturity and learning to follow the leadership of the Holy Spirit are one and the same.

There are places in the Bible where believers are referred to as "children of God," and there are places in the Bible where they are referred to as "sons of God." I use this fact to make a point that although we love our children no matter how mature they are, there is a difference in what we can trust our little children with and what we can trust to our grown sons and daughters. There is a difference between the liberties and the privileges and the responsibilities that we can give to mature sons and daughters.

We come into the kingdom of God as little children, even babies, in Christ. Then we learn about our covenant and about being joint heirs with Christ, and we hear about the wonderful things God wants

> God has a lot of good plans for us.

to do for us. But if we never grow up, even though all of those things may be set aside in an account for us, we will never get to enjoy our inheritance.

We bought our son a car before he turned sixteen. It sat in the garage for six months. Our intention was to give it to him, but if he had never learned to drive, we would never have given him the car. Likewise, God has a lot of good plans for us. He has a storehouse full of blessings for each of us, but we have to mature and grow up in order to have them. One of the primary signs of being mature in the Lord is our willingness to be led by the Spirit of God.

Dave and I appreciate the fact that our grown sons and daughters know what we want and what we don't want, what we approve of and what we don't approve of. We don't have to run around with a list of rules and regulations, always giving them laws to follow. When they were little, we had a list of do's and don'ts for them, but the longer they lived with us, the more they came to know and follow our hearts.

GOD WANTS US TO TRUST HIM

The more time we spend listening to God, the more aware we become of how He wants us to behave and how He wants us to act:

> For all who are led by the Spirit of God are sons of God. For [the Spirit which] you have now received [is] not a spirit of slavery to put you once more in bondage to fear, but you have received the Spirit of adoption [the Spirit producing sonship] in [the bliss of] which we cry, Abba (Father)! Father! The Spirit Himself [thus] testifies together with our own spirit, [assuring us] that we are children of God. And if we are [His] children, then we are [His] heirs also: heirs of God and fellow heirs with Christ [sharing His inheritance with Him]; only we must share His suffering if we are to share His glory. (Romans 8:14-17)

Share His suffering? The bottom line is anytime our flesh wants to do one thing and the Spirit of God wants us to do something else, if we choose to follow the Spirit of God, our flesh is going to suffer. We don't like that, but the Bible simply says that if we want to share Christ's glory, we have to be willing to share His suffering.

I can still remember suffering through those early years of walking in obedience when I thought: *Dear God, am I ever going to get over this? Am I ever going to get to the point where I can obey God and not hurt while I'm doing it?*

I like to encourage those who are just beginning to heed the voice of God that once the fleshly appetite is no longer in control they will get to the point where it is easy to obey God—the place where they actually *enjoy* obeying God. In

Romans 8:18 Paul said, "I consider that the sufferings of this present time (this present life) are not worth being compared with the glory that is about to be revealed to us and in us and for us and conferred on us!"

In modern language Paul was saying, "We suffer a little now, but so what! The glory that will come from our obedience far outshines the suffering we endure now." That is good news. Whatever we may go through is absolutely nothing compared to the good things that God is going to do in our lives as we continue to press on with Him.

A true sign of maturity is demonstrated in the way we treat other people. The Bible is a book about relationships: our relationship with God, our relationship with our self, and our relationship with other people. Most would agree that the biggest challenge is getting along with other people.

In Galatians 5:15 Paul said, "If you bite and devour one another [in partisan strife], be careful that you [and your whole fellowship] are not consumed by one another." Paul wrote this to born-again, baptized-in-the-Holy Ghost Christians, yet he had to constantly remind them how important it was for them to get along with each other.

If people make us mad, the Word of God in us will start prompting us to forgive them. It's not easy to do, but we have to choose whether we are going to fulfill the desires of the flesh or whether we're going to be led by the Spirit.

Our flesh can get all stirred up and make us want to throw a screaming fit, but if we are led of the Spirit, we will suffer on Christ's behalf and choose to forgive. That's the suffering to which Paul was referring in Romans. Sometimes we get the suffering message all out of kilter and out of balance.

True Bible suffering is not poverty, disease, or disaster. Jesus came to heal, deliver, and set us free from that kind of suffering. Satan attacks us with those things, and we may have to take them for a season while we are waiting for God to deliver us; but that's not the kind of suffering that God wants us to endure permanently. He wants us to be long-suffering with each other.

If we get into strife, our fellowship with one another can become consumed. We're to walk and live habitually in the Holy Spirit, laying down the habit of hurting people. If we walk in the flesh, we won't get along with anybody, because the bottom line is we all like to have our way about every-thing. The flesh is selfish and self-centered. If we walk in the flesh, we will never act like Jesus.

God teaches us what is right, and all day long, every day, seven days a week, we have to choose the right thing over the wrong thing. Until the last trumpet sounds, and Jesus comes to get us, we're going to have to say no to self and yes to God.

> We have to choose the right thing over the wrong thing.

Like the horse with the "reining ear" always tuned toward his master, we must be willing to follow the Lord in *all* His leading, not just the leadings we feel good about or happen to agree with. We won't always like what we hear Him tell us.

We must realize that in order to follow God, the flesh must be told no, and when that happens the flesh suffers. It is also important to understand that there may be times when we are galloping full speed ahead in one direction when suddenly the Master tells us to *stop and instructs us to go in another direction.*

In Galatians 5:16 the apostle Paul told us, "But I say, walk and live [habitually] in the [Holy] Spirit [responsive to and controlled and guided by the Spirit]; then you will certainly not gratify the cravings and desires of the flesh (of human nature without God)."

If we follow the leading of the Spirit, we won't satisfy or fulfill the desires of the flesh that lead us away from God's best. This verse doesn't say that the desires of the flesh are going to disappear and go away. But if we choose to be led by the Spirit, we won't fulfill the desires of the flesh—and the devil won't get his way.

We will sense a war going on in us as we choose to conform to God's leading. Our flesh is never going to want what the Spirit wants, and even when our spirit wants to follow the Lord the appetites of our flesh will tempt us to disobey God. As long as we're here on the earth our flesh and our born-again heart will *not* be in natural agreement (see Romans 13:14, Galatians 5:17). So we have to learn to obey the Spirit of God and tell our flesh to submit.

GOD WANTS TO GOVERN OUR LIVES

God wants to be in charge of the government of our lives. When we are led by the Spirit, we will fulfill the just requirements of the law. When I follow the leading of the Spirit, I know that I am pleasing the Lord.

If I get mad at Dave and the Holy Ghost tells me to apologize, if I do so, then I please the Lord. If I am tempted to gossip about somebody, but I feel that little signal from the Holy Ghost telling me to get out of the conversation, if I stop my tongue immediately, I am being obedient. If I am speeding down the highway and the Holy Ghost says,

"You're exceeding the speed limit," if I ease up on the gas pedal, I am honoring God.

If we aren't going to be obedient to God and allow Him to govern our lives in that which is little, then He will never make us rulers over much. Many people want to be in charge of big things of life but they don't want to pay attention to God in the little things.

Remember what I said earlier: "*If you're not willing to hear God in one area, it may render you unable to hear in another.*" We cannot pick and choose what we will and won't hear. God wants to govern our lives; it is important to turn the reins of our lives over to Him.

Paul consistently taught people to be led by the Spirit. He was not ministering the law, but the Spirit. He spent a lot of time teaching the difference between law and grace. He said of God:

[It is He] Who has qualified us [making us to be fit and worthy and sufficient] as ministers and dispensers of a new covenant [of salvation through Christ], not [ministers] of the letter (of legally written code) but of the Spirit; for the code [of the Law] kills, but the [Holy] Spirit makes alive. Why should not the dispensation of the Spirit [this spiritual ministry whose task it is to cause men to obtain and be governed by the Holy Spirit] be attended with much greater and more splendid glory? (2 Corinthians 3:6, 8)

Paul was saying that the dispensation of the Spirit, or the new covenant, will cause men to do two things: first of all, to obtain the Holy Spirit (to have the Holy Spirit in their lives), and second, to be governed by the Holy Spirit in their lives.

That's the pattern all ministers of the gospel should follow:

to cause people to receive Christ, and to receive the Holy Spirit into their lives. But many people pray a sinner's prayer and then go back to living the way they have always lived without much change. They obtain the Spirit of God in their lives, but they don't let Him govern their lives on a daily, moment-by-moment basis.

Their failure or refusal to listen for God creates a barrier between them and the blessings of God. If they would simply obey their conscience, they would please God and have the abundant life He wants them to enjoy. But people do what they want to do, or they do what everybody else is doing, instead of following the leading, the promptings, and the guidance of the Holy Spirit. But all those who learn to be governed by the still, small voice of God will see blessings pour into their lives and will have the delight of knowing that they are pleasing God.

Questions for Discussion

1. What does it mean to hear the still, small voice of God in your spirit? Have you experienced this?

2. How do you know God's still, small voice is not your own emotion or desire?

3. Describe a time when the Spirit reminded you of something practical. How did the situation turn out?

4. What is a reining ear? Do you have one? How can you cultivate a reining ear?

5. If a person's conscience can become too dull, how can the Holy Spirit convict that person of sin? Have you had this experience before?

6. What is the communion and fellowship of the Holy Spirit? How have you felt it in your life?

7. What do you believe God is leading you to in response to this chapter?

PART TWO

~

Learning to Obey

My mother and My brothers are those who listen to the Word of God and do it!

—JESUS IN LUKE 8:21

8

Obedience Keeps Our Conscience Tender

◦───◦

God may speak to us in a dozen different ways, but if we harden our conscience, or heart, and refuse to obey Him when He speaks to us, we will miss out on blessings that He wants to give to us. I can remember when every little thing that God wanted me to do, or everything that I was doing He *didn't* want me to do, became a wrestling match between us. It would take weeks, sometimes months, and sometimes even *years* of God dealing with me before I would get it through my thick head that He wasn't going to change His mind.

When I finally gave in to His way, things always worked out to bless me beyond my imagination. I put myself through unnecessary agony by not listening to and obeying God's voice. I could have just done what God told me to do the first time and saved myself a lot of trouble.

Most of us tend to be stubborn and set in our ways, even if our ways aren't working. We can, however, learn to be tender toward God and become sensitive to His voice and the leading of the Holy Spirit. Our spirit man within is designed for communion with God. He speaks through both our intuition and our conscience to keep us out of trouble and to let us know what is right and what is wrong.

Some things may be wrong for one person but right for

another, so we need individual direction from God. Of course, there are general guidelines that apply for everybody; we all know that we're not to lie, cheat, or steal, for example. But there are certain things that might be okay for my friend that wouldn't be okay for me. God has different plans for each of us, and He knows certain things about us that we don't even know about ourselves.

We may not understand why God tells us not to do something when everybody else is doing it, but if our conscience is tender, we clearly know when God is prompting us *not* to do it. The bottom line is, we don't have to know the *why* behind everything—we just need to learn to obey.

Soldiers in training for battle are sometimes required to do ridiculous things that don't make sense. They learn to obey quickly without question. If they are on the front-lines of battle, and their leaders give them a command, they could get killed if they turned to ask why. In the same way, God wants us to learn to trust Him and just obey.

Our conscience works like an inward monitor that beeps when we step out of line. Mature Christians learn to say, "I have a check in my spirit about this. Let me pray about it and see how the Lord leads me." Nonbelievers may wonder what that means.

But when we abide in the Lord, and He is in us, we can quickly sense His disapproval if we are not supposed to go forward with a plan. I have sensed this hesitation in my spirit when shopping, talking, or making plans to do something. Everything seems fine, and then suddenly a sense of caution rises up and lets me know to back off until God gives me a clear direction.

God doesn't scream at us or push us the way He wants us to go. He *leads* us, like a gentle shepherd, inviting us to follow Him to greener pastures. He wants us to get to the point where that little hint of caution is enough to cause us to ask, "What are You saying here, Lord?" The minute we feel that little discomfort or lack of peace, we will know we need to seek God's direction before making a decision.

The Bible says if we will acknowledge God in all of our ways, He will direct our paths (see Proverbs 3:6). Acknowledging God just means that we have enough respect for Him, enough reverential fear and awe of Him, to care what He thinks of our every move.

A good way to start each day would be to pray:

Lord,
I care about what You think, and I don't want to be doing things that You don't want me to do. If I start to do anything today that You don't want me to do, please show me what it is so that I can stop it and do Your will. Amen.

Our conscience corrects and reprimands us to make us uneasy anytime we fall short of the glory of God. We must learn to follow what it tells us regarding both our intentions and our actions—not just *after* we've done something, but when we are *intending* to

> Our conscience works like an inward monitor that beeps when we step out of line.

do something. Our conscience will let us know that it may not be right.

We must be careful to remain sensitive to God's truth, because His Word says that the tendency to ignore His voice will increase in the last days. First Timothy 4:1 says, "But the [Holy] Spirit distinctly and expressly declares that in latter times some will turn away from the faith, giving attention to deluding and seducing spirits and doctrines that demons teach." Verses 2 and 3 warn that some people's consciences will be seared (cauterized), and they will become liars and hypocrites teaching false doctrines that they don't even practice themselves.

If a wound is cauterized, it becomes scar tissue, without feeling. Likewise, when a person's conscience becomes seared or cauterized, it becomes tough and numb to what should be felt. People should feel regret when they inflict pain on others, but there are people in the world who don't seem to have any empathy or sympathy left in their souls.

When people hurt us, we can let scars harden our heart toward them, but if we do that we will lose our own sensitivity to the good things that God wants to do for us. Instead we should pray that those who hurt us will develop a tender conscience toward the voice of God, and that we will remain sensitive to His voice ourselves. Our prayers will not override other people's free will, but we can ask God to work in their lives and ours so that all of us will be sensitive to His leading. This simple prayer can keep our conscience tender toward God so we can be expectant of His guidance:

> *Father,*
> *I pray in the name of Jesus for myself and my loved ones who have seared, hardened, cauterized consciences. I ask that You do a work to break that hardness off of us. Please soften our hearts toward You. Give us tender hearts that are responsive to Your leading, so we can immediately sense what You're saying to us and do what You want us to do. In Jesus' name I ask You to help us to be tender hearted and sensitive to the Holy Spirit. Amen.*

If we expect to hear from God, we must listen for His voice and keep an ear bent for sounds of His leading. We must also be quick to obey if we want to hear from Him often. Our sensitivity to His voice in our inner man can be increased by obedience as well as decreased by disobedience. Disobedience breeds disobedience, and obedience breeds obedience. I have found that the more obedient I am, the easier it is to be obedient again. And the more disobedient I am, the easier it is to be disobedient.

Some days we can tell as soon as we wake up that we're going to have what I call a "flesh day." We start the day feeling stubborn and lazy. Our first thoughts are: *I'm not cleaning this house,*

> If we expect
> to hear from God,
> we must listen for
> His voice.

I'm going shopping. I'm not staying on this stupid diet either. I'm eating what I want to eat all day, and I don't want anybody in my face bugging me about it. If they do, I'm going to tell them what I think.

If we *feel* that way when we wake up, we have a decision to make. We can follow those feelings or we can pray, "God, please help me, quick!" Our feelings can come under the lordship of Jesus Christ if we ask Him to help us straighten out our attitude.

I know all about flesh days; I know we can start out acting bad, and it can go from bad to worse. It seems that once we give in to a selfish attitude and follow our flesh, it's downhill to a wasted day. But every time we obey our conscience, we widen the window that God can use to lead us by His Spirit. Every time we follow the leading of our conscience, it lets in more light the next time. Once we enjoy knowing that God will truly lead us to a better plan, it gets easier to obey Him promptly.

Seeking God for answers is a developed skill, and witnessing His involvement leads to a fruitful lifestyle. Many people don't see God because they are not seeking Him. Our spiritual eye sees with a conscience filled with God's light:

> The eye is the lamp of the body. So if your eye is sound, your entire body will be full of light. But if your eye is unsound, your whole body will be full of darkness. If then the very light in you [your conscience] is darkened, how dense is that darkness! (Matthew 6:22-23)

Many people's lives today are filled with dense darkness because they have not heeded the voice of conscience. Their conscience was meant to guide them, but they can no longer see the right way to go because they have snuffed out the little bit of light that they were given. It's miserable to have thoughts filled with darkness and heaviness.

People can't be happy when there is no light on their path to the future. With a dark conscience they don't like themselves, or anybody else. Nothing seems to work out for them, and it's all a result of not obeying God.

They learn that happiness cannot be purchased over the counter or packaged in bottles or cans. Money cannot buy a permanent ticket to happiness. But a good, clear conscience is of great value. It fills our lives with light when others grope in darkness.

My conscience still functions right even when my mouth is going in the wrong direction. It demands positive responses to negative situations. If I talk to Dave in a way that I shouldn't, or if I gossip about somebody or complain about something, I sense the Holy Spirit nudging my conscience back into the light of God's love. My conscience demands that I straighten up my talk, but I can agree to do what it says to do, or I can choose to ignore it.

If I answer my conscience with anything other than the justice it demands, it will speak more softly the next time. Each time the voice of conscience is rejected, it becomes softer and softer, more difficult to hear. If I mistreat somebody, my conscience demands that I apologize. If I refuse, the next time I mistreat someone, it becomes even easier for me to ignore my conscience and continue disobeying.

We are not obeying our conscience if it tells us to turn off a TV movie that we want to see, but we give an excuse and continue watching it. We often try to override the voice of conscience with the excuse that "everybody else is doing it." One of the main reasons people get into sin is because everybody else does.

> Don't gamble that something is going to work out.

You may be getting ready to marry an unbeliever, and your conscience is beeping loud alarms, because you know the Word says, "Do not be unequally yoked with unbelievers" (2 Corinthians 6:14). But you ignore it. Why would you be surprised if you wind up in trouble?

Some people ignore the warning signals that God gives them because they are afraid of being the only one set apart, alone, without friends or family. Out of fear they choose to do the wrong thing, and then later they wish with all of their heart that they had never acted against their conscience.

Don't gamble that something is going to work out if you don't have God's approval. The Bible says that Jesus is the Author and the Finisher of our faith (see Hebrews 12:2). I learned that He is not obligated to finish anything that He didn't author. A lot of times we start something and then get mad at God if He doesn't come through and finish it.

People struggle because they start works on their own and pray that God will bless something He never led them to do in the first place.

God Will Talk to Us about Relationships

If we listen, God will speak to us concerning our marriage, our friendships, and our business associations. He may ask us to sever friendships or relationships with people who can tempt us away from His plan for our lives. If we spend time with someone who is selfish and self-centered, we may soon spend all our time thinking about what we can get for ourselves.

God may encourage us to make friends with someone who is a giver. Before long we will be givers too. It is exciting to spend time with someone who really hears from God, someone who truly senses what the Holy Spirit is saying and doing. We can also tell when we're with someone who is dull in their spiritual hearing. The Bible says that iron sharpens iron (see Proverbs 27:17), and we can sharpen our ability to hear the right things by being with people who practice listening for God's voice and obeying Him.

The Holy Ghost is in a position of authority over us, and since He speaks through our conscience, we should submit to its authority. Our own mind, without the influence of the Holy Spirit, will lead us to death: "Now the mind of the flesh [which is sense and reason without the Holy Spirit] is death [death that comprises all the miseries arising from sin, both here and hereafter]. But the mind of the [Holy] Spirit is life and [soul] peace [both now and forever]" (Romans 8:6).

First Corinthians 2:13-15 says that the natural man does not understand the spiritual man, meaning that our reasoning mind does not understand our spiritual heart. A person absolutely cannot obey the Spirit without heeding the voice of conscience. The more spiritual the believer is, the more he listens to the voice of his conscience. The believer's conscience should indeed be his very good friend.

The Holy Ghost doesn't try to reveal things to me that I'm not ready to handle. If God revealed in one swift blow everything that's wrong with us, we would be devastated. I still remember the first time God revealed to me that it was hard for people to get along with me. I thought everybody else had a problem, but not me.

One day I was praying for Dave to change, and the Holy Ghost came to me and said, "Dave isn't the problem." God showed me that some of my attitudes were wrong, and some of the ways I acted were wrong. I cried for three days! That was in 1976, but it marked the beginning of major changes in my attitude and actions and ultimately my life.

I love that God speaks directly and precisely to me. I welcomed change after I received the infilling of the Holy Ghost. By now God has shown me many things that would have had me crying for years if He had shown them to me all at once. God is so good to deal with us about one thing at a time.

Perhaps you can think of something you did a few years ago that would bother your conscience if you tried to do it now. It may not have bothered you five years ago, but because God has talked to you about it, you would not think of doing it anymore.

God speaks to us about issues, works with us to bring

correction, and then lets us rest for a while. But eventually, as long as we're still listening, He will always talk to us about something new.

We used to walk through life on a wide and reckless path, but now we are guided down that narrow path. I remember saying to God once, "It seems like my path gets narrower all the time." I remember feeling that the path God was leading me on was getting so narrow that there was no room on it for me. No wonder Paul said, "It's no longer I who live, but Christ who lives in me" (see Galatians 2:20). When Jesus comes to live in us, He takes up permanent residence and slowly expands His presence until there is more of Himself and less of our old selfish nature.

We cannot operate properly in faith if we have a guilty conscience about not obeying what we know God wants us to do. Such conviction affects our faith and our worship of God. The apostle Paul talked often about his conscience, saying, "I am speaking the truth in Christ. I am not lying; my conscience [enlightened and prompted] by the Holy Spirit bearing witness with me" (Romans 9:1).

> We cannot operate properly in faith if we have a guilty conscience.

Whatever Paul did, he was accustomed to checking to see if his conscience was bearing witness of God's approval. Paul said he knew he was doing the right thing because the Holy Ghost enlightened his conscience. Paul obviously lived with "a reining ear."

We need to live the same way.

If our conscience does not bear witness, if we don't believe that God is in agreement with what we plan to do, we should not proceed, even if we can't explain why we feel something isn't right. I'm not talking about basing our decisions on feelings, but there is a sense of uneasiness when God is speaking through our conscience to keep us from stepping off the narrow path of His best for us. Our obedience to the voice of God causes us to be a blessing to the people around us.

GOD WILL TALK TO US ABOUT BALANCE

Listening to the Holy Spirit will keep us balanced in every area of our lives. The Spirit will tell us when we're spending too much, or even not spending enough. Some people are extravagant, and some are stingy; neither one represents balance. First Peter 5:8 states that we are to be well balanced in order to keep Satan from taking advantage of us.

Some people do too much for their kids, and that's why their kids are in trouble. Well-intentioned parents can make everything too easy for their children, preventing them from growing up with a sense of responsibility and dependence on the Lord.

When our children were small, there were times we wanted to give them something, but we felt uncomfortable about it. We learned to pay attention to our intuition and wait until we had peace. At times we would have to say, "I don't have peace about this." If they were upset, we encouraged them to pray that God would reveal what was right concerning the situation. Even children can learn to wait for peace to guide them.

Our children are now grown, and they're all sensitive to the voice of the Holy Spirit, so we can do quite a bit for them now. They always have good attitudes and also want to do things for us. We enjoy great relationships with them.

You don't need to make excuses to anyone for waiting on the Holy Spirit to direct your decisions. Choose to be led by peace. I believe that's the way Paul lived. When people judged Paul, he responded by boldly saying that he commended himself in the sight and presence of God to every man's conscience (see 2 Corinthians 4:2).

When accused, I believe that Paul checked his conscience to see if he felt conviction in his heart. Most of us check our logic or our feelings. We check with our friends, but often fail to check with God. When the accuser comes, we should simply ask God for the truth, saying, "Okay, Lord, did I do something wrong?"

If we didn't do wrong, we can resist the accuser and move on. If we did do wrong, we can repent and still move on. Knowing that God will not condemn us, even if the accuser is right, gives us the freedom to turn to God for confirmation about any doubt we may have. God wants to put condemnation to death. He wants us to be free and not under bondage. He wants peace to govern our lives and keep us balanced.

Sometimes when people feel accused, it may not be their conscience convicting them of guilt. Their feelings of guilt may be the residual effect of some leftover problems from the past. A good example is a girl who had an alcoholic father who always put her down. He said terrible things to her all the time, and as a result she grew up feeling she was worthless and of no value. She is now a sweet girl who loves the Lord and has a precious family, but because of her sense of guilt she will not do anything for herself.

She won't buy herself anything. She won't take vacations. She won't treat herself to any pleasure at all. I talked to her about this issue over the years, and I can see that she has made some progress. She is realizing that out-of-balance self-denial is not God's will for her. It is a result of the way her father treated her.

After discovering that her conscience is clear before the Lord, she still finds it difficult to do anything nice for herself. When shopping she often puts things in her cart, and then puts them back on the shelf. Her husband will say, "Why are you putting that back? I thought you needed it." But if she feels that she can do without it, she puts it back.

> Be careful not to confuse feelings with God's leading.

After years of walking with God, she still feels she doesn't deserve nice things because she isn't worthy of them. Her conscience approves, but her mind will not get into agreement with it because of the things in her past. But deep down inside she knows that God wants to bless her.

I share her story because so many people can relate to her feelings. Many people have a sense of guilt, but it's not necessarily their conscience speaking to them. We need to be careful not to confuse feelings with God's leading. God wants us to enjoy life.

In situations like this, I have learned not to simply follow the feelings or my mind but to practice taking a moment to sense what is deep in my spirit. The Spirit of Truth is in our spirit and will guide us into all truth as we wait on Him.

I understand why some people become unbalanced and feel it is wrong to be happy. As a child, anytime I was having fun, I was made to feel guilty. We children weren't allowed to enjoy anything. If we looked as if we were having fun, we would be told, "What are you doing? Get in here! You don't need to play."

Because I grew up in an abusive home, I had to deal with a lot of guilt. I had to learn the truth about conviction for an offense against God by reading and studying the Word to know exactly what He wanted from me. I came to understand that God does not want me to feel guilty about the things that happened to me that I couldn't help.

For years I felt that everything in my life should be work, work, work. As long as I was working, as long as I was accomplishing something, as long as I was doing what everybody wanted me to do, I didn't feel guilty anymore. But that was not God's voice of balance speaking to me.

We may feel like working, but our conscience may be telling us to stop and just have fun. If we listen to our conscience that has been enlightened by the Holy Spirit, it will tell us to relax and enjoy ourselves.

I'll never forget when my kids were trying to get me to watch a movie with them. They kept saying, "Mom, come on! You don't have to work all day and pray the rest of the time. We know you love God. Come in here and watch a movie with us. Let's pop some popcorn and have some fun."

I finally took my body in there, laid it on the couch, and ate popcorn and watched a movie with my children. We had sodas, and everything was good, but I was feeling guilty. I thought, *Come on, Joyce, the soda is diet, the popcorn is low fat, and the movie is Disney. What are you feeling guilty about?*

It wasn't my conscience speaking to me; it was those old wounds from my childhood. If I had checked with God, I would have known that it was not wrong to take time to be with my family. There's nothing wrong with taking a day off. Theres nothing wrong with having fun. There's nothing wrong with playing golf with my husband. There's nothing wrong with any of that. But I couldn't shake the feeling of guilt because of the way I was raised.

People who have the most trouble obeying their conscience are often people who are insecure because they were abused. They don't know who they are in Christ because they are so afraid of making their Father, God, mad at them. They don't have any liberty or freedom. They live in a prison, a little box, feeling bad about every move they make.

Jesus said, "I came that you may have and enjoy your life, and have it in abundance (to the full, till it overflows)" (see John 10:10). Stop checking with your head and feelings, and start checking with the Holy Ghost on the inside of you. You have to fight against anything that is not from God.

A tender conscience will put you on the path to real joy in the Holy Ghost. Resist guilt and condemnation and feeling bad about every move you make, by drawing near to God.

I have learned to simply ask God to tell me if I am doing something wrong. So many times the Lord will say, "Do all that's in your heart. I'm with you in all that you do. Go have a good time. Have a nice day. The work will be here when you get back."

One day Dave asked me to play golf, and I started to say no, and then thought, *Why not?* I knew that God wanted me to go with Dave that day. God doesn't want me to be lazy and neglect my responsibilities, but He also doesn't want me to feel that all there is to life is work.

It actually took me years to learn how to rest. I was a workaholic and made myself sick more than once by over-working and not resting. Even though I was doing "kingdom work," I still could not ignore God's laws of rest without paying the penalty. I have been amazed at the good health I have enjoyed once I learned to rest properly and not feel guilty about it.

The Bible says to stand fast in the liberty in which Christ has made us free and not to be ensnared again in a yoke of bondage, which we have once put off (see Galatians 5:1). If we want to live in freedom and liberty, we must be determined to do so. The devil will to try to make us feel guilty every time we turn around.

Many people have been so damaged emotionally that they actually feel guilty about almost everything. They have a false sense of guilt and responsibility. I was one of those people, and you may also fall into that category. If so, what can be done?

According to Isaiah 61:1, Jesus died to open prison doors and set captives free. That Scripture is actually referring to the prison of sin, guilt, and condemnation. Jesus died so that our sins could be forgiven and completely removed along with any sense of guilt and condemnation.

> But He was wounded for our transgressions. He was bruised for our guilt and iniquities; the chastisement [needful to obtain] peace and well-being for us was upon Him, and with the stripes [that wounded] Him we are healed and made whole. (Isaiah 53:5)

This Scripture tells us that Jesus died for our sin and guilt. It is not His will for us to remain trapped in either. If you are like I was, and you need deliverance from a false sense of guilt, begin to pray specifically for balance in that area and study what the Bible says about your right to freedom.

Study the love of God and learn that the Lord really does want you to enjoy your life, which is not possible when you are continually loaded down with guilt. Of course, we are to be sincerely sorry for our sins, but the Bible says there is a time for mourning and a time for rejoicing (see Ecclesiastes 3:1,4): "Weeping may endure for a night, but joy comes in the morning" (Psalm 30:5). It is normal to feel

> The Lord really does want you to enjoy your life.

guilty when we first realize that we have offended God or hurt another person. But we become unbalanced when we keep the guilt even after we have repented of the wrong and believe God has forgiven us of it.

I have written several other books that will help you in this area. The *Root of Rejection* and *How to Succeed at Being Yourself* are ones I would recommend. The main thing I encourage you to do is to make a decision that you absolutely will not settle for a lifetime of guilty feelings that make you miserable and prevent you from enjoying life.

God never speaks words to make us feel bad about ourselves. True godly conviction is a positive thing that moves us into a new level of holiness. The devil's condemnation presses us down under a heavy burden so that we can't even hear from God. We need to resist him through prayer:

Father,
Your Word says that You want us to enjoy our lives so that our joy may be made complete in You. The thief comes to kill, steal, and destroy, but Jesus came that I may have and enjoy life, and have it in abundance, to the full and until it overflows. Thank You, Lord.

I ask You, Father, that I may have balance in my life, and that it may be full of joy. Give me a tender conscience that is sensitive to Your voice. Give me peace and freedom to enjoy people, my job, my family, and most of all my relationship with You. Amen.

QUESTIONS FOR DISCUSSION

1. Is there something God has told you not to do that everyone else seems to be doing? What is it? Are you standing fast to what He said to you? What can you do to hold firm?

2. Who in your life is like iron sharpening you? What can you do to cultivate that relationship?

3. Are you like iron sharpening iron for someone else? Who? In what ways can you further develop this part of your life?

4. Is there anyone in your life God is leading you to sever friendship with? Are you walking obediently?

5. Can you think of something that used to be a habit or practice five years ago that you wouldn't dream of doing in the present because God talked to you regarding that issue? What is it? How did He deal with you?

6. How does our obedience to the voice of God cause us to be a blessing to the people around us?

7. Do you find yourself feeling guilt about something in your past? Is it a false sense of guilt? If so, how? Spend some time in prayer asking God to help you overcome this feeling of guilt.

8. What do you believe God is leading you to in response to this chapter?

9

We Can Know Only in Part

There may be times when we just can't see through the darkness that seems to be closing in around us. It is in those times of endurance and patience that our faith is stretched, and we learn to trust God even when we can't hear His voice.

We can grow in our confidence level to the point where "knowing" is even better than "hearing." As I often say, we may not know what to do, but it is sufficient to know the One who knows. We all like specific direction; however, when we don't have it, knowing God is faithful and ever true to His promise, and that He has promised to be with us *always*, is comforting and keeps us stable until His time is right to speak to us more specifically (see 1 Corinthians 1:9, Matthew 28:20).

God has said, "*I* will bring the blind by a way that they know not; *I* will lead them in paths that they have not known. *I* will make darkness into light before them and make uneven places into a plain. These things I have determined to do [for them]; and I will not leave them forsaken" (Isaiah 42:16).

The Hebrew word translated "blind" in this verse is used both literally and figuratively.[1] There are many people who have 20/20 natural vision, but spiritually they are blind—and deaf. If you feel that you are just stumbling around in the darkness and don't know what to do, I encourage you to take that promise from God in Isaiah for yourself. God wants to turn your darkness into light. He has determined to do good things for you, and He will not leave you forsaken.

Many Christians memorize Proverbs 3:5-6 which says, "Lean on, trust in, and be confident in the Lord with all your heart and mind and do not rely on your own insight or understanding. In all your ways acknowledge Him, and He will direct and make straight and plain your paths." But they tend to forget that trust is for the times that they can't get answers as quickly as they want them.

It isn't necessary to *trust* God when we have full understanding and knowledge of what He is doing on our behalf. The Hebrew word translated "trust" in verse 5 means to be bold, confident, secure, and sure.[2] Trust is needed in those times when, for whatever reason, we are not hearing from God as clearly as we would like.

Before we hear from Him, we need to learn to rely on His character, ability, and strength during the times we are not hearing from Him. If we will trust Him during those times, He promises to make clear the way we should go.

We will all enjoy (and suffer) a mixture of times in our lives when we may be certain of something in one area of which we have been seeking God, and yet uncertain in another area. We will always have new temptations to face. But we must learn to trust *all* situations to the Lord, even when He seems to be silent.

God made a promise to Abraham that He would bless his heirs, and we are heirs to the promise by faith in God's grace through Jesus Christ (see Galatians 3:29): "This mystery is that through the gospel the Gentiles are heirs together with

Israel, members together of one body, and sharers together in the promise in Christ Jesus" (Ephesians 3:6 NIV).

Truth from God's written Word is an anchor to our souls when we become temporarily blinded by sudden storms in life. We can always hear from God through His written Word. It never changes or wavers in its intent for us. Even if His Word does not speak to our *specific* situation, it does speak about God's character, and it tells us He will always take care of us and provide a way for us.

The Word teaches that our knowledge is fragmented, incomplete, and imperfect. We know in part and we prophesy in part (see 1 Corinthians 13:9-10). So this tells me that there will never be a time in my life or yours when we

> He promises to make clear the way we should go.

can say, "I know everything about everything that I need to know. I have every answer for my life right now. There is nothing more that I need to know."

Now some of us may think that we know it all! But we know in part, and that is why trust is still needed no matter how much God tells us, or how clearly He speaks to us.

He *leads* us. He doesn't push us. He doesn't hand us a map and send us on our way without Him. He wants us to keep our eyes on Him, and follow Him one step at a time. Step by step. Step by step.

GOD GUIDES US ONE STEP AT A TIME

Abraham learned to trust God to lead him one step at a time. His story of faith begins in Genesis 12:1: "Now [in Haran] the Lord said to Abram, Go for yourself [for your own advantage] away from your country, from your relatives and your father's house, to the land that I *will* show you."

God gave Abraham step one, not step two. He basically told him that he wasn't getting step two until he had accomplished step one. This is so simple, but so profound: God gives us direction, *one step at a time.*

But you may be like many people who refuse to take step one until they think they understand steps two, three, four, and five. If so, it is my hope that you will be inspired to go forward in God's plan for your life by trusting Him with the first step. Understanding that His will for you is revealed a step at a time should build your confidence to do at least what you know already to do. After the first few steps, your faith will grow because you will realize there is always sure footing beneath each step He instructs you to take.

When God spoke to Abraham, He asked him to take a difficult step. He said, "Abraham, pack up your tent, leave this country that you are familiar with, leave your family, leave all your relatives, and go where I lead you. Trust Me, this is for your advantage."

It might not have felt to Abraham that moving would be to his advantage at that time. There is no evidence in the Bible that he was discontented or having any problems with his relatives. He might have liked them all just fine. But God told him to pack up and go to the place that He was yet to show him.

When we obey God, we are blessed. People miss out on blessings because they don't obey what God clearly tells them to do. God lays out a good plan for our lives so that we will walk in it. He shows us the way to go, and we are to walk that direction. Sometimes God may be gracious enough to carry us part of the way. But there comes a time when the carrying is over, and He says, "Now walk!"

> Faith often requires action.

God wants a body of people who will obey Him, and He wants people who will obey quickly. The Lord doesn't want us to argue with Him for three or four weeks before we will do some simple little thing. He wants us to trust Him and take the first step He calls us to take.

People often pray for "great faith," yet they don't understand that faith grows as we step out to do things that we don't have any experience in or perhaps don't totally understand. I don't believe anyone is automatically a person of great faith; faith becomes great through experience. It develops as it is used.

In Luke 17:5 the apostles said to the Lord, "Increase our faith." Jesus answered as recorded in verse 6, "If you had faith (trust and confidence in God) even [so small] like a grain of mustard seed, you could say to this mulberry tree, Be pulled up by the roots, and be planted in the sea and it would obey you."

I believe what Jesus meant was, "If you people had any faith, you would be doing something." One of the ways we release our faith is by doing something. Faith often requires action. The apostles were doing nothing in this situation, and yet they wanted great faith.

There are times when God does not want us to take action, because He wants us to wait for Him to take action.

However, even trust is active rather than passive. We should be actively trusting God, praying, and confessing His Word in our situation while we wait on Him to act on our behalf.

Abraham became a man of great faith by taking steps of obedience, even when He did not totally understand the steps he was being asked to take.

God had to deal with me for an entire year before I was willing take a step of faith and obey Him concerning the ministry we are now doing. I was not purposely being disobedient. I just wanted to be real sure I was doing the right thing and that I was really hearing from God and not being led astray. The decision was a major one, and fear was fighting against my faith.

God spoke to me about some things concerning the future of my ministry. At the time I was working on a church staff and had what I considered to be a very good position. I did, however, have dreams and visions that I felt were from God of doing many other things in ministry that could not be accomplished if I remained in my current position.

God was speaking to me about leaving my job and taking my ministry to the north, south, east, and west. I even had many confirming words from others who did not even know what God was speaking to me. In addition, my husband had been telling me for some time that he felt I needed to step out into some new things and see what God would do. But I was afraid to take the step into the unknown.

I had to be obedient to leave a position of security and step out into the unknown to find out what God would do next. I had heard the Lord speak: "This season in your life is complete, I am finished with you in this place." I had a mixture of excitement and fear. I wanted to go, but did not want to take a chance on being wrong and losing what I had. I am sure at this point you know what I am talking about.

Sometimes God gets finished with something, and we're not finished. My spirit wanted to step out, but my flesh wanted to stay. I had soul ties to the people at the church, and I liked the security of knowing I would get a paycheck regularly and have a place to minister. I had to be willing to invest what I had in order to have what God had planned for my future.

It wasn't easy to obey, but God reminded me of His promise to Abraham: "And I will make of you a great nation, and I will bless you [with abundant increase of favors] and make your name famous and distinguished, and you will be a blessing [dispensing good to others]" (Genesis 12:2).

We can read that promise and think, *Oh, hallelujah!* But we can't forget that God required a sacrifice of obedience from Abraham in order to receive that promise. Abraham had to leave the place where he was, the place where he was comfortable. He had to leave his father, and all of his relatives, and just start moving in faith to the place that God said He would show him.

But did Abraham worry about it? Hebrews 11:8 says, "[Urged on] by faith Abraham, when he was called, obeyed and went forth to a place which he was destined to receive as an inheritance; and he went, although he did not know *or trouble his mind* about where he was to go." Abraham just started moving in faith.

I finally obeyed God too. I would like to be able to say that like Abraham, I did not trouble my mind about where to go, but in all honesty that was not the case. We needed to set up weekly meetings around the St. Louis, Missouri, area to replace the one we had at the church where I worked.

We wanted to be obedient to what we believed God had said to us, which was to "take your ministry and go north, south, east, and west." However, no one wanted to rent us space for the meetings. We had to be diligent and continue pressing on for what seemed to be forever, although in reality it was not that long.

Nobody knew us outside the St. Louis area, so all we knew to do was go to the north, south, east, and west in St. Louis. Eventually we did rent space in banquet centers in each area, and we held either weekly or monthly meetings. Even though we had taken step one in obedience, we still had to persevere.

> The devil took advantage of our lack of experience.

I expected God to miraculously move in major ways in response to my act of obedience, but things did not go the way I expected. Looking back, I know now they occurred properly, but I could not see that at the time. We often see more clearly and have better understanding with hindsight than we do when we are actually going through things.

We heard "no space available" so many times that it became very discouraging. As he usually does, the devil took advantage of our lack of experience in these areas and told us regularly that we had made a mistake and would surely make fools out of ourselves.

Dave had greater faith than I did and regularly encouraged me to press on. Eventually, we did find space to hold all of our meetings. They were successful and provided a foundation for the beginning of our ministry, Life In The Word.

Now we go north, south, east, and west all over the world. As a matter of fact, as I am writing this section of the book, I am returning from a major Life In The Word convention in Africa where I have the privilege of being on television teaching God's Word.

I enjoy watching or reading biographies of various people who have succeeded in ministry, entertainment, or business. Without fail, almost every one of them has "paid their dues," so to speak. What I mean is that in the early days of their quest they had to be very determined not to give up or quit. They endured many failures before having any success.

Occasionally, we see what I call "shooting stars," people who quickly rise to the top of their profession without going through all the difficult early days, but they normally don't last too long. They come out of nowhere and disappear just as quickly. Character is developed during difficult times. Our call and desires are tested when we are told no time after time and still remain determined.

I am told that Abraham Lincoln ran for several public offices and was defeated several times before he was elected to the office of president of the United States. Many people would have given up, but not him. Thomas Edison, who invented the electric light, had about a thousand experiments fail before he succeeded.

Only determined people succeed. Just because we take a step of faith does not mean that we will avoid the rest of the process. God usually builds slow and solid, not fast and fragile.

DON'T BE AFRAID OF MAKING A MISTAKE

As I have said, when I stepped out to obey God, I worried that I was making a terrible mistake. Many times I argued with God: "What if I am wrong? Lord, I have a good job here. I have a good ministry at this church. I have been here for five years, and things are good. God, what if I am wrong? If I am wrong, I will lose everything that I have spent five years working for!"

I learned that even when we are in a place of obedience, we often have no way in the natural of knowing for sure whether we are right or wrong. We have nothing more than faith to help us take that first step. We are not going to know for sure that what we are doing is the right thing until after we have done it and then look back to see if God was there to anoint our efforts.

Sometimes we may be wrong. That thought seems frightening, so we think, *I'd better just stay here where it's safe*. But if we do that, we will soon be miserable, if God has truly told us to move forward.

I have discovered that if our heart is right, and we do the best we know to do when we hear from Him, God will redeem us and honor our steps of obedience. If we move in childlike trust to obey what we believe in our heart He has told us to do, even if that decision is wrong, God will take that mistake and work it out for our good. His word says that He makes all things work together for good to those who love Him and are called according to His design and purpose (see Romans 8:28).

Many people are afraid to move because they think that if they make a mistake, God will be angry with them. But this is where trusting His character is so vital to walking in faith. People who are too afraid to obey are so miserable anyway that they couldn't get any worse off by stepping out and trying to do what God is telling them to do.

I loved my job at our home church. I didn't leave there because I wanted to leave, but God's anointing lifted off of me to be there, and I became miserable until I obeyed Him. I realized that I would only find peace if I tested out what I believed He had told me to do. It was the only way to find out if I was right or wrong about hearing His voice.

So now, I exhort you with this truth: Don't spend all your life playing it safe! Safety is very comfortable, but it may be keeping you from God's perfect plan for your life.

I remember one time when I was trying so hard to hear from God, and I was afraid that I was going to make a mistake. It wasn't long after I had been baptized and filled with the Holy Spirit and I had just started hearing from God. Being led by the Spirit was new to me, so I was scared because I didn't have enough experience to know whether I was really hearing from Him or not.

I didn't understand that God redeems us from our mistakes, if our hearts are right. God was trying to get me to step out in something, and I kept saying, "Lord, what if I miss You? What if I miss You? What if I miss You? Oh, I'm so scared! God, what if I miss You?"

He answered simply, "Joyce, don't worry; if you miss Me, I will find you." Those words, tucked away in my heart, gave me courage to do what I believed He was telling me to do, and they have encouraged me to step out in faith many times since then.

If you want God's will in your life more than anything else, if you've done everything you know to do to hear from Him, then you have to take a chance, step out, and believe.

It may not be a major decision like the one I was trying to make then, or like the one Abraham had to make. It may be a minor issue that God has impressed upon you to do. But whatever it is, the same principle applies: He leads us

> You have to take a chance, step out, and believe.

step by step. God's guidance is progressive. You will find out where He wants you to go—one step at a time.

GOD'S DIRECTION MAY SEEM ILLOGICAL

In my conferences I often ask people to raise their hands if they know they have not taken the step that God has put in front of them to take. Hundreds of people lift their hands in confession. They are waiting to see God's whole blueprint, but seeing the outcome before we obey doesn't require faith: "Faith is being sure of what we *hope* for and *certain of what we do not see*" (Hebrews 11:1 NIV). Faith pleases God. But the assurance is in our heart, not in our circumstance. Once we have a manifestation of what we desire in our circumstance, we no longer need faith in that area.

I took a long time before I obeyed God and left my previous job to begin our ministry. It's a serious decision to let go of one rope without even seeing the next rope to grab. It's irrational, and our minds fight against it. I waited, and waited, and waited, even though God was giving me all kinds of confirmation that I had heard from Him.

It makes me think of a woman who has traveled with us to do special music. She was involved in a great church, serving on the worship team, and heavily involved in their women's ministry. But God began to put it on her heart to lay those things down. God told her: "I don't want you involved in this anymore. You need to spend more time with Me." She didn't understand what God was doing, but one by one He asked her to give up responsibilities she had enjoyed.

She was doing a lot of good things that were blessing people. But at the same time she was believing God for better and greater things. Those new things were not happening, and they would not happen until she obeyed God. She had to leave the good place where she was in order to attain a higher calling.

Soon she found herself sitting at home, not doing anything, with no ministry, kind of lonely. God spoke to her and said, "Start going to Joyce's meetings." She had four little children, seven, five, and three-year-old twins. She had to drive about forty-five minutes to get to our meetings. But God told her to come.

I knew who she was because she had led worship at some special meetings we had held at our home church. I knew she had an excellent voice, but God hadn't impressed upon me to ask her to sing for us.

After about six months of seeing her faithful commitment to be at our meetings, I said to her, "If you are going to be here all the time, do you want to sing and minister?"

She replied, "I really didn't come with the purpose of singing in your meetings; I just felt that God told me to be there. I wanted good teaching, and so I came." But she said she would sing whenever we felt led to include her. At first it was only once every few months, but God led us to His plan for her step by step. I had been praying for somebody to go on the road with us to do special music. And God sent her to us.

This woman had a dream and a vision, but she didn't know how God could work things out for her to travel with four little kids. It's amazing what God can do when He's ready. It took two years of being faithful and refusing to give up her dream before God moved her into His promise to place her in her heart's desire, but she stuck it out and followed Him step by step until His plan for her came to pass.

We all need to learn to "stick it out" until God's promise comes to pass. If she had held onto the good ministry she had, she would never have progressed to see her heart's desire being fulfilled, as she eventually did with us. We make the mistake of holding on to good things that keep us from the better things God has in mind for us. This woman worked with us for a few years and then stepped out again to wait for God to do even greater things through her. Yes, we arrive at our destination one step at a time, not all at once.

Something that was once the will of God may not continue to be His will forever. He is progressive, and He leads us on to higher places. God prunes us and cuts away things that are no longer bearing the kind of fruit He desires us to bear (see John 15:1-8). This cutting away is often painful and not immediately understood, but it is necessary for us to grow into the fruit-bearing believers in Jesus Christ that He wants us to be.

Sometimes we are so entangled and engrossed in what we are doing that we don't hear God when He is telling us to move on or step out. We get so busy we don't take time to examine the root of our dissatisfied feelings. I remember that I was becoming very dissatisfied with my position at the church, but I was so busy doing my job there that I did not take time to examine why I felt the way I did.

God used my pastor to provoke me to seek God. As he put it, he realized something was "not right" with me. He came to my office one day and said, "Joyce, what's wrong with you? You seem very distant and even uninterested in what is going on at the church."

Out of my mouth came these words, "Well, maybe I'm not supposed to be here any longer." The words shocked me. I could not believe I had said what I had just heard myself say. I realize now that thought had been in my spirit for a while, but

> Take time to listen to God.

I was so afraid to think it that I was pushing it down and ignoring what God was placing in my heart.

Even though my pastor did not initially want me to leave, God used him to wake me up. After prayer and waiting on God to hear what He was saying, we agreed it was time for me to step out and find out what God wanted to do in my life.

God was talking, but I was so busy that I was not listening. I encourage you not to make the same mistake I did. Take time to listen to God, and when you sincerely believe He is speaking to you, take the steps of obedience He requires.

And remember that progress requires investment. I had to give up, or "invest," the job I had. The woman who eventually sang in our conferences had to "invest" the job she had and spend almost a year just being faithful before God gave her more specific direction. God takes what we are willing to give up for Him, and multiplies it back to us in a bigger and more wonderful way than we could ever have imagined.

BE DILIGENT TO LISTEN AND OBEY

If we want God's will to operate in our life, we must be diligent and keep doing whatever He has made clear for us to do until He tells us, "Don't do that anymore."

We have a great ministry now, but we are many years down the road from where we started. I couldn't even begin to describe all the steps that we took to get where we are now. Step by step we obeyed the voice of God, doing the things that He said to do even though they were hard. I wanted to give up two or three thousand times, and I probably cried a swimming pool full of tears.

But God's plan unfolded step by step. Following God is like climbing a mountain. If God showed us how high the mountain really is that He wants us to climb, we might be afraid to take the first step. We might argue that we're not ready, that we're not at all prepared to go all the way to the top. So He covers the top of the summit with a cloud, and all we can see is the step before us.

That first step looks manageable, so we take it. And then we take another step, and another, and another, until one day we find ourselves at the top of the mountain without even realizing where we were headed when we began. Then we are very glad we took the journey.

I have spent time getting this message of trust established in your heart because I believe it is vital to understand why God calls for faith with each step. You may think that you are not hearing from God because you don't see the whole picture, but trust that He is showing you all that you need for today. Do what is in front of you to do, and even if you are not hearing perfectly, God will honor your obedience and will complete His full plan for you.

I recall a woman who came to me complaining that she could not hear from God, that He was not speaking to her even though she was seeking Him about some things. He told me that there was no point in speaking to her about doing something else until she had done the last thing He had told her, which she had not done yet.

In God's plan for us, we cannot skip steps that we don't like and move on to other ones. We cannot skip the hard steps or the ones that require sacrifice. I repeat: Following God's plan for our life requires investment.

We must sacrifice *self-will* to have *God's will;* we must sacrifice *our way* to find *His way.* Don't be afraid of sacrifice; it eventually sets us free to be all we desire to be.

Questions for Discussion

1. What does it mean to trust God?

2. Do you trust God at all times? Are you trusting Him now in your present circumstances? Are there areas in which you need to trust Him more? What are they?

3. How do you go about trusting God more? What Scriptures can you use to do so?

4. What is a small step has God directed you to take recently? Are you resisting because He hasn't told you the whole plan?

5. How does action release faith? Have you experienced this in your own life?

6. Is there something in your life currently that you need to invest in in order to make progress? Is there a sacrifice you need to make to find His way?

7. What do you believe God is leading you to in response to this chapter?

10
God Opens and Shuts Doors of Opportunity

We all need to hear from God each day, about many different issues, but there are critical times in our lives when we especially need to know that we are hearing clearly from Him. God wants to speak to us, but we have to be careful that we don't develop a closed mindset about *how* He has to speak to us. As I pointed out earlier in this book, God has many ways through which He may choose to speak, but whichever way He chooses, He does promise to direct our paths.

It's not always easy to know if we are hearing from God or if we are hearing from our own emotional reasoning. Some people say it took them years to learn how to hear from God, but I believe that's because there hasn't been enough clear teaching on how He communicates to His people. God wants us to know He is willing to lead us and guide us as a good shepherd leads His sheep. He will speak directly to our hearts, but if we are deaf to His voice, He will find other ways to lead us.

Sometimes God speaks by opening or closing a door to something we want to do. Paul and Silas tried to go into Bithynia to preach the gospel and minister to the people there, yet the Spirit of Jesus prevented them (see Acts 16:6-7). We do not know exactly how that occurred; it is possible they simply lost their peace. I sense they actually tried to go into that province in Asia Minor, and God somehow kept them from doing so.

Dave and I know from experience that God can open doors of opportunity that no one can close, and He can also close doors that we simply cannot open. I pray that God will open only the doors through which He wants me to pass. I may sincerely think something is right to do, when it may be wrong; therefore, I depend on God to close doors I am trying to walk through if I am in fact making a mistake: "A man's mind plans his way, but the Lord directs his steps and makes them sure" (Proverbs 16:9).

I spent many years of my life trying to organize things that I wanted to do. The result was frustration and disappointment. I know now to depend on God to open doors for me that agree with His perfect plan. God will give us favor and make things easy for us when we seek His will and His perfect timing.

In writing to the church of Philadelphia, the apostle John, inspired by the Holy Spirit, said, "These are the words of the Holy One, the True One, He Who has the key of David, Who opens and no one shall shut, Who shuts and no one shall open" (Revelation 3:7).

Sometimes the only way to discover God's will is to practice what I call "stepping out and finding out." If I have prayed about a situation and don't seem to know what I should do, I take a step of faith. God has showed me that trusting Him is like standing before the automatic door to a supermarket. We can stand and look at the door all day, but it won't open until we take a step forward and trigger the mechanism that opens the door.

There are times in life when we must take a step forward in order to find out, one way or the other, what we should do. Some doors will never open unless we take a step toward them. At other times we may take a step and find that God will not open the door. If we trust Him for guidance, and the door opens easily, we can trust that He is leading us to enter into the opportunity before us. In 1 Corinthians 16:9 Paul stated that God had opened a wide door of opportunity for him and his companions. He also mentioned that there were many adversaries, so we must not mistake opposition for a closed door.

Paul and his coworkers Silas and Barnabus did not sit and wait for an angel to appear or a vision to be given

> Some doors will never open unless we take a step toward them.

to them while praying for direction. They took steps in the direction they felt was correct. Many times God did open the door, but there were times when He closed the door. This did not discourage them. They were not afraid of "missing God." They were men of faith and action. They also knew to back off quickly when it became evident that God was not permitting them to follow their own plan.

TEST YOUR OPTIONS

People ask often, "How do I find my ministry?" Some spend many immobile years waiting to hear a voice or receive supernatural direction. I tell them to step out and find out, as I mentioned earlier. In the early years of my journey with God, I wanted to serve Him. I felt He had placed a call on my life, but I did not know exactly what to do. Being the bold type, I began to try different acts of service.

For example, I worked in the nursery at church and quickly found that I was *not* called to children's ministry. I got involved in a street ministry, and although I did it faithfully for a season I had no real grace on me for it, so I found that I was not called to street ministry. However, I came alive inside when I had any opportunity to share the Word with people on any level. I found joy in teaching, and it was obvious I was good at it.

God gives each of us gifts for ministry to others. I don't believe He calls us to do things we despise or that are a burden to us. This does not mean that God won't ask us to do things we don't particularly want to do, but God will give us grace to do it when we step out and try.

Don't spend your life in so much fear of making a mistake that you never do anything. Remember, *you cannot drive a parked car.* You need to be moving if you want God to show you which way to go. He leads one step at a time; if you take one step forward, and it's the wrong way, He will let you know before you go too far. Step out and find out which doors God will open and which ones He will close.

There are times when it is better to do *something*, rather than continue doing nothing. Faith acts even when unsure; without faith it is impossible to please God. The example of Paul and Silas trying to go into Bithynia and being prevented by the Spirit was life changing for me. Taking this biblical example, I was no longer afraid to take steps. I knew I could trust God to keep me from going places that were not in His plan for me.

A missionary I know went to a wise man for counsel about what he should do. He explained that he knew he was called to the mission field, but he didn't know where to go. Should he go to India, Africa, or Mexico? He stated that at times he would pray and see black faces. Other times he would see red or yellow faces. He was waiting for God to give him direction, but he had been waiting for a long, long time.

The wise man said, "Well, brother, do something, lest you do nothing." I believe this was sound advice. It motivated the man to step out and find where he had the grace to serve, the place that filled him with peace. When there is a calling on our lives to minister to the rest of the body, we do not have peace when sitting still.

I do not want to mislead you. There certainly are times when we should wait on God, pray, and not take immediate action. But there are also times when the only way we can discover God's will is by stepping out in faith. I took baby steps at first and found that little steps won't cause big trouble if we are wrong.

We can test the waters. Just as we put our toe in the swimming pool to see if the water is cold or warm, we can take a small step toward what we think God wants us to do and see if the path is warm and inviting or cold and dark. I encourage you to take one step; if God opens the door, then take another step. If He closes the door, then back off, try another direction, or wait a while. Always pray and step out again.

> The only way we can discover God's will is by stepping out in faith.

When Dave and I felt that God was calling us to begin a television ministry, we began to take steps. We could not do it without money, so the first thing we did was write to the people on our mailing list asking friends and partners of our ministry to give financially toward helping us start a television ministry. We felt God had placed a certain amount of money in our hearts that we would need to begin, and that is exactly how much came in.

We took another step. We hired a producer, which God also had to provide. A man had applied for a job as a television producer three months before God spoke to us. We had told him we did not have a television ministry and would not be able to use his services. We remembered the man and realized that God had provided for us before we even knew we had a need.

The next thing we did was buy time on a few stations once a week. As they paid for themselves, and we saw good fruit, we bought more time. Eventually, we went on daily television and now have a worldwide daily program that prayerfully is helping millions of people.

We took baby steps at first. Although we don't live by circumstances, it is not wrong to see whether God is showing favor in certain circumstances to lead us in a certain way.

GOD'S WAYS ARE NOT OUR WAYS

There are certain things that God must do in order for things to work for us. We may be able to manipulate some things, but not all things. For example, Dave and I could not produce a television program and begin to air it without money. We had no way of getting enough money on our own, so God had to provide it. Had we written to our friends and partners and not received the money, we could not have taken another step. This was a circumstance in which God had to get involved.

We often teach people not to pay attention to their circumstances, and that teaching has value. We walk by faith, not by sight or feelings (see 2 Corinthians 5:7). Yet, there are certain things *God must do* first in order for us to fulfill our calling.

Suppose a woman prays and feels she should work to help with the family expenses. She decides to get a job, but she has two small children. If she cannot find a babysitter, she cannot go to work. That is a circumstance that God must take care of in order for her to move forward. If I were in her circumstance and could not find someone to care for my children, I would doubt that going to work was God's answer at that time for my life.

In 1977 God told me to stop working and prepare for the ministry to which I felt He was calling me. By that time I knew I wanted to teach God's Word worldwide, but God knew I needed preparation by spending time set apart with Him. I made good wages at my job and enjoyed many benefits. I wanted to obey God, but I was afraid we would not have enough money. I eventually quit my full-time job and got a part-time job.

God had not told me get a part-time job. He had told me to *quit* working and trust Him for provision. Each month we were already forty dollars short of having enough to pay our bills. If I did not work, we would not have any money for extra expenses such as car repairs, clothes, or unexpected needs.

So I shared a job with another woman; one week I worked two days, and the next week I worked three days. I thought this arrangement left me plenty of time to prepare for ministry, but I did not realize that a major part of the preparation was learning to lean entirely on God and be delivered from my independent nature. I was good at taking care of my own needs and providing for myself, but I had to learn a new way of living.

Nothing seemed to go right at this new job. When I touched equipment, it broke down. I felt uncomfortable and rejected by the other workers. Then unusual things began to happen. One day I noticed the office manager copying pages from a book and asked what the book was. She said, "My book on witchcraft."

I got weak in the knees as I realized the situation I was in. I thought, *God has put me here to help this woman,* so I tried to talk to her about the error of her ways. I actually saw a demonic manifestation on the woman's face. Her skin turned an ugly yellow color, and her expression suddenly looked evil. From that day forward, my circumstances only got worse. I worked on a bookkeeping machine, and it continually broke down, but no one could find anything wrong with it. It worked for other operators, but not for me.

One day the office manager came to me and said, "Joyce, you're fired!" I was not the type of person who got fired. I had always been known as a good worker and a dedicated employee. I think it safe to say that God closed that door. I had disobeyed Him by taking a part-time job. God is not interested in part-time obedience. Since I was in disobedience, Satan was able to lead me into what was intended to be a trap for my life and possibly the end of my ministry before I even saw the beginning of it.

Being fired was a circumstance I could not ignore! God worked through that circumstance to let me know without a doubt that He did not want me to work at anything except the task of preparing for ministry.

God proved Himself to Dave and me by supernaturally providing for us month after month for six years. During those early years of preparation and teaching Bible studies in homes, we had continual financial needs, and we saw the faithfulness of God firsthand. I remember needing shoes for my children and finding new tennis shoes at a garage sale for twenty-five cents. I needed new dishcloths, and a friend came to my door saying, "I hope you don't think I'm crazy, but I felt that God told me to bring you a dozen dishcloths." Those years were hard but wonderful, because we learned how to trust God!

I don't suggest following circumstances alone. We should also consider peace and wisdom, which are major ways that we hear from God. In other words, when I got fired from my part-time job I could have gone looking for another job, but I had no peace about it. I am sure I had no peace the first time, but I ignored it because I was not ready to depend totally on God.

Following circumstances alone can definitely get us into real trouble. Satan can arrange for circumstances as well as God can, because he has access to this natural realm. Therefore, if we follow circumstances alone without considering other ways we hear from God, it can lead us into deception.

> God is not interested in part-time obedience.

We know that we cannot go against God's Word. We must be led by peace and walk in wisdom. It is easy to do a quick "inner check," to test the barometer of peace in our heart before trusting our circumstances to lead us. Yet, we cannot totally ignore circumstances as one of the ways God speaks to us.

The safest way to hear from God is to combine biblical methods of being led by the Spirit, and allow them to serve as a check for one another. A woman may desire to be with a married man at work because she is strongly attracted to him. She may even think it is God's will for them to be together. But of course what she thinks is wrong, because God's Word clearly condemns adultery or even lusting in the heart for someone. Coveting what belongs to another person is wrong, according to the Word of God.

Satan may set up circumstances that continually place this woman with the man she is attracted to, and she can begin to think in error that God is putting them together. After all, the man has shared with her that he is having trouble with his wife at home.

Strong desire (lust) can easily deceive people. If this woman is led by her circumstances alone, she can quickly ruin her life. If she compares her circumstances to God's Word, she will know to disregard the circumstances.

> We should thank God that His ways are not our ways.

Our oldest son David, who manages our World Missions Department, recently came to me wanting advice on who to hire to fill a job opening he had. He felt God wanted him to offer the job to someone he would not have chosen naturally. He tried to fill the job with several seemingly qualified people, only to have each one turn the position down. He said, "It *appears* that God wants the person I would not have chosen."

God has said in His Word, "My thoughts are not your thoughts, neither are your ways My ways" (Isaiah 55:8). The individual God placed on David's heart was the only one who was genuinely interested in the job. We knew this was another example of God helping us hear from Him through open and closed doors. God does not always give a job or a task to the most qualified person. Often a person's heart attitude is more important than experience or credentials, especially in ministry positions.

I have discovered that God often seems unreasonable. What He chooses to do does not always make sense to us; it does not always fit into our balance of reason. We have a tendency to want things to make sense, but God wants us to learn to be led by our trust and not by our understanding.

We should thank God that His ways are not our ways. My life would have turned out badly if God had given me my way in many situations. It is wise for us to pray, "Your will be done, Lord, not mine." I often tell the Lord what I would like to have, but follow it up with, "However, if You know it is not right for me, please don't give it to me."

His thoughts are above our thoughts. He sees the end from the beginning. All His ways are right and sure. In the natural we can think something makes sense, but it may not be what God wants at all. You and I can hear accurately from God. We only need to apply the guidelines from His Word, and we will not be deceived.

Questions for Discussion

1. What do you want to hear from God about? Be specific.

2. Have you tried stepping out in faith only to watch God shut that door? Describe your experience. Has that experience encouraged you to step out more often in faith, knowing God will correct your steps as you trust Him? Has this experience discouraged you in any way?

3. Are you in the regular habit of testing your options? Describe an experience in which you have done so.

4. Is there an area in your life that you are in part-time obedience to? What is keeping you from full-time obedience? Pray for strength to make that adjustment.

5. Is God speaking to you through your current circumstances? If so, what is He saying to you?

6. What are areas in which you are asking God for something, but still need to affirm that His thoughts and ways are not your thoughts and ways? Is every part of your life submitted to His Lordship?

7. If God seems unreasonable to us, does that give us the right to disobey what He has said? How do you deal with God's seeming unreasonableness?

8. What do you believe God is leading you to in response to this chapter?

11

Hindrances to Hearing God

Some people have said to me, "Well, God just never talks to me." But I am convinced that it is more likely that they never listen, or that they have become desensitized to God's voice. God makes many attempts to speak to us through His Word, natural signs, supernatural revelation, and internal confirmation, all of which we have discussed in earlier chapters. But there are some obstacles to hearing His voice that may need to be removed from our hearts.

One way to miss hearing from God is by being too busy, as I have mentioned. We get so busy that we have no time to hear from God. We can even become too busy with religious activity. In the early days of my walk with the Lord, I was very enthusiastic and anxious to serve Him, so I signed up for anything that seemed even remotely interesting to me. The fruit of my trying was that I quickly discovered what I was *not* anointed to do. It is still better to try something rather than do nothing forever; at least by the process of elimination we can learn what God wants us to do. We learn what we are good at and what we are not good at, what we enjoy and what we don't enjoy.

I can get up in front of thousands of people and minister the Word without feeling uncomfortable at all. But when I was testing my options for ministry, I quickly learned that I was not anointed for children's ministry, and even the children would agree. I also was *extremely* uncomfortable when I worked in street ministry. Going door to door, or walking up to people on the street, and trying to minister to them was not comfortable for me.

I used to feel bad about that, thinking I was just a coward or afraid of what people would think of me, but I have since learned that there are people who are gifted and called to do everything. I know people who are called to street ministry, and they are as comfortable doing that as I am doing what God has called me to do.

Those days of trying different ways to serve were good days in some ways because I did begin to discover where my anointing was. When I taught Bible studies, I loved it. It excited me. I saw good fruit. It didn't seem like work at all. But when I did other things that I was not anointed to do, it was not that way.

My busy life was also a drawback in that I didn't take time to really be sensitive to God's voice. As a result, I often spent frustrating time in "works of the flesh." Works of the flesh are things we do without God's power flowing through us. They are difficult, they drain us, and they produce no joy or fulfillment. They are often good things, but not God things.

I remember once feeling very proud and smug that I was "working for God." But the Lord said, "You are working *for* Me, but you don't spend any time *with* Me." This was a sobering thought that began to wake me up to what was really important to God and what wasn't. He wanted my attention, not just my works.

People can literally burn out on religious activity as they struggle to serve God under the law instead of seeking an intimate, conversational relationship with the Lord. Jesus said that His yoke is easy to carry and His burden is light (see Matthew 11:30). Anyone who is feeling worn out and

> He wanted my attention, not just my works.

wasted from the work they are doing for God is probably spending too much time serving and not enough time sitting at His feet to hear what He wants to say to them (see Luke 10:38-42).

Many Christians are still under the Old Testament law and are missing out on the benefits of the New Testament's dispensation of grace. We are called to relationship, not to religious activity with no relationship.

RELIGIOUS IDEAS KEEP US FROM HEARING GOD

I believe that religious activity can keep us from hearing God. Let me explain what I mean by "religious." It is a term widely used today, and I could be thought to be rude if I didn't explain what it means to me. Religious people are frequently those who follow formulas and do good works to earn God's favor but who don't have a close personal relationship with Him. God does not initiate religious works; they are done for God and usually without God.

Jesus did not die so we could have religion; He died so we could be one with God through Him, so we could have a deep personal relationship with the Triune God: Father, Son, and Holy Spirit.

Jesus was actually very upset with the religious people of His day. He said they were "whitewashed tombs full of dead men's bones" (see Matthew 23:27). They followed rules and regulations and made laws for others to follow, but they did not attend to the more important matters such as really helping people out of right motives.

The following passage in Matthew 23:23-28 shows how Jesus felt about religious activity. In it He said:

> Woe to you, scribes and Pharisees, pretenders (hypocrites)! For you give a tenth of your mint and dill and cummin, and have neglected and omitted the weightier (more important) matters of the Law—right and justice and mercy and fidelity. These you ought [particularly] to have done, without neglecting the others. You blind guides, filtering out a gnat and gulping down a camel! Woe to you, scribes and Pharisees, pretenders (hypocrites)! For you clean the outside of the cup and of the plate, but within they are full of extortion (prey, spoil, plunder) and grasping self-indulgence. You blind Pharisee! First clean the inside of the cup and of the plate, so that the outside may be clean also. Woe to you, scribes and Pharisees, pretenders (hypocrites)! For you are like tombs that have been whitewashed, which look beautiful on the outside but inside are full of dead men's bones and everything impure. Just so, you also outwardly seem to people to be just and upright but inside you are full of pretense and lawlessness and iniquity.

The scribes and Pharisees were the most religious people of their day, yet they were not pleasing to God. God has always been more interested in the condition of people's hearts than the works of their hands.

Religious people set up rules to demonstrate what they believe is a sign of holiness. They try to make other people follow those rules. They are legalistic and rigid, not realizing that holiness is the result of a changed heart from spending personal time with God.

If we aren't sensitive to God's mercy, and if we aren't merciful to others, we will lose our sensitivity to God's voice. Legalistic people have one way of doing things. They believe that anyone who doesn't live their way is wrong.

Jesus has empathy for people who have been abused by religious law and oppressed by that kind of religious leadership. He wants to see people healed and restored so that they can know that God is good, that He is full of mercy and is long-suffering, slow to anger, and ready to forgive. God gives grace freely, which is His power to help us do what we cannot do on our own. When He tells us to do something, He doesn't leave us powerless; He gives us what we need to do it.

When Jesus said, "Come unto me, all ye that labour and are heavy laden" (Matthew 11:28), He was talking to people suffering from spiritual burnout. He wants to comfort those who are worn out from trying to serve and who are feeling like failures. There

> If we aren't sensitive to God's mercy, we will lose our sensitivity to God's voice.

are thousands and thousands of people in the church today who are in this overworked and underfed condition. People want to have a powerful relationship with God and have done everything that so-called religion has told them to do, and yet they still find themselves empty.

In their desire to please God, they have replaced *seeking* God with *working* for Him. God wants us to do kingdom works, which are things He *leads* us to do; but He does not want us to be busy in religious activity, thinking He is pleased with our sacrifices which He did not ask us to make. How can people do the works of God if they have not taken time to hear from Him that they should do them?

The Bible says that we must be born again (see John 3:1-8)—it doesn't say that we must be religious. We must let Jesus come into our lives and sit on the throne of our hearts to rule and reign over every step we take. When He tells us to go a certain direction, He will also issue to us the power we need to do what He has told us to do. Jesus will never say, "Just do it!" He always gives us the power to do whatever He tells us.

The greatest hindrance to hearing from God is trying to get to Him through works instead of through a personal relationship with Him by being born again and fellowshipping with Him regularly. People can go to church for years and do religious things all their life without ever knowing Jesus as the Lord of their life.

It is frightening to realize that there are probably thousands of people sitting in churches every week who won't go to heaven. As I often say, "Sitting in a church won't make a person a Christian any more than sitting in a garage will make them a car."

In Matthew 7:20-23 the Bible states that there are people who will say in the judgment, "Lord, Lord, we have done many mighty works in Your name," and He will say to them, "I never knew you; depart from Me, you who act wickedly [disregarding My commands]" (v. 23). People can be doing good works and yet disregarding God's commands if they are not taking the time to spend with Him and hear His instructions.

If you are not sure you have been born again, if you have never acknowledged Jesus as the Lord of your life, if you desire to have an intimate relationship with Him so that you can hear His voice, begin a new life by simply and sincerely praying this prayer:

Father in heaven,
You loved the world so much You gave Your only begotten
Son to die for our sins so that whoever believes in Him
will not perish, but have eternal life. Your Word says we
are saved by grace through faith as a gift from You.
There is nothing we can do to earn salvation.

I believe and confess with my mouth that Jesus Christ
is Your Son and the Savior of the world. I believe He died
on the cross for me, bearing all of my sins and paying the
price for them. I believe in my heart that You raised Jesus
from the dead.

I ask You to forgive my sins, and I confess Jesus as my
Lord. According to Your Word, I am saved and will
spend eternity with You! Fill me with Your Holy Spirit to
live in me and guide me in Your ways. Give me ears to
hear Your voice so that I may follow You from this day
forth. Thank You, Father. I am so grateful! In Jesus'
name, I pray. Amen.

If that was the first time you ever prayed that prayer, I encourage you to read the following verses of Scripture to confirm in your heart this new intimate relationship with God that you now have: John 3:16; Ephesians 2:8-9; Romans 10:9-10; 1 Corinthians 15:3-4; 1 John 1:9; 4:14-16; 5:1,12,13.

God will give you the power and the strength you need to serve Him in righteousness and holiness. Jesus is not a hard taskmaster. In His Word He has said:

Come to Me, all you who labor and are heavy-laden and overburdened, and I will cause you to rest. [I will ease and relieve and refresh your souls.] Take My yoke upon you and learn of Me, for I am gentle (meek) and humble (lowly) in heart, and you will find rest (relief and ease and refreshment and recreation and blessed quiet) for your souls. For My yoke is wholesome (useful, good— not harsh, hard, sharp, or pressing, but comfortable, gracious, and pleasant), and My burden is light and easy to be borne. (Matthew 11:28-30)

Jesus was saying, "I am good, and My system is good— not harsh, hard, sharp, or pressing." Religious rules and regulations can be harsh, hard, sharp, and pressing. You can easily get overburdened if you don't know how to do everything that you feel is expected of you. But Jesus is saying to you here: "I'm not that way. My system is not that way. It's not hard, harsh, sharp, and pressing, but it's comfortable, gracious, and pleasant."

Religion tells us what to do, but it doesn't tell us how to do it. If God didn't give me the power to run a ministry like Life In The Word, I would be in *way* over my head. But it's not hard for me. I'm comfortable doing what God has equipped me to do. I wouldn't be equipped with any power to get it done if I were trying to serve God because of some religious conviction and just doing works without hearing from Him.

Rules leave us on our own and make us feel guilty when we can't live up to what is expected of us. But when we do good works because of a personal leading from God, we are both motivated and empowered to serve Him.

If someone asks us, "What religion are you?" we should talk to him or her about our personal relationship with Jesus instead of what particular church we attend.

I like to answer that question with, "Thank you for asking; I don't have any religion, but I do have Jesus." We

> Religion tells us what to do, but it doesn't tell us how to do it.

need to get accustomed to asking people, "Do you know Jesus? Is He your Friend? Do you have a personal relationship with Him?"

Jesus leads us to a place that is comfortable, gracious, and pleasant. I believe it's easy to serve God if we learn to hear *from* Him before we struggle to do things *for* Him that He never asked us to do.

Before you start getting busy doing good works, take time and seek God about whether they are His works, which He is leading you to do, or whether you are just doing things in an effort to please Him. If you discover that you are involved in works of the flesh and that there is no real anointing from God on you to do them, don't be afraid to lay them down and seek God about His will for your life.

HARD-HEARTEDNESS KEEPS US FROM HEARING GOD

As we have seen, in His Word God says of His people, "I will give them one heart [a new heart] and I will put a new spirit within them; and I will take the stony [unnaturally hardened] heart out of their flesh, and will give them a heart of flesh [sensitive and responsive to the touch of their God]" (Ezekiel 11:19).

When we give our lives to God, He puts a sense of right and wrong deep within our conscience. But if we rebel against our conscience too many times, we can become hard-hearted. If that happens, we need to let God soften our hearts so that we can be spiritually sensitive to the leadership of the Holy Ghost.

I was very hard-hearted before I began really fellowshipping with God. Being in His presence regularly created the new heart in me that Jesus died for me to have. Without a heart sensitive to the touch of God, we will not recognize many of the times He is speaking to us. He speaks gently, in a still, small voice, or with gentle conviction about a matter.

Those who are hard-hearted and busy "doing their own thing" will not be sensitive to God's voice. I am grateful that He has softened my heart with His Word, because a hardened heart cannot receive the blessings that He wants to give.

If you don't relate to having a hard heart yourself, perhaps you have to deal with hard-hearted people and need to know how to pray for them. As I have said, I pray that my conscience will remain sensitive to the Lord. Before I began listening for God to direct me, I could mistreat somebody, and God would have to deal with me, and deal with me, and deal with me about it before I would admit that my behavior was wrong.

I am not that way anymore; God has changed me, because He is in the business of changing people. Now when my conscience nudges me to apologize to someone, I quickly act to make things right again.

My older son was really hard-hearted too, and I have watched God change him. Now he is so tenderhearted, he loves ministering to hurting people. If he says or does anything that he senses might hurt someone's feelings, he can hardly wait to go back and apologize.

When we talk about learning to hear from God, we don't mean just listening for God to tell us what to do; often He tells us what *not* to do. In other words, if we are taking an action or behaving in a way that is not pleasing to Him, we need to discern that He is not pleased with us and be willing to make an adjustment.

God changes people. It's a promise in His Word. He says, "I will take that stony and unnaturally hardened heart out of you and I will give you a heart of flesh, a heart that is sensitive to the touch of your God" (see Ezekiel 36:26).

Having a hard heart causes a lot of problems. For example, Jesus said that He was not in favor of divorce because divorce is the result of hard-heartedness (see Matthew 19:1-9). I also believe that most divorces are because of the hardness of someone's heart. Either one party is so hard-hearted he or she won't wait for God to change their spouse, or else one party is so hard-hearted that the other one just can't endure it any longer.

I was very difficult to get along with in the early years of our marriage. I was hard-hearted from being repeatedly abused in my childhood. However, Dave had a strong relationship with God and was willing to pray for me and wait for God to change me. Dave heard God say, "Pray and wait," and I am eternally grateful that he did.

If we had both been hard-hearted, I am sure we would not be married today. There are times when divorce is the only answer to a situation, but it should be the exception, not the rule. There are far too many divorces today.

I have even heard that the divorce rate is greater among those who claim to be Christians than those who don't— which is sad. As His children, God gives us a new heart— His heart—and we should learn to be more merciful and long-suffering, as He is. He gives us His heart so that we can ultimately learn to represent Him, doing the same thing He would do in any given situation.

Hard-hearted people break marriages and friendships too

quickly and thus, lose out on the richness of God's purpose and plan for their lives. Just think what Dave and I would have missed had he given up on me in those early years. Because he didn't do that, we are

> As His children, God gives us a new heart— His heart.

now helping millions of people worldwide through the ministry opportunities God gives us. If we had not been faithful to God and to one another, we would have missed that blessing, and God would have had to choose someone else.

God begs us not to harden our hearts, indicating that to do so is a choice of our own will:

> Therefore, as the Holy Spirit says: Today, if you will hear His voice, *Do not harden your hearts,* as [happened] in the rebellion [of Israel] and their provocation and embitterment [of Me] in the day of testing in the wilderness. (Hebrews 3:7-8)

When we hear from God, we have the choice to respond with humility and trust, or to harden our heart and ignore Him. Regrettably, when people don't get what they want, or when they go through trials and tests, many of them choose to harden their heart.

That's exactly what happened to the Israelites when they were making the trip through the wilderness. God led them into the wilderness so that He could prove to them that He would do good for them and that they could trust Him (see Deuteronomy 8:2-3). He had great things planned for them, but He tested them first to see if they were really going to believe Him. That is why He tells us not to harden our heart as they did.

Don't let trials make you bitter; let them make you better. In Hebrews 3:9-11 the Lord says:

Your fathers tried [My patience] and tested [My forbearance] and found I stood their test, and they saw My works for forty years. And so I was provoked (displeased and sorely grieved) with that generation, and said, They always err and are led astray in their hearts, and they have not perceived or recognized My ways and become progressively better and more experimentally and intimately acquainted with them. Accordingly, I swore in My wrath and indignation, They shall not enter into My rest.

Many problems affected the children of Israel because they had hardened their hearts. They wouldn't learn the ways of God, and so they couldn't progressively get better; consequently, they couldn't enter the rest of God. In verses 12 and 13 the writer of Hebrews says:

[Therefore beware] brethren, take care, lest there be in any one of you a wicked, unbelieving heart [which refuses to cleave to, trust in, and rely on Him], leading you to turn away and desert or stand aloof from the living God. But instead warn (admonish, urge, and encourage) one another *every day*, as long as it is called Today, that none of you may be hardened [into settled rebellion].

People with hard hearts are rebellious and refuse correction. They have difficulty hearing from God, and they have difficulty in relationships. They are not willing to see other people's viewpoint; they don't understand other people's needs and usually don't care. They are self-centered and can't be moved with compassion.

Actually, considering all the problems that arise from having a hard heart, it seems prudent to me to begin aggressively seeking God to soften our hearts and to help us be sensitive and tender to His touch, responsive to Him.

I have personally made the subject of sensitivity to the Holy Spirit one of prayer and seeking. I want to be sensitive to the needs and emotions of others. I want to recognize quickly when I am not behaving the way God desires. I would like to recommend that you consider doing the same thing.

Repent of any hard-hearted attitudes God may be convicting you of. Ask Him to help you in this area and to change you. Greater sensitivity will help us hear from God promptly and clearly. We become better and better when we recognize that God's ways are above our ways and say to Him, "God, I want Your way in my life; teach me Your ways, O God."

A WORLDLY VIEWPOINT KEEPS US FROM HEARING GOD

The Word of God teaches us that as believers we are in the world but not *of* the world (see John 17:13-18), which means that we cannot have a worldly view of things:

> Do not be conformed to this world (this age), [fashioned after and adapted to its external, superficial customs], but be transformed (changed) by the [entire] renewal of your mind [by its new ideals and its new attitude], so that you may prove [for yourselves] what is the good and accept-

able and perfect will of God, even the thing which is good and acceptable and perfect [in His sight for you]. (Romans 12:2)

It requires a constant vigilance not to become like the world in its ways and attitudes. Watching too much graphic violence in the form of entertainment can sear or harden our conscience. Many people in the world today are desensitized to the agonies

> Greater sensitivity will help us hear from God promptly and clearly.

that real people suffer due to all the violence that is seen in movies and on television. Some people claim it is not a problem to watch violence because it is "just a movie or a TV show and not really happening," but it still affects us.

We can get to the point where we have no empathy when we hear reports of real tragedies or when we hear of terrible things happening to other people. When my uncle died, someone said to my aunt, "Well, praise the Lord anyway." That person's inability to empathize with my aunt's pain hurt her at a time in which she was already in great distress. Those were insensitive words spoken from a hardened heart, not compassionate words from God.

I remember when hearing of a rape or a murder on the evening news was shocking. Now, it is so frequent that it barely affects us emotionally. Dave told me that the first time his family heard of a paperboy being robbed, it was shocking news. The world has changed so much since then that such an incident would actually be considered minor today and might not even be mentioned at all.

The news media frequently delivers negative reports, often with unemotional accounts of tragic events, and many times we listen with unemotional responses. We hear of so much violence nowadays that we hardly notice it or pay any attention to it. This is understandable, but not acceptable. Evil is progressive and will continue to increase if we don't aggressively come against it.

I believe this is all part of Satan's overall plan for the world. He wants us to have a hard-hearted viewpoint, not really caring about people or their needs. As Christians we should pray for those who are hurting and vow to fight against the apathetic ways of the world's attitudes. Single-handedly we may not be able to solve all the problems in the world today, but we can care—and we can pray.

Jesus said, "The Sprit of the Lord is upon me to preach good news" (see Luke 4:18). I believe that there are still more good things going on than bad if somebody would report them. I am not saying that we should never turn on the news broadcast or read the newspaper, but I am saying that we should not dwell on the world's reports or conform to its viewpoint. We need to listen to what God says about current events in our lives and pray as He leads us to intercede for others who are affected by them.

UNFORGIVENESS KEEPS US FROM HEARING GOD

Long-lasting abuse can cause a person to harden his or her heart. This hardness is a survival tactic to protect the one being mistreated while enduring cruelty, which can sometimes last for years. Numbness to pain helps victims survive abuse; they simply shut off their feelings. But when emotions are turned off for years, it takes a toll on people's health.

Those who have refused to feel anything for a long time are afraid to feel anything again, because all they remember is horrible pain. The pain caused by abuse can be too much to bear if not faced with God's redemptive power to heal the hurt.

Eventually, emotional pain must be dealt with in order to let godly emotions flow in our lives again. It is difficult to change a hard heart into a tender one, but all things are possible with God (see Matthew 19:26). It requires a willingness to work with God and patience to get those feelings turned back on.

If you have been a victim of abuse, don't stay in that bondage. Don't continue to treat your symptoms by staying hard-hearted. You are not really protecting yourself from further pain. Hard-heartedness is not from the Spirit of God. God created us to have feelings. We know that even Jesus wept (see John 11:35).

> God will give you the power to forgive, if you ask Him to do so.

Anytime you open up your feelings, you will be vulnerable to feeling pain, but it will be different when Jesus the Healer is living on the inside of you. Anytime you get hurt, He will be right there to take care of that wound. Forgiveness is the only thing that will set you free from the pain of abuse. God will give you the power to forgive, if you ask Him to do so.

I certainly understand how personal problems or a series of disappointments can harden the heart. As a result of the abuse I had suffered, I was bitter, sour, and negative. When Dave and I got married, my motto was, "If you don't expect anything good, then you won't be disappointed when it doesn't happen." But I have come a *long* way!

Anytime bitterness tries to take hold of you, refuse it. You are not the only one going through difficulties. The devil backs us off in a little corner where we believe we are the only one with problems. We think, *Why me? Why me?* But sooner or later everyone goes through abuse of some sort.

I don't mean to sound unsympathetic, but no matter how bad your problem is, there is somebody who has a worse problem than you do. I have gone through some hard things in my life, but it is nothing compared to what I hear from others.

A woman worked for me whose husband walked out on her after thirty-nine years of marriage and just left her a note. What a tragedy it was for her! I was so proud of her when she came to me after a few weeks and said, "Joyce, please, please pray for me that I will not get mad at God. Satan is tempting me so severely to get mad at God. I can't get mad at God. He's the only friend I have. I need Him!"

That hardness of heart was trying to come on her because her life had not turned out the way she wanted. She had served God, made sacrifices, and prayed, but God had not met her need the way she had wanted.

People have a free will, and we can't control their free will—even through prayer. We can pray that God will speak to them and do everything He can to lead them to do the right thing, but the bottom line is that He has to leave them free to make their own choice. If someone makes a bad choice that hurts us, we shouldn't blame it on God. If we will keep a good attitude, if we will resist embitterment, God will bless us anyway.

I know a man who prayed that his sick son would not die. He exercised his faith and really believed that his son would live. His son did die, and the man became really bitter toward God. His heart became hardened because he didn't get what he wanted.

One day he finally said to God, "Where were You, God, when my son died?"

And God said to him, "I was at the same place I was when My Son died."

Think of what it must have been like for God the Father to watch His son Jesus suffer all that He went through so that we could be delivered from sin and despair and set free to the blessed hope that we have today.

Those who have been seriously abused need to forgive their abusers in order to recover from the pain that has been inflicted upon them. But many people have unforgiveness in their hearts from much milder offenses than abuse, and they need to forgive their offenders also.

Unforgiveness, bitterness, resentment, or offense of any kind can render us unable to hear from God. The Word of God is very clear on this subject: If we want God to forgive our sins and offenses against Him, we must forgive others their sins and offenses against us.

Ephesians 4:30-32 teaches us that it grieves the Holy Spirit when we harbor negative emotions in our heart, such as anger, resentment, and animosity. When we hold unforgiveness for any reason, frequently or for a long time, it hardens our heart and prevents us from being sensitive to God's leading in our life.

I heard someone say that holding unforgiveness is like taking poison, hoping your enemy will die. Why spend your life being angry with someone who is probably enjoying his or her life and does not even care that you are upset? Do *yourself* a favor—forgive those who hurt you! Give yourself the gift of forgiveness.

LEGALISM CLOSES OUR EARS TO THE VOICE OF GOD

I have mentioned how religious ritualism interferes with a Spirit-led life, but I would like to discuss the topic of legalism a little more thoroughly, because I believe it is still one of the greatest hindrances to hearing from God.

First of all, I don't believe that we can experience joy if we are not being led by God's Spirit, and we cannot be led by the Holy Spirit and live simultaneously under the law. A legalistic mentality says that everybody has to do exactly the same thing, the same way, all the time. But the Spirit of God leads us individually, and often in unique, creative ways.

The written Word says the same thing to everyone and it is not a matter of private interpretation (see 2 Peter 1:20). What this means is that the Word of God does not say one thing to one person and another thing to someone else. However, the direct leadership of the Holy Spirit *is* a personal issue.

God may lead one person not to eat sugar because He knows of a health issue in his or her life, but that may not be the rule for everyone. People who are legalistic try to take God's word to them and make it a law for everyone.

I once heard that by the time Jesus was born, the scribes and Pharisees, the religious leaders of His day, had turned the Ten Commandments into two thousand rules for the people to follow. Imagine trying to enjoy your life while having the burden of following two thousand rules, most of which were man made!

Jesus came to set captives free. We are not free to do whatever we feel like doing, but we have been set free from legalism and are now free to follow the leadership of the Holy Spirit.

Isaiah prophesied of Jesus, saying, "The Spirit of the Lord God is upon me, because the Lord has anointed and quali-fied me to preach the Gospel of good tidings to the meek, the poor, and afflicted; He has

> Jesus came to set captives free.

sent me to bind up and heal the brokenhearted, to proclaim liberty to the [physical and spiritual] captives and the opening of the prison and of the eyes to those who are bound" (Isaiah 61:1).

The Word says, "Now the Lord is the Spirit, and where the Spirit of the Lord is, there is liberty (emancipation from bondage, freedom)" (2 Corinthians 3:17). Jesus wants us to have liberty and not legalism. If the Son has set you free, you are free indeed (see John 8:36).

- Free from sin
- Free from manipulation and control
- Free from fear of what others think of you
- Free from comparing yourself with everybody else
- Free from competition with others
- Free from selfishness
- Free from legalism
- Free to be an individual
- Free to be who you are
- Free! Free! Free!

In Christ, we have been liberated and set free from the manipulation and control of narrow-minded, Pharisee-like people who think their way is the only way to do any-thing.

I hate that spirit, yet I was like a Pharisee for so many years, giving orders, getting mad at everybody who didn't do everything as fast as I thought they should, the way I thought they should. I was harsh, hard, sharp, and pressing.

But when I first read Matthew 11:29-30 in *The Amplified Bible*, I meditated on Jesus' words until they were settled in my heart:

Take My yoke upon you and learn of Me, for I am gentle (meek) and humble (lowly) in heart, and you will find rest (relief and ease and refreshment and recreation and blessed quiet) for your souls. For My yoke is wholesome (useful, good—not harsh, hard, sharp, or pressing, but comfortable, gracious, and pleasant), and My burden is light and easy to be borne.

I confessed these words over and over, "I will not be harsh, hard, sharp, or pressing, but I will be gentle, meek, humble, and lowly."

I had to get that concept into my own hard heart. I studied the definition of the word "meekness" from Vine's Greek dictionary. The gist of it is that meekness is Christ's own gentle and soothing disposition and is an "inwrought grace of the soul."[1]

It was such a powerful explanation that I literally tore the page out of the book and carried it in my wallet. There were times when I wanted to let somebody know how upset I was with them, but instead, I would get out that definition of meekness and read it again.

My point is that getting rid of my hard heart wasn't easy. Hard-heartedness is not mastered overnight. I personally had to work at overcoming it for years before I sensed that true meekness was finally "worked into my soul."

Keeping your heart tender won't just happen—you must consciously cooperate with the Holy Ghost and let Him do the work in you that needs to be done. This is of great importance: We are not to be legalistic. If we are, we need to ask God to change us and to give us a heart of flesh that is sensitive to His voice.

If you are legalistic or hard-hearted, pray this prayer sincerely:

Lord,
I don't want to be legalistic or hard-hearted. I want my conscience to be alert so I can know when You approve or disapprove of what I am doing or about to do. I don't want to hurt people's feelings either consciously or unconsciously.

I want to have compassion on hurting people and to give them real encouragement, not some flippant religious answer that doesn't really meet their need or that leaves them more wounded than they were before. I want to be sensitive to Your touch and to Your ways. Amen.

GRACE REMOVES OUR HINDRANCES FROM HEARING GOD

Romans 14 is a good chapter to study if legalism is hindering your ability to hear from God. It calls for real balance, explaining that what is wrong for some people may not be wrong for others. The difference is whether they are acting upon or against their own personal convictions from the Lord.

It makes religious people mad when we do not follow all their rules and still have a good relationship with God. As I have said, the written Word of God has rules that are the same for everyone. For example, it says not to lie; therefore, nobody has the right to lie. It says not to murder, and nobody is exempt from that instruction. But the written Word of God does not tell us how long to pray daily; it just tells us to be sure we are actively pursuing prayer.

The Bible tells us to study God's Word regularly, to meditate on it day and night (see Joshua 1:8). That obviously does not mean without interruption; otherwise, we could not get anything else done. The Bible therefore does not say exactly how much we should read the Bible or pray daily. Yet, there are many people who still make rules in these areas.

I have heard people actually say, "If you're not praying at least one hour every day, then you're missing God's will." They base this teaching on the Scripture in which Jesus said, "Can you not pray with Me one hour?" (see Matthew 26:40). But Jesus was talking to His disciples about a specific situation, not making a rule for all times.

Praying one hour a day certainly is a good goal. It is a good pattern to follow for discipline purposes, but to make a law out of it is wrong. These areas and others like them are ones in which we are to be personally led by the Holy Spirit. It is fine if people hear a teacher or preacher suggest something and feel led to do it, but they should not be made to feel guilty if they don't do what someone else does.

> The written Word of God has rules that are the same for everyone.

When Jesus spoke from the cross saying, "It is finished!" (John 19:30), He meant that the system of legalism was finished, that now, not just the religious priests can go into the presence of God, but that all people can speak to God and hear His voice.

Before Jesus died on our behalf, the only way to receive God's promises was by living a perfect, sinless life (by being very legalistic), or by offering a blood sacrifice for sin. When Jesus died and paid for the sins of mankind with His own blood, the curtain of the temple which separated people from the presence of God in the Holy of Holies was torn from the top to the bottom (see Matthew 27:50-51). That event signified that God tore that curtain in half from heaven downward, inviting us to come into His presence freely—no more sacrifices, no more legalistic rules. Even ordinary people who don't do everything right all the time can now enter freely into the presence of God.

The whole issue of behavior is not about whether we never make a mistake, but whether we obey God. A legalistic attitude leaves us with a hard heart, but a personal relationship with God makes us sensitive, tender, and responsive to His touch (see Ezekiel 11:19).

The Word confirms that this new covenant of grace, this liberty to approach God, was His idea:

> Therefore, brethren, since we have full freedom and confidence to enter into the [Holy of] Holies [by the power and virtue] in the blood of Jesus, by this fresh (new) and living way which He initiated and dedicated and opened for us through the separating curtain (veil of the Holy of Holies), that is, through His flesh, and since we have [such] a great and wonderful and noble Priest [Who rules] over the house of God, let us all come forward and draw near with true (honest and sincere) hearts in

unqualified assurance and absolute conviction engendered by faith (by that leaning of the entire human personality on God in absolute trust and confidence in His power, wisdom, and goodness), having our hearts sprinkled and purified from a guilty (evil) conscience. (Hebrews 10:19-22)

Freedom from legalism is not a call to lawlessness. It is a responsibility for each of us to learn to hear from God for our own lives.

Questions for Discussion

1. What are the hindrances to God? What happens to those who fall prey to those hindrances?

2. Can you identify any of these hindrances in your own life? Which ones? How can you overcome them?

3. What are your motives for ministry? Are they pure?

4. Why do you think people get caught up in working for God instead of seeking God? If applicable, describe a time in which you felt or acted this way. At the time, what were you feeling?

5. Is there any reason believers should experience burnout? Explain.

6. Are you burnt out on ministry? Have you worn yourself thin doing things for God instead of spending time with God? If so, what can you do to begin to change this?

7. Have you chosen to harden your heart toward God? In what ways? Have you taken steps to overcome this? What happened?

8. How does watching violence on TV affect you personally? Your family?

9. As you examine your own life, are there man-made laws you follow (like certain times to pray or length of time

spent studying the Word)? Where did you find these laws? Can you find correlation in the Word to support them?

10. What do you believe the Lord is leading you to in response to this chapter?

12

Keep Your Receiver Deceiver Free

To hear from God we must first believe that we *can* hear from Him. Many people *want* to hear from God, but they don't really *expect* to hear from Him. They tell everyone, "I just can't hear from God; He never talks to me."

These people have too much static in their "receivers" to hear Him clearly. Their ears are jammed with too many messages coming from ungodly sources. Consequently, they have a hard time discerning what God is really saying to them.

It doesn't do any good for God to speak to us if we do not *believe* we are hearing from Him. The deceiver, the devil, doesn't want us to think that we can hear from God. He doesn't want us to believe, so he sends little demons to stand around and tell us lies day and night that we can't hear from God.

But we can answer, "It is written, God has given me the capacity to hear and obey Him" (see Psalm 40:6). The Word declares that *all* believers have the capacity to hear *and* obey God and to be led by the Holy Spirit. Jesus heard clearly from the Father all the time. Many people who were standing around Jesus when God spoke to Him only heard what they thought was thunder (see John 12:29). If you are having trouble hearing from God, I encourage you to take a few moments every day and confess your faith in hearing from Him. As you confess what you believe in your heart, you will develop faith and expectancy to hear Him.

I frequently confess: "I hear from God. I am led by His Holy Spirit. I know my Father's voice, and the voice of a stranger I will not follow. I am led and guided by the Holy Spirit, even unto my death. God will guide me all the days of my life. He will guide me and give me the answers that I need."

TRUSTING GOD OPENS OUR RECEIVERS

If we live God's way, if we choose to serve Him, we can avoid weeklong wrestling matches with Him. Wisdom tells us to let God do with us what He wants, so that we don't keep going around and around the same "mountain" all the time (see Deuteronomy 2:3 KJV). I have met people who have been circling the same obstacles and issues for twenty or thirty years. If they had simply obeyed God in the beginning, they would have moved on with their lives long ago.

No matter how much we may enjoy where we are when God finds us, He will not let us stay there and become stagnant. He has new places to take us and new lessons to teach us. He wants to keep us full of life, full of growth, and full of His plan.

God has said to us, "If you don't pay attention to Me, if you ignore Me and do not give heed to My reproof, I am going to cry out to you. I will try to help you, but if you continue to give Me a deaf ear, you will come to Me in a panic when you get in trouble" (see Proverbs 1:24-28). God is merciful and long-suffering, but the time comes when we have to realize that we just need to be obedient to Him.

When Bible teachers talk grace, everybody loves them. When they teach how much God loves people in the midst of their messes, everybody loves them. But I believe you will also love me for teaching you obedience. If you don't have a good mix of all of God's Word, you will get out of balance and get in trouble.

Jeremiah 10:23 says, "I know that [the determination of] the way of a man is not in himself; it is not in man [even in a strong man or in a man at his best] to direct his [own] steps."

We don't have the ability to run our own lives in our best interests. Only God knows what is best for us in the long run. Once I started serving Him, I knew He could do anything, so I gave Him my list of what I wanted done. I thought I could tell God how He should run my life. I thought I had a great plan and that because God is so mighty, He could bring my plan to pass. I found out that even with God's help I still couldn't make my plan work.

> God is merciful and long-suffering.

Jeremiah said that it is not in a man, not even a strong man, to direct his own steps. We are not capable of running our own lives. We need God's wisdom and guidance as well as His strength and power, so we should listen to what He has to say.

God is looking for people who will demonstrate the glory of His presence in their lives. They will be people who obey Him in every little thing. Obedience keeps us from defiling our conscience and keeps us living for God's glory.

Isaiah 11:2 says, "The Spirit of the Lord shall rest upon

Him." We know that this is a prophecy about Jesus, but if the Spirit of Jesus is dwelling in us and living through us, then we will enjoy all that is upon Him. We will have wisdom, understanding, counsel, might, and knowledge.

Problems dissolve in the presence of these virtues. We don't have to wait years to understand something if we are obedient to the leading of the Spirit. The Lord will give us quick counsel and might if we are reverential and submissive toward Him. He will neither judge us by the sight of His eyes, nor decide by the hearing of His ears (see Isaiah 11:2-3).

People who want to have understanding, who want to hear from God, who want to have wisdom and knowledge imparted to them, must have reverential fear and awe of God. Reverential fear is to know that God *is* God and that He means business. He has called us His friends, even His sons and daughters, but we're to respect Him and honor Him with reverential obedience.

If we want to hear from God, we need to reverence Him. If we want understanding, we need to be desperate to hear from Him. I don't want to buy equipment for our ministry without hearing from God. I don't want to go to speaking engagements if God is not sending me. I don't want to hire one person to work on my staff if God hasn't told me to do so.

Every week Dave and I desperately need to hear from God about many things. We need to hear from God about how to handle people and numerous situations. Our constant prayer is, "What should I do about this? What should I do about that?"

A hundred things happen every week in which Dave and I have to be of quick understanding and make God-driven decisions. If we don't obey God on Monday, our

> If we are unwilling to hear in one area, we may be unable to hear in others.

week can be in chaos by Friday. Therefore I am determined that I am not going to live in disobedience.

People are concerned about the specific will of God for their life, wondering what He wants them to do: "Lord, should I take this job, or do You want me take another job? Do You want me to do this, or do You want me to do that?" I believe God wants to give us that kind of specific direction, but He is even more concerned about our obedience to His general will for our lives. If we are not obeying the guidelines He has already given us in His Word, it will be difficult to hear what He has to say about His specific will for us. Remember, if we are unwilling to hear in one area, we may be unable to hear in others.

OBEDIENCE OPENS OUR RECEIVERS

We need to pray and obey God's leading. Our obedience is not to be an occasional event; it is to be our way of life. There's a big difference between people who are willing to obey God daily and those who are only willing to obey in order to get out of trouble. God certainly shows people how to get out of trouble, but He bestows abundant blessings on those who decide to live wholeheartedly for Him and who make obedience to Him their lifestyle.

Many people obey God in the big issues, but they aren't aware that obedience in the little things makes a difference in His plan for their lives. The Bible says plainly that if we are not faithful in the little things, we will never be made rulers over much. There is no sense in God telling us to do some major thing if we are not going to be faithful to do the little things. It is very important to be obedient in the smallest of things.

Proverbs 1:23 says, "If you will turn (repent) and give heed to my reproof, behold, I [Wisdom] will pour out my spirit upon you, I will make my words known to you."

God says He will make His words known to us if we listen to Him when He corrects us, and if we obey when He tells us to stop doing something. He will open up wisdom to us, and we will have more revelation than we could ever imagine.

All we need to do is to be obedient to what God has told us to do. He will reveal treasures from His Word that are hidden within it. We have not even scratched the surface of all there is to know about God. In all the years there has been teaching and preaching, since the time that Jesus was here, we have not even scratched the surface of the revelation that's in the Word of God. If we obey Him, He will make His will clearly known to us. He will speak living words (His *rhema*) to us, His personal word for our lives.

The following verses present a sobering destiny for those who choose to go their own way, ignoring fellowship with God and obedience to Him:

Because I have called and you have refused [to answer], have stretched out my hand and no man has heeded it, and you treated as nothing all my counsel and would accept none of my reproof, I will also laugh at your

222

calamity; I will mock when the thing comes that shall cause you terror and panic—when your panic comes as a storm and desolation and your calamity comes on as a whirlwind, when distress and anguish come upon you. Then will they call upon me [Wisdom] but I will not answer; they will seek me early and diligently but they will not find me. Because they hated knowledge and did not choose the reverent and worshipful fear of the Lord, would accept none of my counsel, and despised all of my reproof, therefore shall they eat of the fruit of their own way and be satiated with their own devices. For the backsliding of the simple shall slay them, and the careless ease of [self-confident] fools shall destroy them. But whoso hearkens to me [Wisdom] shall dwell securely and in confident trust and shall be quiet, without fear or dread of evil. (Proverbs 1:24-33)

I do not believe that God will refuse to help us just because we fail to obey Him perfectly in every single thing. But I do think we need to consider the seriousness of ignoring the grace of God that is available to us. His mercy is available, but the Word says that a day of calamity will come like a whirlwind, and that those who have ignored Him now will not be able to find Him when they call out to Him.

I believe that God pours grace and mercy into the lives of sincere people who are wholeheartedly seeking Him and are not knowingly or willfully disobeying Him. Yet, there are lots of people who call themselves Christians who are not obeying God and are not listening to Him. We can get so confident in a "buddy system" with the Lord that we forget we are dealing with God Almighty.

If we are not paying attention to what He says, how can our lives be anything other than a wreck? If a person is in a mess, it is because he or she didn't pay attention to God in the past. The only way that person can ever get out of that mess is to repent and obey God's wisdom from this day forward.

Jesus said, "If you love Me, you'll obey Me" (see John 14:23). Whenever I study about hearing from God, I keep coming back to the fact that we won't hear from Him clearly if we are not obeying Him. Without obedience we have a guilty conscience. As long as we have that guilty conscience, we cannot have faith and confidence to stand in God's presence (see 1 John 3:20-24).

Paying attention to God's Word should be the goal of our lives. Making money should not be our life goal. Being a big business tycoon should not be the goal of our life. Reaching the top of the corporate ladder should not be our life goal. Amassing great amounts of money and owning houses and cars and clothes should not be the goal of our life.

The Bible tells us plainly that without faith and confidence, no matter what blessing God is trying to get to us, we will not receive it (see James 1:5-7). If we don't behave ourselves, God doesn't stop giving. His nature never changes, no matter what we do. He *is* love (see 1 John 4:8); love is not something that He turns on and off depending on our behavior. But when we know that we have done wrong, and don't repent, we're not able to receive from God.

As soon as we do something wrong, the deceiver will send condemnation to try to interfere with our ability to hear God. There is no condemnation for those who are in Christ Jesus (see Romans 8:1), and we are not going to do everything perfectly. But if we don't know the truth, we won't be free to enjoy God's forgiveness and blessings.

Thank God for the blood of Jesus that blots out our sins from God's eyes. It cleanses us from the power of sin and removes the condemnation that it brings. I spent many years trying to bounce back from feeling the condemnation of disobedience. I finally grasped a higher plan—that is to do what God says to do from the start. Obedience is a better plan. I discovered that if I would just be obedient, then I wouldn't have to struggle from feeling bad about disobeying God.

Obey God in every little thing, and you will enjoy an excellent life. Be diligent in your obedience; go the extra mile, and do every little thing that God tells you to do. Learn to live your life before God, and not before man. Do all the little things that God tells you to do, even though nobody else may ever know. Put your grocery cart back in the stall where it belongs instead of leaving it out in the middle of the parking lot. Why? Because the owner of the property has put up a sign saying, "Please return carts here," and God has said to submit to authority (see Titus 3:1).

> Jesus said, "If you love Me, you'll obey Me."

The flesh says, "Well, everybody else leaves their carts everywhere; why should I put mine up?" Because our standard is not others—our standard is Jesus. When I compare myself to everybody else, I don't look too bad. But if I compare myself to Jesus, I am humbled and ask God to help me! Until Jesus comes to get us, we need to compare ourselves to Him and the standard of holiness that He holds up for our lives.

We have a lot of work to do in order to measure up to His standard. While we have no reason to take pride in our own flesh or our personal achievement, our effort toward excellence will keep us sensitive to God's voice.

THANKFULNESS OPENS OUR RECEIVERS

God's general will for us is to "thank [God] in everything [no matter what the circumstances may be, be thankful and give thanks], for this is the will of God for you [who are] in Christ Jesus [the Revealer and Mediator of that will]" (1 Thessalonians 5:18). We don't need to worry about whether it is God's will that we go to the mission field until we have learned to obey His will right where we are.

Thankfulness keeps our ears open to hear God. The Bible says we are to thank God in everything, not *for* everything, but *in* everything. That means that no matter what is going on in our life, we are not to complain, murmur, grumble, or find fault. God doesn't want to hear us whine because whining is evidence that we have no faith in His ability to make things better.

He would rather hear us say, "Well God, this is definitely a sacrifice of praise, but I give thanks to You because You are great and mighty; even in the middle of this mess, You are still great and mighty." God honors us when we demonstrate that kind of faith. He will speak to our receptive ears and lead us out of trouble.

People who grumble and complain from daylight until dark never hear God, because to hear Him they must quit complaining! It took me years to discover that fact. I grumbled and complained and murmured and found fault with everybody, and then was jealous because everybody else was getting a word from God.

"Why isn't anything good happening to me?" I would groan.

Dave kept telling me, "Joyce, good things aren't going to happen in our life until you get stable."

Then I would get mad at him for telling me that and would snap back, "You don't have any compassion at all!"

I wanted him to get negative along with me, but we really would have been in a mess if he had agreed with me. Finally, I learned that if I wanted to hear from God, I had to quit complaining. The Bible says it is God's will for us to thank Him in everything.

Sometimes I thanked Him with tears running down my face, sitting on the edge of my bed and crying, "God if You want to know the truth, I want to go somewhere and have a screaming fit! But I am going to obey You because I have done everything else, and nothing else works. You said to thank You in everything. Thank You, Lord. Thank You that You are still God and that You are still on the throne. Thank You that You are doing good things, even though I am in an awful mess. Thank You, thank You, thank You that I am saved."

After telling us to thank God in everything, the next verse says, "Do not quench (suppress or subdue) the [Holy] Spirit" (1 Thessalonians 5:19). I believe we quench the Holy Spirit through complaining. We need the Holy Spirit to work in our lives. The more thankful we are, the more freedom the Holy Spirit has to work in our situation. It's natural to complain, but it is supernatural to give thanks when we are tested and tried by life's circumstances.

> People who grumble and complain from daylight until dark never hear God.

ASKING GOD FOR ANSWERS OPENS OUR RECEIVERS

"If any of you is deficient in wisdom, let him ask of the giving God [Who gives] to everyone liberally and ungrudgingly, without reproaching or faultfinding, and it will be given him" (James 1:5). The context of this verse has to do with enduring trials.

If we need help, we are to ask God with confidence, and He will not judge us. He will not find fault in us for asking. He often broadcasts His answers to us in many ways, but if our receivers are jammed with unbelief, we can't receive them. Without faith we won't be listening for His answer. The Word explains that when we ask God for something, we must ask in faith with no wavering, no hesitating, and no doubting (see James 1:6). God wants us to be totally confident in Him to manifest His power and love in our lives. He doesn't ask us to live perfectly; He just asks us to trust Him and obey Him.

In answer to our plea for help, God may convict us of our need to apologize for offending someone. If we don't do it because of our embarrassment or pride, our guilt will stand in the way of our hearing from God. We shouldn't be surprised if every time we come to God for wisdom in a new area, we only hear the last thing He told us to do. We need to swallow our pride and just do it. Every time I have finally obeyed God, I have been greatly rewarded, both with relief and with a renewed relationship with Him and the people from whom I have been estranged through my disobedience.

Now I have reverential fear and awe of God and am obedient to His instructions. If God tells me to apologize to somebody, I go and do it. Sometimes it is hard, and sometimes it is embarrassing. Pride is lumpy; it doesn't go down easy. I would much rather that person came to me and fell all over me with apologies, but if God tells me to go, I go because I have developed a reverential fear and awe of the mighty God I serve. I know I can't give God some flimsy excuse for disobedience and expect to hear clearly from Him and operate in His anointing.

Another thing God may instruct us to do is to bless someone by giving them something that belongs to us. I encourage you not to fall in love with your belongings, then you won't be so oppressed when God tells you to get rid of them. I agree that it's hard to give things away if God tells you to do so, but it's more difficult to stand before Him with a guilty conscience than to just follow through and be a blessing to someone. We need to keep a right attitude toward things; having the peace of God and being able to hear from Him is much more important than holding on to things.

WHOLEHEARTED ATTENTION
OPENS OUR RECEIVERS

Everything that we take in through our ears and our eyes is either going to prosper us or poison us. Our hearts are like radios, and if we want to pick up God's message to us, we cannot tune in to all the other junk that is going on around us. God is broadcasting the assurance of His love for us, but there can be too much interference around us to hear Him speak.

We need to be quiet and peaceful in order to hear Him. Peace comes by obeying God to the very best of our ability and by the cleansing power of the blood of Jesus. Sometimes we depend on the cleansing power of the blood, yet we fail to understand the extreme importance of obedience.

We are to seek the Lord wholeheartedly. Many Christians only have a halfhearted interest in the pursuit of God. They want God to take care of them, but they don't really want to make the sacrifice of time and devotion it takes to grow in knowledge of Him and His Word—and they don't want to commit time to pray.

God told Abraham, "I will make a covenant with you. I will make your name famous. I will make you rich. I will do things for you that nobody else could do. I will give you a child in your old age. But here's your part; you must walk *wholeheartedly* before me" (see Genesis 12-15). Abraham fell on his face before God. He knew he was standing in the presence of an awesome God who meant business.

> We are to seek the Lord wholeheartedly.

Abraham understood that God had a plan for his life. God wanted Abraham and his heirs to prosper. God wanted good things to happen to him. That promise was passed on to all who would accept Jesus as their Lord. God wants us so happy that people will look at us and say, "That man serves a mighty God who cares for him; nobody else could make those things happen in that man's life but God."

God's glory is a wonderful exchange for our wholehearted devotion. Our full attention on God will keep the static out of our receivers so we can receive every good thing that He is trying to give us.

A PURE HEART KEEPS OUR RECEIVERS STATIC FREE

Jesus said, "Blessed are the pure in heart, for they shall see God" (see Matthew 5:8). If we have a pure heart, we will enjoy having clarity. We will see clearly God's plan for our lives. We won't feel aimless or confused. We will know that it is not God's will for us to feel guilty or condemned.

First John 3:21 confirms, "Beloved, if our consciences (our hearts) do not accuse us [if they do not make us feel guilty and condemn us], we have confidence (complete assurance and boldness) before God, and we receive from Him whatever we ask, because we [watchfully] obey His orders [observe His suggestions and injunctions, follow His plan for us] and [habitually] practice what is pleasing to Him."

If our conscience doesn't condemn us, we can receive what God is sending out to us. If disobedience is causing our conscience to be clouded, it's time to get rid of that static in our receivers. To keep our hearts pure before the Lord, we need to let Christ make His home in us and make His desires our desires.

As I wrote in the beginning pages of this book, Jesus said, "Be careful what you are hearing. The measure [of thought and study] you give [to the truth you hear] will be the measure [of virtue and knowledge] that comes back to you—and more [besides] will be given to you who hear" (Mark 4:24).

We are to use selective hearing when searching for a word from God. The Bible says that in the latter days many false prophets will rise up and tell people what their itching ears want to hear. People will search for one teacher after another who will tell them something pleasing and gratifying. To suit their own desires, they will turn away from hearing the truth and will wander off into listening to myths and man-made fictions (see 2 Timothy 4:3-4).

Never before have we seen such an influx of psychics vying for a ready ear. Television shows feature mediums who claim to be connecting with departed loved ones. They are communicating with familiar spirits who tell half-truths about the past and then lie about the future. God's Word clearly says, "Turn not to those [mediums] who have familiar spirits or to wizards; do not seek them out to be defiled by them. I am the Lord your God" (Leviticus 19:31). This is a serious command! Spiritualism, divination, and witchcraft are all forbidden in the Word of God.

God says that He will set His face against anyone who turns to mediums and spiritists to prostitute themselves by following them (see Leviticus 20:6-7). Yet Christians still read horoscopes and consult psychics and wonder why they don't have peace.

Many people, including some who consider themselves to be Christians, participate in practices that God considers vile and evil. They innocently think there is nothing wrong with such practices. Multitudes of people in the world consult the stars before making a decision, even for things as simple as when to cut their hair. However, a careful study of God's Word shows clearly that these things are an abomination to God. Even wearing and depending on "good luck charms" is an affront to God. Our faith must be in God alone, not God plus a lot of other things. Those of us who believe in Jesus Christ don't need to depend on luck; we can trust God that He will bless us.

Some religions teach people to worship nature—the stars, the moon, the sun, rocks, trees, and other things that

God has created. Why worship the stars when you can worship the One who made the stars? Why look to the stars for direction and advice when God's Spirit desires to lead you? God demands first place in our life; He is a jealous God, and we should always go to Him, not to things created by Him.

> Keep your heart pure and be careful what you listen to.

It is wrong to seek guidance for our life through anything other than God Himself. It offends God when we seek these other sources. No one who does so will ever have the peaceful, joy-filled, and prosperous life God intended for him or her to have. If you have been involved in any activity of this sort, I strongly encourage you to thoroughly repent, ask God to forgive you, and turn away completely from such practices.

Keep your heart pure and be careful what you listen to. Just as you can't tune in to two stations at once, neither can you serve two masters (see Luke 16:13). You may have to choose new friends if they are filling you with static contrary to the Word of God. You may have to change television stations at home, and choose new radio stations while you are riding in your car. Pay attention; if negative talk is filling the sound waves around you, make a change in your listening habits. Make sure that negative talk is not coming out of your own mouth.

The Word of God tells us that:

Immorality (sexual vice) and all impurity [of lustful, rich, wasteful living] or greediness must not even be named among you, as is fitting and proper among saints (God's consecrated people). Let there be no filthiness (obscenity, indecency) nor foolish and sinful (silly and corrupt) talk, nor coarse jesting, which are not fitting or becoming; but instead voice your thankfulness [to God]. For be sure of this: that no person practicing sexual vice or impurity in thought or in life, or one who is covetous [who has lustful desire for the property of others and is greedy for gain]—for he [in effect] is an idolater—has any inheritance in the kingdom of Christ and of God. (Ephesians 5:3-5)

There may be things in your life that need to be cut off, given up, and pruned back so that you can receive from God. You may even need to pay attention to the self-talk that goes on in your inner being. To hear from God you need to be willing to live on holy ground, and that means to keep your thoughts in line with God's Word. Focus on the truth that God has a plan for your life that includes many, many blessings. It is not possible to have God's blessings and continue to pursue desires of the flesh. So God will deal clearly with each of us to let us know what needs to be done to make our receivers free to hear Him. When He speaks, we are to obey Him quickly with reverence and honor because He is a holy God, and He desires to work holiness in us. He will reward us openly if we will obey Him secretly in the hidden realms of our hearts (see Matthew 6).

We must not strive with God; instead we are to let Him have full reign in our life. If we let Him lead, guide, and direct us, we will not miss or regret the plan He has for us. If we continue to resist Him, we will grieve all the days of our life because our inner man will know that we have missed His best.

TUNE OUT THE VOICE
OF ERROR

As believers it is our right and privilege to hear God speak to us. God gives us a discernment to know His voice over voices of deception. He parallels this discernment with the instinctive nature of sheep that recognize the voice of their shepherd.

Jesus taught this parable about a good shepherd: "The sheep listen to his voice and heed it; and he calls his own sheep by name and brings (leads) them out. When he has brought his own sheep outside, he walks on before them, and the sheep follow him because they *know his voice*" (John 10:3-4). Then He said, "I am the Good Shepherd; and I know and recognize My own, and My own know and recognize Me" (John 10:14).

If we truly belong to God, we will *know* His voice from the spirit of error. We will know that what we have heard is something that is in His nature to say. We will know that what He has said does not contradict His Word, or wisdom, or common sense.

It grieves me to hear from people who say, "God told me to do this," yet, it is obvious that a good shepherd would never tell them to do what they are doing. An example comes to mind of a young woman who for a while came to all of our conferences. She slept in her car, and we learned that she was deep in debt, without income. Yet, she believed God had *told* her to forsake all and come to our meetings.

We tried to tell her that God's voice of wisdom would not tell her to sleep in her car, because it isn't safe. Common sense says that we need to find work and pay our bills if we are in debt. A good shepherd would not have led this woman into a dangerous situation in which she had to beg for bread. She finally admitted that she lied about many things, which is evidence that she was following a spirit of error.

So people ask, "How can I be sure I am hearing from God?" The Word says that we just *know* His voice from others. We will know the difference between His voice and the voice of deception if we truly know His character, nature, and the history of how He has led others before us. Jesus said of His sheep, "They will never [on any account] follow a stranger, but will run away from him because they do not know the voice of strangers or recognize their call" (John 10:5).

Along with the gift of hearing God's voice, we are given the gift of discernment to know that it is truly God. If He speaks, He will also give us discernment to know it is God so we can trust when He is telling us to go forward or when He is telling us to wait.

To avoid the spirit of error, we simply need to look into God's Word. There we see a mirror of the glory of the Lord, and looking at His glory transforms us into His very own image "in ever increasing splendor and from one degree of glory to another" (2 Corinthians 3:18). The more we study and learn the Word, the more we will let its power flow through our life.

> We will know the difference between His voice and the voice of deception.

Spend time with God. Proverbs 4:20-23 says, "My son, attend to my words; consent and submit to my sayings. Let them not depart from your sight; keep them in the center of your heart. For they are life to those who find them, healing and health to all their flesh. Keep and guard your heart with all vigilance and above all that you guard, for out of it flow the springs of life."

Questions for Discussion

1. Do you believe that you can hear from God? If not, try joining me in this confession:

   "I hear from God. I am led by His Holy Spirit. I know my Father's voice, and the voice of a stranger I will not follow. I am led and guided by the Holy Spirit, even unto my death. God will guide me all the days of my life. He will guide me and give me the answers that I need."

2. Why do you think we're not able to receive from God when we walk in disobedience?

3. In what ways are you living before man instead of living before God? What does the Word say about this?

4. Is there an area of your life where you find yourself grumbling and complaining versus thanking God in all things? What would God have you do in this situation?

5. What is your understanding of the importance of obedience? How is this understanding reflected in your life? How does your understanding align with the Word of God?

6. How do you keep your full attention on God? In what ways are you already doing this? What areas do you need to work on?

7. What is the purpose of holiness and obedience? Should we pursue holiness and obedience for the sake of obtaining rewards from God? Why or why not?

8. What do you believe the Lord is leading you to in response to this chapter?

13

Sanctify Your Ears unto the Lord

God's Word promises that He will do a redemptive work in us to show us how to be led of His Spirit. First Thessalonians 5:23-24 explains:

> And may the God of peace Himself sanctify you through and through [separate you from profane things, make you pure and wholly consecrated to God]; and may your spirit and soul and body be preserved sound and complete [and found] blameless at the coming of our Lord Jesus Christ (the Messiah). Faithful is He Who is calling you [to Himself] and utterly trustworthy, and He will also do it [fulfill His call by hallowing and keeping you].

The Lord will teach us how to hear from Him. He will preserve our spirit, soul, and body, and He will lead us to a holy, sanctified life in Him.

Many people do not understand that we are a tri-part being: a spirit, soul, and body. We are a spirit, we have a soul, and we live in a body. God promises to take care of all three parts that make us who we are.

Many Christians make the mistake of thinking that God cares only about the spirit. But He wants us to be whole in mind (emotions) and body too.

I remember looking at myself in the mirror one night

when I was getting ready for a meeting. I said, "God, I belong to You, not to anybody else. I'm Dave Meyer's wife, and in that sense I belong to him, but in reality I belong to You."

As a Christian, you belong to God too. Jesus bought you with the price of His own life (see 1 Corinthians 6:20). You have a destiny to fulfill in a plan that God has designed specifically for you. There is something God wants you to do, something that God wants you to enjoy. You are not an accident. You were planned in the heart of God. He formed you in your mother's womb with His very own hand. His plan for you is revealed through the work of the Holy Spirit, whom Jesus sent to live inside of you.

If you are not familiar with the indwelling presence of the Holy Spirit, I encourage you to read my book *Knowing God Intimately*. In it I share in great detail how to receive the Holy Spirit into your everyday life and enjoy the awareness of His presence deep in your heart.

We are to work with the Holy Spirit to carry out the plan that began to operate in us when we accepted Jesus as our Lord and Savior. Our new birth begins in our spirit, is carried out through our soul (mind, will, and emotions), and is finally visible to other people through a demonstration of His glory in our physical lives.

God's glory is expedited by our knowledge of how He wants to work in us, and what we should do to fulfill His plan. We have to discern the difference between the leading of the Holy Sprit and the desires of our flesh. We won't lust for things our bodies crave if we follow the Spirit. We won't be led to the destructive desires of our human nature, if we make a habit of listening to the Holy Spirit and doing what He tells us to do (see Galatians 5:16-17).

We may as well stamp "disaster" across our foreheads if

we spend our lives doing whatever we feel like doing. Our feelings are fickle and can take us in a thousand different directions away from God's plan for us. Desires of the flesh won't disappear, but if we walk in the way the Spirit leads us, we won't fulfill the desires and lusts of the flesh. We will make choices that will lead us to abundant peace, joy, and righteousness (see Romans 14:17).

Every time God speaks to us, and we act like we don't hear Him, our hearts become a little more calloused until it becomes very hard for us to hear Him. Eventually, our stubbornness dulls our ability to hear at all. Each time we turn our back on what we know is the right thing to do, we become a little more obstinate until we are totally deaf to His leading.

> There is something God wants you to do, something that God wants you to enjoy.

In the sixth chapter of Jeremiah, the Lord told Jeremiah to warn His children of the impending destruction of the city that was full of oppression.

But the prophet responded, "To whom shall I [Jeremiah] speak and give warning that they may hear? Behold, their ears are uncircumcised [never brought into covenant with God or consecrated to His service], and they cannot hear or obey. Behold, the word of the Lord has become to them a reproach and the object of their scorn; they have no delight in it" (v. 10).

How tragic to see that God wants to protect and provide for His people, but they are not able to hear His voice because their ears are uncircumcised.

The most powerful Scripture in the New Testament about hearing from God is John 5:30 in which Jesus said, "I am able to do *nothing* from Myself [independently, of My own accord—but only as I am taught by God and as I get His orders]. Even as I hear, I judge [I decide as I am bidden to decide. As the voice comes to Me, so I give a decision], and My judgment is right (just, righteous), because I do not seek or consult My own will [I have no desire to do what is pleasing to Myself, My own aim, My own purpose] but only the will and pleasure of the Father Who sent Me."

Jesus had a sanctified, circumcised ear. He didn't do *anything* unless He heard the Father's voice concerning it. Imagine how different our lives would be if we asked God *before* we stepped out instead of calling on Him to rescue us from the messes we get ourselves into when we go our own way without His counsel.

God's Word shows us clearly that we need to listen for His voice and commit our ears into a covenant with Him, letting Him sanctify and circumcise our ears so that we can hear Him. Many times God clearly shows us what to do, but we don't do it because we don't like His plan. We can even pretend spiritual deafness when we don't like what we clearly hear Him say. Our fleshly appetites can hinder our acceptance of God's truth.

We can come face to face with truth and still not accept it. I admit that truth is much easier to accept when it concerns someone else and their lives than when it concerns us and our own lives. We have a plan for how we want our lives to go, and we have a way that we want to work out our plan. Most of the time we want God to make our plan work instead of listening to God for His plan. We should pray first and get God's plan, not plan first and then pray for God to make our plan work.

ASK GOD TO SANCTIFY AND CIRCUMCISE YOUR EARS

If you are not hearing the voice of God speak to you, I encourage you to ask the Father to sanctify and circumcise your ears to be sensitive to His leading. "Sanctify" means to set apart for a sacred purpose, and "circumcise" means to cut away the flesh. In asking God to sanctify and circumcise your ears, you are asking Him to make your ears sensitive to hear what is holy and right and to remove worldly temptations that distract you from His greater plan for your life.

In other words, ask God to give you ears that hear what He wants to say, not just what you want to hear. Ask for sanctified ears that are anointed to hear His voice with clear discernment, and circumcised ears to accurately hear His voice without the interference of fleshly desires.

> Ask God to give you ears that hear what He wants to say.

In Exodus 29, we read the story of how God sanctified Aaron and his sons to be priests in His sanctuary, the Tent of Meeting. God specified to Moses in great detail the ritual required to ordain Aaron and his sons for service before the Lord.

Moses was to cover Aaron and his sons with the ram's blood on their right ears, and the thumb of their right hands, and the great toe of their right feet, and then dash the rest of the blood around the altar. Then anointing oil was to be sprinkled upon Aaron and his garments and on his sons and their garments in order to sanctify them and make them holy (see vv. 20-21).

This ceremony is a physical picture of our own spiritual sanctification as priests unto the Lord (see Revelation 1:5-6). The shedding of Christ's blood for the wages of sin sanctifies those it covers, and the anointing of the Holy Spirit, represented by the oil, is poured out to empower for service those who are made righteous by the blood of Jesus.

It is significant that God instructed Moses to put the blood on the right ear, the right thumb, and the right great toe, because in the Bible the right side signifies the side of power. It was a ceremony with meaning that speaks a message to us today. The ear was anointed so the priest would hear clearly and not be deceived, the thumb so that what he laid his hand to do would be right and blessed, and the right toe so that everywhere he went would be correct and sanctified. This is God's desire for each of us.

We can hear, take action, and go in directions that are safe and divinely led. Just as Aaron and his sons were set apart for God's use, we believers are set apart for holy use too. Christ's blood sanctifies us for service to the Lord, and the Holy Spirit empowers us for good works.

A SANCTIFIED EAR HEARS GOD'S PLAN

We need to wake up to the spiritual realm of our lives. We need to get more comfortable fellowshipping with the Holy Spirit and hearing what He has to say to us. Many people still don't understand the work of the Holy Spirit in their lives. They may be curious about the supernatural or the unseen realm, but if they don't know what the Word of God says, they can be easily deceived about what is really happening in the spirit realm around them.

As surely as we have a physical body, we also have a spiritual body. When we understand where God is taking us, it helps us trust Him to lead us in the way we should go. First Corinthians 15:39-42 explains that while we begin life in our physical bodies, they will someday perish and decay. But as born-again believers, our spiritual bodies will be resurrected as imperishable and immune to decay.

God has made eternity quite clear in His Word. We are immortal through our faith in Jesus Christ, and we will spend more time in our spiritual bodies in heaven than we will in our physical bodies in this life. It seems wise to find out as much as we possibly can about our spiritual life rather than concerning ourselves about this temporal existence in which we presently live.

First Corinthians 15:44 tells us that one day our physical bodies, sown in dishonor and humiliation, will be raised in honor and glory. Our infirmities and weaknesses will be resurrected in strength and endued with power.

Even though he went through tremendous trials and tribulations, Paul did not become discouraged because he looked not to what was seen, but to what was unseen (see 2 Corinthians 4:18). We need to follow his example. Instead of looking at what we see around us, we need to look at what the Holy Spirit is doing. Through sanctified, circumcised ears He will lead us to focus on God's answers instead of our problems.

Two people can read the Word, and the person with carnal, fleshly ears will hear it differently from a person with circumcised ears. For example, John tells us, "Beloved, I pray that you may prosper in every way and [that your

> He will lead us to focus on God's answers instead of our problems.

body] may keep well, even as [I know] your soul keeps well and prospers" (3 John 2).

Less mature, carnal Christians (still lured by physical pleasures and appetites) may get excited about the promise of prosperity and healing, because that is all they hear in this Scripture. They think, *Wow! Praise God! He wants us to prosper and be in health!*

But mature believers who have sanctified ears that are sensitive to God's holy intent will also hear the part of the verse that says, "even . . . as your soul keeps well and prospers." They hear with understanding that God is going to give them prosperity and healing *in correlation* with how their souls are prospering.

I have developed a habit over the last few years of stopping frequently to see what I sense is in my spirit. Our soul (or mind) can be full of anxiety; an inner voice of self-talk may be screaming doubts into our thoughts, such as:

- You're not going to make it!
- This isn't going to work!
- This idea is stupid!
- Nobody cares what you're doing!
- You're not even hearing from God anyway!
- Why don't you sit down and shut up!

Negative thoughts can pound our heads to the point that we feel like giving up. But if we will pause and ask, "Lord, what do You have to say about this?" deep within our spirit, where the Holy Spirit dwells, we will sense His answer rising up with faith and promise and truth that sets us free from all the anxiety our mind has been feeding us.

I remember a specific instance when it really helped me to check to see what the Spirit was saying. I had completed a meeting and had worked very hard to ensure that it would be good and helpful to the people. Although they seemed to enjoy the meeting, I kept hearing in my head that "no one was blessed, and most wished they had not even come."

I felt like a miserable failure, which I knew was not God's will for me, so I got still and quiet and listened to see what the Holy Spirit would quicken to me in my spirit. I instantly heard the still, small voice, the knowing that is deep inside of us, say, "If the people did not want to be here, they would not have come; if they were not enjoying it, many of them would have left. I gave you the message, and I never give anyone bad things to preach, so don't allow Satan to steal the joy of your labor."

Your head may say, "God does not love you," but if you listen to your spirit through sanctified ears you will hear, "God loves you unconditionally and has a great plan for your life."

We hear from God through our spirit, not our mind. No wonder God says, "Let be and be still, and know (recognize and understand) that I am God" (Psalm 46:10).

So when the devil is pounding my mind, feelings, and emotions with unbelief and fear, I close my eyes for just a minute and say: "Lord, what is the truth?"

Then I just *know*. I know I am not going to quit doing what He has told me to do. I know I am not going to give up the plan He has laid out before me. I know I am indeed hearing from God. I know God has called and anointed me, so I am pressing on to the finish line.

As you learn the difference between the functions of your spirit and the functions of your soul and body, you will find it easier to discern when the devil is trying to wear away your enthusiasm, and when you need to rebuild your energy through fellowship with the Holy Spirit.

LISTENING AND OBEYING DETERMINES OUR ETERNAL DESTINY

The spiritual part of man lives forever, either in heaven or in hell. To live in hell is to live in total separation from God, which would be the most awful existence. We cannot comprehend how horrid it would be to live in total separation from the presence of God. To be separated from Him means to be completely disconnected from any form of comfort, grace, provision, protection, and most of all intimate fellowship.

Even unbelievers now enjoy a measure of the presence of God in the earth, though they don't realize it. But in hell there will not be any peace, just the loneliness of total darkness.

Eternity is forever, and we need to be more concerned with eternity than most of us seem to be right now. One day a trumpet will sound, and Jesus will return for us (see 1 Thessalonians 4:16-17). We will know then that the time we spend seeking Him and leading others to Him *now* will have been worth it.

There is nothing of greater value in which to invest our time than learning to hear the voice of God speaking to our spirit. The Bible says, "For the Word that God speaks is alive and full of power [making it active, operative, energizing,

> Eternity is forever, and we need to be more concerned with eternity.

and effective]; it is sharper than any two-edged sword, penetrating to the dividing line of the breath of life (soul) and [the immortal] spirit, and of joints and marrow [of the deepest parts of our nature], exposing and sifting and analyzing and judging the very thoughts and purposes of the heart" (Hebrews 4:12).

When God speaks, He divides the thoughts of our soul from the truth in our spirit and brings to life His purposes in us. When I became a student of the Word, I didn't know when I was operating in the soul and when I was operating in the spirit. I didn't know when I was operating emotionally until I studied God's Word and learned to operate by faith in His promises.

When I wanted something, I just tried to make it happen. I tried in all the wrong ways. If I wasn't getting my way, I pouted and threw fits. Sometimes I wouldn't talk to Dave for days on end, hoping to manipulate him to give in and give me what I wanted. All I cared about was what *I* wanted. I was carnal, selfish, self-centered, and extremely miserable because I was all wrapped up in myself.

Many people get into a relationship with God hoping that He will give them what they want. Their life prayer is a list of everything *they* want. Consequently, they remain baby Christians all their life. They slip in the door of heaven when they die, but they never have victory in this life, because they haven't learned to listen to God and hear what He wants for them.

We cannot walk in the flesh and have victory or be truly happy! We cannot spend our life seeking to satisfy our own appetites and still affect anybody else's life in a positive way.

It is not possible. If we follow the leading of the Holy Spirit we will not fulfill the lusts of our flesh (see Galatians 5:16).

GOD RESTORES OUR SOUL

For a period of time, I rebuked whatever I didn't want because I thought it must be from the devil. I rebuked until my "rebuker" was just totally worn out! But then I discovered that a lot of what I was trying to rebuke was from God. Many of the things that I did not like or want were things God had allowed for my growth and development.

Many Christians say, "God told me," when what they heard wasn't from Him at all. That's why it is so important to know whether the voice we are listening to is from our soul or our spirit.

Psalm 23 says that God restores our soul. Our soul is our unique personality free to choose what it will believe. We process the knowledge we have gained in our mind and make decisions according to what we believe.

Our soul doesn't tell us what God wants; it reports only what it knows about our own desires. Our soul tells us what we feel; our spirit tells us how God feels. Our soul tells us what *we* think, not what God thinks. What we want, think, and feel can be very different from what God wants, thinks, and feels. But as we communicate in our spirit with God, a work can be done to transform our soul to think like Christ. Our soul *needs* to be renewed and refreshed to think like the mind of Christ.

We can allow a Holy Ghost invasion into our lives. We can be so filled with the Spirit of God that we allow Him into every room in our life. He can get into our thoughts, emotions, and even our will. To renew our thoughts, we need new information from God's Word and from His voice speaking directly to our spirit.

Philippians 2 teaches us to work out our salvation with fear and trembling by shrinking from whatever might offend God or discredit the name of Christ (see v. 12). When our feelings run amuck, we need to keep them from running our lives. We need to submit our will to what God tells us to do through His Word to us.

If we don't feel like going to church, we go anyway. If we don't feel like giving that hundred-dollar offering God told us to give, we do it anyway. If God tells us to give away items we feel like keeping, we give them away with joy. I have discovered that if I

> All He wants
> from us is
> our own
> obedience.

want to be happy, and if I want to have an anointing on my life, then I must be obedient to the voice of God. I don't always have to know *why* God wants me to do something. I just need to know *what* He tells me to do—and then do it!

"Walking in the Spirit" is a phrase that charismatic believers have used loosely in the past few decades. What it means to me is to hear God speak and do whatever He tells me to do. We can point our finger when we see that other people aren't obeying God, but all He wants from us is our own obedience.

I remember when God started dealing with me to be more patient. I knew He wanted me to ask Him to work more patience in me, but I didn't pray for that because I knew what would happen if I did. So I said, "No, I'm not praying for that yet." I was smart enough to understand that to develop patience I would have to go through trials that I didn't want to endure.

We were in the final stages of restoring a fifty-two-year-old house, and I was eager to see it finished, when finally in obedience to God's prompting, I asked Him to teach me patience. I prayed for Him to perfect my faith and to keep me from lacking any good thing.

Of course, we needed to close on the house we were in before we could move into our new house; that's when everything started going wrong. Contractors didn't show up to finish their projects, the wrong sink and countertop were delivered, furniture was delivered to us that we didn't choose. I had a lot of opportunity to learn patience in those last weeks before the house was finished. God knew it was a perfect opportunity for me to learn to be long-suffering.

I told the supervisors at the building site, "You all better be glad I'm saved!" My soul was stirred up! It seemed to me that everyone on the job ought to have been able to get things done, but they just said, "There's nothing we can do. We're doing all we can. That's just the way it is in the industry."

That was so hard for me to hear. My soul needed to be restored. It takes much longer to get calmed down than it does to get upset. I'm much more patient now than I used to be, but at the time I wished I had waited until the house was finished before I asked God to teach me about patience! God has done a good work in me now. I have changed a lot, but that test stretched my soul.

GOD AWAKENS OUR SPIRIT WITHIN US

We communicate with God through our spirit. Jesus said that we must worship God in spirit and in truth (see John 4:24). Our spirit intuitively senses God's presence and receives revelation when there is a better way to do something.

The mind receives head knowledge, but the spirit receives a deeper sense of knowing, which many people try to describe by saying, "It was just in my heart." There are things we know because we have learned them, but there are also things we know that we haven't learned because the Holy Spirit communicates them to us through our own spirit. For example, sometimes when I'm preaching, I will say things that I haven't thought of before. I'm as surprised as anybody else at the profound wisdom in the teaching.

Our conscience is also part of our spirit man. When our spirit is made alive to the awareness of God, we can fellowship with Him and receive answers from Him through our intuition and conscience. Our spirit and soul should work together, and the body should act as a servant to both.

When the body rules a person's mind and spirit, God's plan for that individual gets turned upside down. Jesus said, "All of you must keep awake (give strict attention, be cautious and active) and watch and pray, that you may not come into temptation. The spirit is willing, but the flesh is weak" (Matthew 26:41).

Jesus was trying to get the disciples to pray with Him, but they kept falling asleep. He was trying to prepare them for the temptation that was coming. He was saying, "Don't sleep, pray! You're going to be tempted beyond what you can bear if you don't pray." He wanted them to do what He was doing.

As Jesus prayed, an angel came and strengthened Him in spirit enabling Him to endure the temptation that was coming against Him. But the disciples didn't pray, they slept, and proved that the flesh is weak.

Our spirit is willing to do what is right, but our flesh will not help us. Our flesh will pull us under if we don't pray and ask God to strengthen us in spirit and to circumcise our hearts to resist temptation. Isaiah 11:1-3 speaks of Jesus, saying:

> There shall come forth a Shoot out of the stock of Jesse [David's father], and a Branch out of his roots shall grow and bear fruit. And the Spirit of the Lord shall rest upon Him—the Spirit of wisdom and understanding, the Spirit of counsel and might, the Spirit of knowledge and of the reverential and obedient fear of the Lord—and shall make Him of quick understanding, and His delight shall be in the reverential and obedient fear of the Lord. And He shall not judge by the sight of His eyes, neither decide by the hearing of His ears.

Jesus didn't make decisions on how He felt, or by what He thought, heard, or saw. He's the One who said, "Lord, let this cup pass from Me; nevertheless Your will be done and not Mine" (see Matthew 26:38-39). It wasn't that He didn't have desires just as we do, but He didn't walk by His will (soul); He walked by what He knew was right in His Spirit.

We need to live in a realm deeper than our bodies, deeper than our souls; we need to live in our deepest place—our spirit, which can communicate with the Spirit of God and accurately hear the way we should go. Jesus made decisions out of this spiritual realm. We get in trouble when we don't make decisions out of this spiritual realm.

People who enjoy a good life are those who walk with God and overcome problems by listening to the Spirit who speaks to their heart. They see things in the spirit, they understand the difference between thoughts from their soul and intuition from their spirit. More and more, little by little, they are obeying the Spirit of God and not yielding to the desires of their flesh, and they are enjoying victory in their everyday lives because of it.

The only time we ever have a victory is when we go through things and learn how to hear from God. Victory comes when we say no to the flesh, die to self, and do what God has said to do—no matter how we feel about it, and no matter what anybody thinks.

> We need to live in our deepest place— our spirit.

David, the psalmist, taught us how to seek God's leading, saying, "I call to remembrance my song in the night; with my heart I meditate and my spirit searches diligently" (Psalm 77:6).

The next time you have a decision to make, don't try to figure it out with your head. Go somewhere to get still and let your spirit search diligently for God's voice. Commit your ears, hands, and feet to Him in prayer:

Lord,
I ask that You anoint my ears to hear Your voice, anoint my hands to work at Your plan, anoint my feet to go only where You lead me. Sanctify me for Your purpose, and circumcise my heart to desire what You desire for me. Amen.

Questions for Discussion

1. Is there an area of your life where you have planned first and then asked God to bless your decision? What do you think you should do in response to this realization?

2. What is the difference between your spirit and your soul? Which are you living according to?

3. What does it mean to renew and refresh your spirit? Does yours need renewing and refreshing? What are some ways in which you can do so?

4. What do you base your decisions on? Emotions, the Word of God, what other people think, or a combination thereof? Why?

5. Describe a recent victory (according to the definition in this chapter of what a victory is) you have had in your own life. How did it make you feel?

6. How do you distinguish between head knowledge and a deeper sense of knowing in your spirit? What are you more prone to?

7. What do you believe the Lord is leading you to in response to this chapter?

14

Enjoy the Spirit-Led Life

⸺⸻

God has an awesome plan to radically and outrageously bless us, but to fully enjoy His plan we must radically and outrageously obey Him. We need God's help to stay on the pathway to His blessings. God knows how to wrestle us to the ground if He has to, and every day I give Him permission to do just that to me.

God puts His Holy Spirit in us to lead us to perfect peace. If we are listening to what gives us peace, we will make wise decisions. The apostle Paul wrote, "Everything is permissible (allowable and lawful) for me; but not all things are helpful (good for me to do, expedient and profitable when considered with other things). Everything is lawful for me, but I will not become the slave of anything or be brought under its power" (1 Corinthians 6:12).

There are many things that we *could* do, and God wouldn't say a thing about them. We refer to this as God's permissive will. He isn't going to give us a divine word about every single move we make. But He will always give us wisdom if we ask His opinion. He is faithful to fill our hearts with peace when we are on the right path, and to remove peace from us when we begin to go astray.

I have a strong personality. For a while, I was concerned that no matter how much I wanted to obey God, I might never be able to walk in His perfect will. But God has shown me that He will keep me in His perfect will if I will pray and trust Him. If I get off track, He will make sure that I get back on it by His grace. I have learned that we can depend on God to help us remain obedient.

Our prayer every morning should be something like this:

God,

I want to walk in Your perfect will all my life. I don't want Your permissive will; I don't want to do anything without Your approval and blessing. If I try to do something that's not Your best for me, please let me feel hesitation in my heart, a check in my spirit, to keep me on the path of Your plan.

Help me to submit myself to You.

Help me not to be stiff-necked.

Help me not to be stubborn.

Help me not to be hard-hearted.

God, I want Your will to operate fully in my life. I've experienced the fruit of my own will enough to know that if I get my way, and it's not what You want, it's going to turn out bad. I'm willing to obey You, but please help me to hear clearly what You are telling me to do. Amen.

If we will pray like that, I believe God will keep us in His perfect will. I've lived life my way long enough to know that my plans aren't as rewarding as God's. I pray that He won't let me get by with anything that isn't in His will for me.

If I'm praying for something that's not covered clearly in the Word of God, if I'm facing a decision that I can't find chapter and verse to lead me through, then I pray:

God,
I want this, but I want Your will more than I want my
own. So if my request is not in Your timing, or if what
I'm asking for is not what You want for me, then please
don't give it to me. Amen.

We can get emotionally driven to do something that seems like it is from God, but after a while we may find that perhaps it is just a good idea that doesn't have a hope without the power of God's anointing. But God is not obligated to finish anything He didn't originate. We can pray about the projects we start, but there is no point in getting mad at God if He won't finish them for us.

The Bible says that we should fix our eyes on Jesus, who is the Author and the Finisher of our faith (see Hebrews 12:1-3). If we keep our eyes on Jesus, and obey His voice, we will enjoy the outrageous blessings of the abundant life He has promised. Hearing God speak to us is life's greatest blessing:

> God is not obligated to finish anything He didn't originate.

Happy (blessed, fortunate, enviable) is the man who finds skillful and godly Wisdom, and the man who gets understanding [drawing it forth from God's Word and life's experiences], for the gaining of it is better than the gaining of silver, and the profit of it better than fine gold. Skillful and godly Wisdom is more precious than rubies; and nothing you can wish for is to be compared to her. Length of days is in her right hand, and in her left hand are riches and honor. Her ways are highways of pleasantness, and all her paths are peace. (Proverbs 3:13-17)

GOD WILL LEAD YOU TO RIGHT DECISIONS

When we listen to God's direction, we make wise decisions that lead to riches, honor, pleasantness, and peace. In other words, as I have said, we will be radically and outrageously blessed. Once Dave and I pray for God to guide us, we just use wisdom and common sense for both minor and major issues.

Wisdom will always lead you to God's best. Wisdom teaches that you won't keep friends if you try to control and dominate everything that goes on in your life and theirs. You won't keep friends if you talk about them behind their back. Wisdom says, "Don't say things about others that you wouldn't want people saying about you."

Common sense will guide you in money matters. You won't get in debt if you don't spend more money than you make. A lot of people never have a fruitful ministry because they think they can run a ministry without good business principles. The Holy Ghost doesn't need to speak in an audible voice to tell us that we can't have more money going out than we have coming in. We'll get in trouble if we do that.

Wisdom will not let us get overcommitted in our time. No matter how anxious we may be to accomplish things, we need to take time and wait on God to give us peace about what we are to do and not do. It has been very difficult for me over the years to learn to say no to speaking opportunities, but I have learned that it is not wisdom to wear myself out trying to do so much that I end up not doing anything in a quality way.

To God, quality is more important than quantity. Many

times wisdom leads us to say no to things that we would like to say yes to, and vice versa. Wisdom may lead us to say yes to something to which we would like to say no. If a friend invites me to do something that is extremely important to her, and I have recently had to say no to her several times, even if I don't really want to accept the invitation it might be wise for me to do so if I value her friendship and want to keep it.

Wisdom is our friend; it helps us not to live in regret. I think the saddest thing in the world would be to reach old age and look back at my life and feel nothing but regret about what I did or did not do. Wisdom helps us make choices that we will be happy with later on. Wisdom has nothing to do with emotions. We must look beyond feelings to know the will of God.

Peter wasn't sure what he should do after Jesus rose from the dead and proved Himself alive to him and the disciples. So he went back to what he was doing before he met Jesus, saying to the others, "I'm going fishing." (I like the King James Version of that verse in which Peter says, "I go a fishing.") The story is in John 21:2-18. The others decided to go fishing with Peter. They fished throughout the night, but caught nothing.

"Morning was already breaking when Jesus came to the beach and stood there. However, the disciples did not know that it was Jesus. So Jesus said to them, Boys (children), you do not have any meat (fish), do you? [Have you caught any-thing to eat along with your bread?] They answered Him, No!" (vv. 4-5). Emotional decisions usually leave us "catching nothing." In other words, they don't provide the kind of results with which we will be satisfied.

"And He said to them, Cast the net on the right side of the boat and you will find [some]. So they cast the net, and now they were not able to haul it in for such a big catch

> Emotional decisions usually leave us "catching nothing."

(mass, quantity) of fish [was in it]" (v. 6).

It's interesting that Jesus didn't call the disciples men, but rather He called them children. He asked them, "Are you doing any good at what you are trying to do?" That is a question we might ask ourselves when we have no fruit (or fish) to show for the long hours we work.

When we fish outside of the will of God, it's equivalent to fishing on the wrong side of the boat. Sometimes we struggle, strive, work, and strain, trying to make something great happen. We try to change things, or change ourselves, or get our ministry started, or make it grow. We try to get more money. We try to get healed. We try to change our spouse, or even try to find a spouse. We can work and work and work and work, but still have nothing to show for our labor.

Have you caught anything? Have you accomplished anything besides getting worn out? If your answer is no, you may be fishing on the wrong side of the boat. If you listen for God's voice, He will tell you where to throw your net.

Just pray:

God,
Whatever You want for me, that's what I want. I surrender my life to You. Your will be done and not mine. Amen.

GOD WILL LEAD YOU TO GOOD WORKS

"When they had eaten, Jesus said to Simon Peter, Simon, son of John, do you love Me more than these [others do— with reasoning, intentional, spiritual devotion, as one loves the Father]? He said to Him, Yes, Lord, You know that I love You [that I have deep, instinctive, personal affection for You, as for a close friend]. He said to him, Feed My lambs" (John 21:15).

Three times Jesus asked Peter, "Do you love me? Peter, do you love me? Do you love me Peter?" Finally, by the third time, Peter was grieved that Jesus kept asking him the same thing. He said, "Yes, Lord, You know that I love You." Then we discover the solemn reason Jesus was asking Peter that question.

"I assure you, most solemnly I tell you, when you were young you girded yourself [put on your own belt or girdle] and you walked about wherever you pleased to go. But when you grow old you will stretch out your hands, and someone else will put a girdle around you and carry you where you do not wish to go" (John 21:18).

God challenged me with that Scripture because I had my own plan and was walking in my own way. If we really want God's perfect will, He may ask us to do things that we do not want to do. If we really love Him, we will let Him have His way in our lives.

I believe that Jesus was showing us that when we were young Christians, and less mature, we went wherever we pleased. As baby Christians, we did what we wanted to do. But as we mature, we are to stretch out our hands and surrender ourselves to God. We must be willing to follow Him to places we may not want to go.

There are many messages that can be taken from this text. If we love Jesus, our bottom line of obedience is to care for those whom He loves. In His words to Peter, Jesus was saying to us, "If you love Me, do something for somebody else, on My behalf."

Jesus said, "If you [really] love Me, you will keep (obey) My commands" (John 14:15). To whatever degree we love Him, to that same degree we obey him. To whatever degree we are obeying God, that's the measure of our love for Him. Our love for Jesus grows as we obey Him.

I'm radically and outrageously in love with Jesus. I love Him more than I did when I first put my trust in Him. Because I love Him, I am willing to obey Him even if it means suffering in the flesh and not pleasing myself.

> So, since Christ suffered in the flesh for us, for you, arm yourselves with the same thought and purpose [patiently to suffer rather than fail to please God]. For whoever has suffered in the flesh [having the mind of Christ] is done with [intentional] sin [has stopped pleasing himself and the world, and pleases God], so that he can no longer spend the rest of his natural life living by [his] human appetites and desires, but [he lives] for what God wills. (1 Peter 4:1-2)

It's important to understand the difference between suffering in the flesh and suffering demonic affliction. Giving up the selfish appetites of our flesh does not mean we are to suffer from sickness, disease, and poverty. Jesus died to deliver us from the curse of sin. But unless we are willing to suffer in the flesh, we will never walk in the will of God.

When we get up in the morning, we should prepare ourselves for the day by thinking with the mind of Christ. We should set our thoughts on walking in God's will all day long. We might even say to ourselves, "Even if I need to suffer in order to do God's will today, I am setting my mind for obedience."

To follow through with our good intentions, we have to love Him enough to let the love of God govern our day. The Word says, "Arm yourselves with this kind of thinking, that I would rather suffer than fail to please God" (see 1 Peter 4:1). If you learn to think like that, you will never intentionally disobey God again.

GOD WILL SPEAK CLEARLY SO YOU WILL NOT DOUBT

God has spoken to His people with clear instruction from Genesis through Revelation. His first words to mankind were filled with the promise of blessing. As soon as He created man and woman, He blessed them and said, "Be fruitful, multiply, and fill the earth, and subdue it [using all its vast resources in the service of God and man]; and have dominion over the fish of the sea, the birds of the air, and over every living creature that moves upon the earth" (Genesis 1:28).

In the first chapter of the book of the Revelation of Jesus Christ, John writes that he heard a voice saying, "I am the Alpha and Omega, the Beginning and the End" (v. 8). The entire book of Revelation is a record of what John was told by the Spirit of God.

When Saul, who had

> We have to love Him enough to let the love of God govern our day.

been persecuting Christians, was on the road to Damascus, a great light shown about him (see Acts 9). The voice of the Lord spoke to him saying, "Saul, Saul, why are you persecuting Me?" And Saul, who was later renamed Paul, said right away, "Lord, what do You desire me to do?" (see vv. 4-6).

It's not difficult to understand why God chose Paul to lead the rest of us into a mature walk with God. First of all, God chose the worst sinner He could find to show us what grace really is. By converting Paul, God demonstrated His miraculous power to put us on the road to blessings. If He could redirect Paul, who was as far away from God's perfect will as he could get, He can also save us from our foolish ways.

Paul was full of religious zeal, but he was persecuting Christians! He was sincere, but sincerely wrong. He genuinely believed that he was doing God a service by capturing and imprisoning Christ's followers. As soon as Jesus corrected Paul, he submitted and asked, "Lord, what do You want me to do?"

When God does speak to us, He wants to hear us say, "Yes, Lord, Your servant hears You. What would You have me do?"

God clearly tells us what He wants us to do in His Word. If you want to hear Him speak to you more clearly, then stay in the Word. He will speak to you through the written (*logos*) Word. He will enlighten Scriptures that will give you relevant living words (His *rhema*) to show you what He wants you to know and do.

There have been times, when I was reading the Bible, searching for direction, that a Scripture seemed to illuminate the entire page. That Scripture then specifically answered my need at that time. The Word came alive, full of meaning, just as if I was in an intimate conversation with God.

The more you know the written Word, the more He can bring to your remembrance Scriptures you need for answers throughout the day. The ideas, thoughts, promptings, and inner witness that we have discussed in this book will always be in line with God's written Word.

One day, I was emotionally hurt over something that had happened. Dave and I had been treated unfairly and unjustly in a certain situation, and I was feeling down about it. I was on an airplane, so I decided to read the Bible. When I opened it to Zechariah 9:12, the words seemed to jump off the page at me. It said, "Return to the stronghold [of security and prosperity], you prisoners of hope; even today do I declare that I will restore double your former prosperity to you."

When I saw that verse, my faith went to a new level. I knew without a doubt that God was speaking to me about my situation. I knew that if I would not give up hope, if I would have the right attitude, that I would see the day when God would give me back double what had been taken from me in that situation.

Almost one year later, to the day, God did an outstanding work and proved Himself true to His promise by restoring double what had been unjustly taken from us, and He restored it through the same people who had mistreated us! God's justice is sweet; don't fail to wait for it.

Jesus taught that a mature heart is like good soil that hears the Word, retains it, and, by persevering, produces a fruitful crop (see Luke 8:15). The Holy Ghost knows exactly what you need to renew your hope. I opened the Bible expecting to get a word from God to help me, but He surpassed my greatest hope by not only comforting me, but by promising to restore my loss. That Scripture is your promise too. Hang on to hope in God's Word. Don't let His promises slip away by not knowing what He is saying. Faith comes by hearing, and hearing by the Word of God (see Romans 10:17).

GOD WILL LEAD YOU THROUGH PEACE

I previously pointed out that God leads His people through peace, but now I would like to elaborate on this subject simply because it is so important. People who do things they don't have peace about have miserable lives and don't succeed at anything. Follow peace!

God leads His people through peace: "And God's peace [shall be yours, that tranquil state of a soul assured of its salvation through Christ, and so fearing nothing from God and being content with its earthly lot of whatever sort that is, that peace] which transcends all understanding shall garrison and mount guard over your hearts and minds in Christ Jesus" (Philippians 4:7).

If you are doing something, like watching television, and all of a sudden you lose your peace about what you are doing, you have heard from God. A lack of peace is God saying to you, "Turn it off. Go the other way. Flee from what you are doing." God's Word says, "Keep and guard your heart with all vigilance and above all that you guard, for out of it flow the springs of life" (Proverbs 4:23).

If we don't have peace, we are not obeying God because we are to let the peace of God rule as an umpire in our heart: "And let the peace (soul harmony which comes) from Christ *rule* (act as umpire continually) in your hearts

> God leads His people through peace.

[deciding and settling with finality all questions that arise in your minds, in that peaceful state] to which as [members of Christ's] one body you were also called [to live]. And be thankful (appreciative), [giving praise to God always]" (Colossians 3:15).

If you lose your peace when you say something, God is speaking to you. It will save you a lot of trouble if you apologize right then. You can say, "I am sorry that I said that. I was wrong to say it; please forgive me."

Anytime we lose our peace, we are hearing from God. I love the move of the supernatural, but there is nothing more powerful than the compass of peace in our heart. God will lead us gracefully by peace. Follow after it: "Strive to live in peace with everybody and pursue that consecration and holiness without which no one will [ever] see the Lord" (Hebrews 12:14).

GOD WILL LEAD YOU BY A STILL, SMALL VOICE

The audible voice of God does not come to us very often. The primary way we hear from God is through His still, small voice within, or that inner witness. The primary reason we don't hear Him is we are just too busy. He says to us, "Let be and be still, and know (recognize and understand) that I am God" (Psalm 46:10).

I mentioned earlier the time Elijah was running from the

death threats of Jezebel and needed to hear from God (see 1 Kings 19). Elijah was a great man of God, but he found himself in a desperate situation. It is meant to comfort us to know that this great prophet of God was a human being with a nature just like ours (see James 5:17). He had the same feelings and affections that we have and a constitution just like ours. Yet he prayed for it not to rain, and it didn't rain for six months. When he prayed for it to rain, it rained (see vv. 17-18). But Elijah wound up in so much fear that he asked the Lord to take his life.

His story shows us that no matter how great our faith may be, we will still need to hear from God at some point in our lives. When we get into trouble, God will come and help us get back on the right path, if we develop a reining ear that listens for His voice. Elijah's story reminds us that God understands our weaknesses, and that even if we make mistakes, we can still pray powerful prayers that God will hear:

As he lay asleep under the broom or juniper tree, behold, an angel touched him and said to him, Arise and eat. He looked, and behold, there was a cake baked on the coals, and a bottle of water at his head. And he ate and drank and lay down again. The angel of the Lord came the second time and touched him and said, Arise and eat, for the journey is too great for you. So he arose and ate and drank, and went in the strength of that food forty days and nights to Horeb, the mount of God. There he came to a cave and lodged in it; and behold, the word of the Lord came to him, and He said to him, What are you doing here, Elijah? He replied, I have been very jealous for the Lord God of hosts; for the Israelites have forsaken Your covenant, thrown down Your altars, and killed Your prophets with the sword. And I, I only, am left; and they seek my life, to take it away. And He said, Go out and stand on the mount before the Lord. And behold, the Lord passed by, and a great and strong wind rent the mountains and broke in pieces the rocks before the Lord, but the Lord was not in the wind; and after the wind an earthquake, but the Lord was not in the earthquake; And after the earthquake a fire, but the Lord was not in the fire; and after the fire [a sound of gentle stillness and] a still, small voice. (1 Kings 19:5-12)

When Elijah heard the voice, he went out of the cave. God asked Him again, "What are you doing here?"

I don't know exactly what the wind, the earthquake, and the fire represent; but I think there's a good possibility that they represent all of the turmoil

> When we have turmoil going on around us, it is very difficult for us to hear from God.

that was going on in Elijah. I imagine his mind was in awful confusion, his emotions were in chaos, and his will was upset.

I'm so happy God rescued Elijah from his sense of failure.

I need that assurance myself. I think one of the reasons so many people listen to me is because I admit all the wrong things I do, and people can relate to making mistakes. When we have turmoil going on around us, it is very difficult for us to hear from God.

One of the things that I think is a problem today is the busy, hurried, frantic, stressful lifestyles that people live. Busyness makes it very challenging to hear from God. One of the best favors you can do for yourself is to find a place where you can be still and quiet.

GET ALONE WITH GOD

Hearing God requires quiet solitude. If you really want to hear the still, small voice of God, you will have to be still. You need to go somewhere and be alone. Find a cave, like Elijah found, where you can simply be still. Jesus said, "Go into your most private room and shut the door" (see Matthew 6:6).

You need extended periods of quiet to seek God. You need to be free of distractions and interruptions. I'm not saying you need this all of the time, but you must have time when you can be alone with God. If not, you are missing His best for you.

In moments alone with God, He will give you a vision of where you need to go. As you take steps toward your destiny, you need to revisit Him frequently to learn the next step to take.

Dave and I have offices in our home where we can pray and study. All of our kids work for us at our main office just a few minutes from our house. They are frequently in and out of our home when they need something. At our main office, our phones ring constantly. Anytime I come out the office door, there is someone there needing to ask me questions. Even with two offices, I don't have a place to get alone and seek God without interruptions.

I have had to find a place where I can go that no one can find me. I give about three people the phone number where I am. They know not to call me for anything other than an extreme emergency.

I have to get alone with God; sometimes I have two or three days alone with Him. I cannot fulfill my calling without that time with Him. I have a job, a mandate, from God to bring a word to this nation and to the world. I need to hear from God. If I am not alone to give Him first place in my life, I cannot hear from God or be led by the Holy Ghost. I have to have time to give the Lord my undivided attention.

You can't wait until turmoil demands that you seek God. No one can find time to spend with Him for you. You have to get decisive and tell people around you, "I have to be alone to seek God."

I kept trying to fit God into all the unsuccessful things that were keeping me busy. One of the best pieces of advice the Lord ever gave me was this: "*Don't try to work Me into your schedule; work your schedule around Me.*" I had to entirely change my approach and put God first. I found that whatever else didn't get done simply didn't need to be done anyway.

When you are alone with God, don't think about your problems. Sit down, get quiet, and answer God's question when He asks you, "What are you doing here?"

Tell Him you want to know what He has for your life.

Ask Him to tell you what He wants you to do.

Ask Him to tell you what He *doesn't* want you to do.

Present yourself to God and listen. You are honoring Him by going to Him. You *will* get an answer from Him. If you don't hear Him speak during your time alone with Him, keep a reining ear turned toward His throne, and in the following days look for ways He answers you.

A young girl said to me, "I don't understand God at all. I spent many hours praying, trying to get a word from Him, and He never said one thing to me." But she added, "Two days later, as I was walking across the kitchen to the refrigerator, God spoke to me about the thing I had prayed about." She wanted to know, "Why didn't He answer me before?"

I said, "I can't answer that, but if we are diligent to seek God and show Him that we want His will, He promises to speak to us. It may not be in our timing, but He will speak to us. I am certain that God will not to speak to us if we don't spend time with Him."

I think that sometimes we try too hard to hear from God. What I mean is that we actually want to hear so badly we get tense about it; we let it make us anxious and almost fearful that He may not speak or we may not hear. This could be one of the reasons we often hear later after we have had a time of seeking Him. Later we are relaxed, just going about our ordinary business, and He is able to speak because then we can hear.

You will hear God speak in a moment of inner and outer silence: "And your ears will hear a word behind you, saying, This is the way; walk in it, when you turn to the right hand and when you turn to the left" (Isaiah 30:21). He will direct your path one step at a time.

God's Greatest Desire

God's greatest desire for His children is that they experience His best in their lives. He wants to have close fellowship with us and to be invited into every area of our lives. He wants to speak to us and lead us in all our decisions by His Spirit.

It is God's will that we hear clearly from Him. He does not want us living in confusion and fear. We are to be decisive, secure, and free. He wants each of us to fulfill our destiny and to walk in the fullness of His plan for us.

Yes, we can hear from God in a personal, intimate way.

Listen, that is the first step toward hearing. Turn your ear toward Him and be still. He will speak to you to tell you He loves you. He cares about your life and what you need. God wants to meet your needs and do more than you could ever think or imagine in order to bless you abundantly (see Ephesians 3:20). He will never leave you or forsake you (see Hebrews 13:5). Listen to Him and follow Him all the days of your life.

> He will direct your path one step at a time.

God's greatest desire is to have a people who worship Him in Spirit and in truth (see John 4:23-24), who follow Him and know His voice (see John 10:2-14). The depth of our personal relationship with God is based upon intimate communication with Him. He speaks to us so that we are guided, refreshed, restored, and renewed regularly.

Romans 14:17 teaches us that the kingdom of God is not meat and drink, but it is righteousness, peace, and joy in the Holy Spirit. God desires that all of His children enjoy a life of right relationship with Him through Jesus Christ, that they have peace and abundant joy. This life is available to you, and I encourage you to settle for nothing less.

You are one of His sheep, and the sheep know the Shepherd's voice—the voice of a stranger they will not follow. You can hear from God, it is part of your inheritance—don't ever believe otherwise!

QUESTIONS FOR DISCUSSION

1. Are you trying to fish on the wrong side of the boat? Are you attempting to do something in your own strength? If so, what will it take for you to obey God's voice in the matter?

2. What does it mean to suffer in the flesh? In what ways are you suffering in the flesh right now?

3. Describe a time when the Word came alive to you and directly answered a specific question you were seeking God for direction about.

4. Do you feel led by peace? How? Give an example.

5. When and where do you find a time and place where you can be still and quiet to hear God? How often are you able to do so? Do you wish it could be more?

6. Ask God to tell you what He wants you to do. Ask God to tell you what He doesn't want you to do. Listen. Record what He says (note that His response may not be immediate).

7. What does it mean to worship God in spirit and in truth?

8. What do you believe the Lord is leading you to in response to this chapter?

NOTES

CHAPTER 1

1. W. E. Vine, Merrill F. Unger, William White Jr., *Vine's Complete Expository Dictionary of Old and New Testament Words* (Nashville: Thomas Nelson, Inc., 1984, 1996), "New Testament Section," p. 111, s.v. "COMFORT, COMFORTER, COMFORTLESS," A. Nouns. No. 5, *parakletos.*
2. Ibid.

CHAPTER 9

1. James Strong, "Hebrew and Chaldee Dictionary," *Strong's Exhaustive Concordance of the Bible* (Nashville: Abingdon, 1890), p. 87, entry #5787, s.v. "blind," Isaiah 42:16, *ivver*, "blind (lit. or fig)."
2. Strong, "Hebrew and Chaldee Dictionary," p. 20, entry #982, s.v. "trust," Proverbs 3:5, *batach*, "be bold (confident, secure, sure)."

CHAPTER 11

1. Vine, "New Testament Section," p. 401, s.v. "MEEK, MEEKNESS," B. Nouns. No. 1. *prautes.*

How to Hear from God
Study Guide

CONTENTS

INTRODUCTION

Learning to hear from God and being led by the Holy Spirit on a daily basis is a very exciting way to live! God desires to speak to us about the plan He has for our lives. His plan is a good one, but we are in danger of missing it if we don't learn how to listen to and obey God's voice.

Jesus told His disciples that He would send them the Holy Spirit to dwell in them and be their Counselor and Helper. He said the Holy Spirit would teach them all things and bring to their remembrance things He had taught them. The Holy Spirit is the Spirit of Truth—He leads God's children into truth, not error (see John 14:26).

God speaks to us in a number of ways. These ways include, but are not limited to: His Word, nature, people, circumstances, peace, wisdom, supernatural intervention, dreams, visions, and what we call the inner witness. The inner witness is best described as a "knowing" deep inside. I believe this is also the "still, small voice" that is described in 1 Kings 19:12.

God speaks to us through our conscience and our desires. At times, He speaks in an audible voice, although this is rare for most of us and nonexistent for many of us.

How can we know that it is God speaking to us? Three things happen:

1. We are filled with faith that God is going to do something wonderful in our life—we may not fully understand what that "something" is, but we are filled with simultaneous feelings of expectation and thanksgiving.
2. We have a new awareness of God's presence with us.
3. We are led into a new level in our relationship with God.

All three of these outcomes of "hearing from God" are wonderful!
What should our prayer be? I suggest something like this:

God, open my ears and sanctify them so that I am sensitive to Your voice. Don't let me be distracted by fleshly desires that keep me from hearing You. Help me to listen and to learn to love times of solitude with You. Don't let me become so busy or live a life so "noisy" that it drowns out what You desire to say to me. Amen.

Hearing from God leads us to the place where our steps are truly ordered by the Lord (see Psalm 37:23). He gives us guidance, and as we follow His voice, we experience the pleasure of living a Spirit-led life—the most satisfying and meaningful life a person can possibly lead! We also live with greater freedom from the deceiver who seeks to lead us astray. We have more focus and more joy.

There is no substitute for hearing God's voice . . . and then obeying it.

USING THIS STUDY GUIDE

The purpose of this workbook is to reinforce the principles taught in my book *How to Hear from God*. You should have a copy of *How to Hear from God* as well as a Bible to work through this book.

This study guide is written in a question and answer format. Here's the way to get the most out of this book:

Step One: Look up the corresponding chapter in *How to Hear from God* and read it.

Step Two: Look up in your Bible the Scriptures designated in the study guide and read them. This is an important step because those Scriptures are the basis of the teaching in that particular chapter.

Step Three: Answer the questions in the study guide by referring to the material in *How to Hear from God* and in the Bible. Once you have finished answering the questions in each chapter, turn to the answer key at the back of the book to check your answers.

I encourage you to:

- *Work at a comfortable pace.* Don't rush to finish quickly. Stay in each chapter until you have a thorough understanding of the material and how it pertains to your life.
- *Follow the three steps above with each chapter in this study guide.* I have tried to set up everything for you, to make it as easy as possible, but the rest is up to you!
- *Use this study guide for individual study or group discussion.* You will likely find in a group discussion that you learn new ways to apply the principles in the book—ideas will have occurred to others that have not occurred to you. Be open to learning from others and gaining wisdom from them.
- *Consistently and steadily work through this book until you have completed the study guide.* Concepts tend to build upon concepts, and you will gain much more from a consistent and thorough study, as opposed to picking up and putting down the material over a long period of time, or interspersing it with other information.

READ YOUR BIBLE EVERY DAY

The Bible used to prepare this workbook is *The Amplified Bible.* You will find as you read the answers to the questions that these answers are often based on quotations from this version of the Bible.

I strongly encourage you to commit time each day to just reading the Word. You may enjoy a certain reading plan. One of the reasons I enjoy *The Amplified Bible* is that it explains the meaning of important words. It is also good to read various versions of the Bible for new insight. There are wonderful reference books available to provide background history of the Word and the cultural implications from the time period in which the Scriptures were written. The important thing is just to read. God can bring to life the answers that are hidden in the pages of His written Word for any trial you may face.

YOUR PERSONAL PRAYERS

At the end of each chapter, you will find an opportunity to write out a prayer. I believe strongly in "spontaneous" prayer—any time, any place, for any purpose! There is also an advantage, however, to personally writing out a prayer to the Lord. Writing a prayer helps you focus on what it is you really desire God to do for you. It helps you clarify your own thoughts, feelings, and needs.

Open Ears, Every Day

As you go about your daily routine in life, I encourage you to focus your mind consciously on various concepts you are encountering in the *How to Hear from God* book and this study guide. Meditate on those concepts. Ask God to show you how to apply those concepts to the particular circumstances, relationships, events, and activities of your personal life.

Opening your ears to hear from God is a process that may take time. So often we allow negative thinking, false conclusions, lies, and worldly perceptions to overshadow our ability to hear clearly from God. The process of hearing is a process of renewal. The more you walk in that process, the greater your ability to hear from God.

1. Read John 14:26, John 15:26, and John 16:7–11.
   a. Whom does the Holy Spirit represent and of Whom does the Holy Spirit testify?_____

   _____

   b. What did Jesus say the Holy Spirit would teach His disciples? _____

   _____

   c. What did Jesus say the Holy Spirit would help His disciples recall?

   _____

   _____

   d. What did Jesus say the Holy Spirit would do to the world?_____

   _____

2. Read 1 Kings 19:12.
   What are the words used in this verse to describe God's voice? _____

   _____

3. Read Psalm 37:23–24 and Isaiah 26:7.
   What is God's promise to us who hear and heed the voice of the Lord?

   _____

   _____

PART ONE

Learning to Listen

Be careful therefore how you listen. For to him who has [spiritual knowledge] will more be given; and from him who does not have [spiritual knowledge], even what he thinks and guesses and supposes that he has will be taken away.

—JESUS IN LUKE 8:18

1
God Talks to People Every Day

~~~~~

Read Chapter 1 in *How to Hear from God*. Then read in your Bible the Scriptures designated below and answer the questions that follow. When you finish, check your answers in the answer key provided at the end of this book.

To Whom Does God Speak . . . and How?

God has spoken to *all* people in their inner consciousness, through creation of the natural world and through creating within man an inner void that only God can fill.

1. Read Romans 1:19–21.

   a. To what part of a person does God make Himself evident? _____

   _____

   _____

   b. What does God reveal about Himself to all mankind through His creation? _____

   _____

   c. What happens when people do not honor and glorify God, even when they know and recognize Him as God? _____

   _____

2. Read Romans 14:12.

   What is required of each of us? _____

   _____

3. Read Isaiah 26:8–9.

   a. What is our heartfelt desire? _____

   _____

   b. Whom does our soul yearn for? _____

   _____

   c. What does our spirit seek?_____

   _____

What Does God Say to All Men and Women?

God speaks to men and women for very specific purposes—He speaks to them so they may know what is lasting and what isn't, so they may carry out His will, so they may live forever, and so He may direct their daily footsteps.

4. Read 1 John 2:17.

   a. What passes away and disappears? _____

   _____

   b. What remains forever? _____

   _____

5. Read Proverbs 3–6.

   What does God promise to the person who seeks to know, recognize, and acknowledge Him? _____

   _____

6. Read Jeremiah 29:11–14.

   a. When does God hear us? _____

   _____

   b. When does God reveal Himself to us? _____

   _____

c. What does God reveal to us when we seek Him and pray to Him?

_____

_____

d. What does the Lord do for us when we find Him? _____

_____

WHAT DOES THE HOLY SPIRIT SPEAK TO US?

God speaks to those who seek to follow the leading of the Holy Spirit in all they do. The Bible says *all* people can hear from the Holy Spirit if they will only seek God and receive Jesus as their Savior and receive the Holy Spirit Whom the heavenly Father sends.

7. Read Luke 11:13.
   To whom does God the Father give the Holy Spirit? _____

   _____

8. Read John 1:32–33 and John 14:15–20.
   a. Who is the One Who baptizes with the Holy Spirit? _____

   _____

   _____

   b. Where does the Holy Spirit reside? _____

   _____

   c. What does it mean to be baptized in the Holy Spirit? _____

   _____

   _____

   d. Why can't the "world" (unbelievers) receive the Holy Spirit? _____

   _____

   _____

9. Read John 16:12–13 and John 14:26.

a. Into what does the Holy Spirit guide us? _____

_____

_____

b. What does the Holy Spirit announce and declare to us? _____

_____

_____

c. What does the Holy Spirit cause us to recall? _____

_____

_____

10. Read John 6:45.

As those who listen to and learn from the Father, Who is our personal Teacher? _____

_____

_____

WHAT DOES THE HOLY SPIRIT KNOW TO TELL US?

The Holy Spirit knows all about us—all about the way we should conduct our lives—and about God's plans and purposes. The Bible gives us examples of men and women who have heard from the Lord, including great details about God's plans and purposes, as well as the consequences of their obeying the Lord's instructions.

11. Read Matthew 10:30, Psalm 139:16, Acts 17:26–27.

What does the Holy Spirit know about us? _____

_____

_____

12. Read Matthew 7:13–14, Deuteronomy 30:19, and Jeremiah 21:8.

   a. How does the Bible describe the "gate" through which the Holy Spirit leads us? _____

   _____

   _____

   b. How does the Bible describe the "way" the Holy Spirit leads us to follow in life? _____

   _____

   c. What critical choice does the Holy Spirit help us to make? _____

   _____

   _____

13. Read Genesis 6:13–17.

   a. In this passage, what did God tell Noah that He was going to do?

   _____

   _____

   b. What did God tell Noah to do? _____

   _____

   _____

14. Read Exodus 7:1–5.

   a. In this passage, what did God tell Moses about Pharaoh? _____

   _____

   _____

   b. What did God tell Moses about Aaron? _____

   _____

   _____

    c. What did God tell Moses that he was to do? _____

    _____

    _____

    d. What did God tell Moses about the way Pharaoh would respond to Moses' message? _____

    _____

    e. What did God tell Moses would be the end result? _____

    _____

    _____

15. Read 1 Corinthians 2:10–13.

    a. What does the Holy Spirit unveil and reveal to us about God? _____

    _____

    _____

    b. Why does the Holy Spirit reveal to us the thoughts of God? _____

    _____

    _____

WHAT ARE GOD'S PROMISES TO LEAD AND GUIDE US?

The Lord promises to be our Shepherd—to lead and guide us in the paths He desires for us to walk. He tells us that we will have the ability to hear His voice. God speaks to us—our role is to listen intently for what He has to say to us and then to obey Him fully.

16. Read Ezekiel 34:11–16.

    In this passage, what does the Lord promise to do for His sheep? _____

    _____

    _____

17. Read 1 John 2:27.

 a. What does this verse say about the permanent source of guidance that we have in the Holy Spirit? _____

 _____

 _____

 b. What does this verse say the anointing of the Holy Spirit teaches us?

 _____

 _____

 _____

 c. What does this verse challenge us to continue to do? _____

 _____

 _____

18. Read John 10:4–5.

 As His "sheep," what did Jesus say about our ability to hear and follow Him? _____

 _____

 _____

19. Read Psalm 46:10.

 What is the best way for us to hear from the Lord? _____

 _____

 _____

20. Read John 2:5.

 What should our response be when the Lord speaks to us? _____

 _____

 _____

PRAYER TIME

As you have read Chapter 1 and have completed this chapter of the workbook, has the Lord spoken to your heart and mind about His desire to speak to you personally on a regular, daily basis?

I invite you to use the space below to write out a prayer to the Lord, asking Him to speak to you about the matters in your life that are of greatest concern to you. Ask Him to speak to you about His plan for your life. Ask Him to give you an open heart to hear what He says. And . . . express your desire to *obey* whatever it is He tells you to do.

_____

_____

_____

_____

_____

_____

_____

_____

_____

_____

2

Create an Atmosphere to Hear from God

Read Chapter 2 in *How to Hear from God*. Then read in your Bible the Scriptures designated below and answer the questions that follow. When you finish, check your answers in the answer key provided at the end of this book.

WHAT DOES IT MEAN TO CREATE AN ATMOSPHERE TO HEAR FROM GOD?

To enjoy the fullness of God's presence, we must consistently maintain an atmosphere conducive to seeking Him, honoring Him, and being faithful and obedient to Him. If we want to hear from God, we must yield our attitudes to the lordship of Jesus Christ and learn to be led of the Spirit in *all* our ways.

1. Read Romans 12:18.

   How are we to live in relationship with other people? _____

   _____

2. Read Hebrews 5:11.

   What does this verse tell us as to *why* we don't seem to hear from God?

   _____

   _____

HOW CAN WE TELL WHETHER IT IS THE LORD WHO IS SPEAKING?

We must know God's character in order to know what is from Him and what isn't.

3. Read Matthew 11:28–30 and Jeremiah 6:16.

a. What does God desire that we do? _____

_____

_____

b. What does God promise to do for those who enter into relationship with Him? _____

_____

c. What do these passages tell us about God's character? _____

_____

d. How does God describe the obligations He places on us? _____

_____

_____

4. Read 2 Timothy 2:13.

What does this verse say about God's character? _____

_____

5. Read Matthew 13:9–16.

a. In this passage, what does the Lord call us to do? _____

_____

_____

b. What keeps us from hearing what the Lord is saying and perceiving what He is doing? _____

_____

_____

c. In essence, why do we fail to know the Lord's desires for us? _____

_____

_____

WHAT ATTITUDES INVITE THE PRESENCE OF GOD?

God speaks to those who have an attitude of honoring Him above all others—
those who continue to have faith that God has spoken to them, those who
wait patiently to hear from God and who have an attitude of obedience.

6. Read Jeremiah 17:5–8.

   a. According to this passage, whom does God bless? _____

   _____

   _____

   b. Who is the person who is cursed? _____

   _____

   _____

   c. What does the Lord promise to the person who puts full trust and
      confidence in Him rather than in "frail man"? _____

   _____

   _____

7. Read Galatians 1:15–17 and Galatians 1:21–24.

   a. What did Paul see as God's message to him? _____

   _____

   _____

   b. How certain was Paul that God had spoken to him? _____

   _____

   _____

   c. What was the result of Paul's allowing God's Word to grow in his
      heart and be manifested in his preaching? _____

   _____

   _____

8. Read Romans 9:1.

What was Paul's "witness" that he was hearing from God? _____

_____

_____

9. Read Judges 6:36–40 and John 20:29.

Gideon required a visible sign from God, and God honored Gideon's request, but it wasn't God's best. How did Jesus respond to those who asked Him for a visible sign? _____

_____

_____

10. Read Proverbs 8:34–36.

a. In this passage, who is the blessed person? _____

_____

_____

b. What happens to the person who finds the Lord's wisdom? _____

_____

_____

c. What is the fate of the person who doesn't wait to hear from God or who sins? _____

_____

_____

11. Read Psalm 40:6.

a. What "capacity" has God given to each of us? _____

_____

_____

b. How does God regard obedience? _____

_____

_____

_____

PRAYER TIME

As you have read Chapter 2 and have completed this chapter of the workbook, has the Lord spoken to your heart and mind about your need to make changes in the "atmosphere" of your life?

I invite you to use the space below to write out a prayer to the Lord, asking Him to help you create an atmosphere in which you can hear from Him. Confess to the Lord any attitudes you may have harbored that are not in keeping with His plans and purposes. Receive His forgiveness and ask Him to help you make the changes you need to make. Ask Him to help you keep a listening attitude—an attitude that honors God, is filled with faith and patience, and is obedient.

_____

_____

_____

_____

_____

_____

_____

_____

_____

_____

3
God Speaks through Supernatural Revelation

⌒

Read Chapter 3 in *How to Hear from God*. Then read in your Bible the Scriptures designated below and answer the questions that follow. When you finish, check your answers in the answer key provided at the end of this book.

GOD'S *LOGOS* AND *RHEMA* WORDS TO US

Of all the other ways that God may speak to us, He will never contradict the written Word, which was originally referred to by the Greek word *logos*. God specifically brings to our remembrance His *logos* for every situation. His *rhema* may not be word for word in the Bible, but the principle will always be supported in the written Word. The Bible confirms whether or not what we are sensing is of God.

1. Read Luke 4:1–13.

   a. When the devil tempted Jesus to turn a stone into a loaf of bread, how did Jesus respond? _____

   _____

   b. When the devil tempted Jesus to worship him, how did Jesus respond?

   _____

   _____

   c. When the devil tempted Jesus to cast Himself down from the temple, how did Jesus respond? _____

   _____

   d. What was the phrase common to each of Jesus' responses? _____

   _____

2. Read 2 Corinthians 10:5.

   a. What is it that we are to refute? _____

   _____

   b. What are we to do with every "thought and purpose"? _____

   _____

   _____

GOD SPEAKS THROUGH WISDOM AND COMMON SENSE

One way to hear from God is through conventional wisdom and common sense. Wisdom discerns truth in a situation, while common sense provides good judgment in what to do about the truth. Wisdom is supernatural because it isn't taught by men, but is a gift from God. The book of Proverbs is a great source of wisdom—I recommend you read at least a few verses from this book every day.

3. Read James 1:5.

   a. What are we to do if we are deficient in wisdom? _____

   _____

   b. What are the characteristics of the way God gives us His wisdom?

   _____

   _____

4. Read Proverbs 2:1–5.

   a. How are we to treat God's commandments? _____

   _____

   b. To what are we to make our ears attentive? _____

   _____

   _____

c. To what are we to direct our heart and mind? _____

_____

_____

d. What is promised to those who "seek [Wisdom] as for silver" and "search for skillful and godly Wisdom as for hidden treasures"? _____

_____

_____

5. Read Proverbs 2:9–10.

In this passage of Scripture, what is promised to those who are righteous, those who are upright and in right standing with God? _____

_____

_____

God Speaks through Dreams and Visions

In the Bible there are many accounts of God speaking to people through dreams and visions, but these are among the least common ways God speaks to us. Not every dream is a spiritual dream. Not everything we "see" is of God. We must test our dreams and visions against the principles of God's Word. We must not believe we are spiritually inadequate in some way if God does not speak to us through dreams or visions.

6. Read 1 John 4:1–3.

a. What are we to do when we have a spiritual experience or are told by someone that he or she is speaking a spiritual truth? _____

_____

b. How do we perceive and recognize the Spirit of God at work? _____

_____

_____

c. How do we perceive that something is not of God? _____

_____

_____

7. Read John 3:27.

What is to be our attitude toward the gifts God gives us? _____

_____

_____

GOD SPEAKS THROUGH PROPHECY

Sometimes the Lord speaks prophetically through other people to reveal His will for our lives. Prophecy is the interpreting of the divine will and purpose through inspired preaching and teaching. Prophecy must be in line with the Word of God, and a personal word of prophecy should confirm something that is already in our heart.

8. Read 1 Corinthians 14:1–4.

a. What does a prophet do? _____

_____

_____

b. What is the purpose of prophecy to the individual person who hears it? _____

_____

_____

c. What is the purpose of prophecy to the church? _____

_____

_____

9. Read 1 Timothy 4:13–16.

What should we do while waiting for a prophecy from the Lord to come to pass? _____

_____

_____

Prayer Time

As you have read Chapter 3 and have completed this chapter of the workbook, has the Lord spoken to your heart and mind about the ways He desires to speak to you through supernatural revelation?

I invite you to use the space below to write out a prayer to the Lord, asking Him to help you be faithful in your daily reading of His Word. Ask Him to speak to you as you read your Bible. Ask Him to make you very sensitive to what He may desire to say to you through conventional wisdom and common sense, through dreams and visions, and through prophecies.

_____

_____

_____

_____

_____

_____

_____

_____

_____

_____

4
God Speaks through Natural Things

⟳

Read Chapter 4 in *How to Hear from God*. Then read in your Bible the Scriptures designated below and answer the questions that follow. When you finish, check your answers in the answer key provided at the end of this book.

THE FIRST STEP IS BELIEVING GOD IS

In the first chapter, we noted that God speaks to *all* people through His creation, His handiwork. The main message of creation to all people is, *God is.* God has given to every person a measure of faith to believe in Him. God rewards all those who seek Him out with the answer to their search—with His very own presence!

1. Read Hebrews 11:6.

   a. What is the necessity for those who "would come near to God"?

   _____

   _____

   b. How does God reward those who seek Him out? _____

   _____

   _____

2. Read Romans 12:3.

   What has God apportioned (or given) to each of us? _____

   _____

   _____

   _____

God Speaks to Us through Nature

The very first words of the Bible are our first lesson of faith, "In the beginning God . . ." Many people acknowledge God exists, but they have not learned to relate to Him on a day-to-day level when they face struggles or difficulties. By grace, God tries to reach us every day, and He places reminders of Himself everywhere. He leaves clues of Himself all around us!

3. Read Matthew 6:28–30 and Luke 12:24.

a. What lesson does Jesus call us to learn about God from observing the lilies of the field? _____

_____

_____

b. What lesson does He call us to learn about God from observing the ravens? _____

_____

4. Read Proverbs 8:29, Job 38:10, and Jeremiah 5:22.
a. What do these verses say about God's creation of the sea? _____

_____

_____

b. What lesson can we learn from these passages? _____

_____

_____

5. Read Job 38–41 and Job 42:2.
What does Job tell us about God's control of all nature—even the things we do not understand? _____

_____

_____

GOD SPEAKS THROUGH OUR NATURAL ABILITIES

God answers many of our questions about our purpose and calling through our natural gifts and abilities, as well as our spiritual gifts and abilities. He leads us to our purpose through the natural skills and unique talents He bestows upon us. Our God-given gifts are skills we easily perform without formal training—and which give us pleasure as we use those skills for the good of everyone around us. We know we are operating in our gifts and calling when what we do ministers life to others.

6. Read Genesis 4:20–22 and 2 Chronicles 2:7–8, 14.

   These passages identify a variety of natural skills and abilities. What are they? _____

   _____

   _____

7. Read 1 Corinthians 12:28.

   What *spiritual* abilities are identified in this verse? _____

   _____

   _____

8. Read Romans 12:4–8.

   a. Why did God give different gifts (faculties, talents, qualities) to the church? _____

   _____

   _____

   b. What are the ministry gifts identified in this passage? _____

   _____

   _____

c. In what ways are we to employ them as we use the gifts below?

• Prophecy _____

_____

• Giving (contributing) _____

_____

• Giving aid and superintending _____

_____

• Doing acts of mercy _____

_____

9. Read John 10:10.

What is one of the major reasons we are given talents and abilities?

_____

_____

GOD SPEAKS TO US THROUGH PEOPLE

God desires that we seek His advice and guidance first and foremost. The best policy is to seek God and let Him choose how and through whom He wants to speak to us. God, at times, will use a person to give us wise counsel in *how* to do something. He also will use people to give us a word of advice that confirms what we already feel in our own spirit. It is very important that those who speak words of advice into our lives are godly people who can speak "a word in due season" to us. If God chooses to speak to us through others, we should humbly receive from anyone He chooses to use.

10. Read Proverbs 15:22–23.

What does this passage say about a word of advice that is spoken at the right moment? _____

_____

_____

11. Read Psalm 1:1–2.

    What kind of counsel must we avoid?_____

    _____

    _____

GOD SPEAKS TO US OUT OF OUR OWN MOUTHS

Many times God speaks to us out of our own mouths. As we speak aloud possible solutions to a problem and their potential outcome, one particular "answer" may settle in our heart.

12. Read Proverbs 16:1.

    Who prompts us to speak out "wise answers"? _____

    _____

    _____

13. Read Psalm 81:10.

    What does God promise to do if we will seek Him and open our mouth wide toward Him? _____

    _____

    _____

14. Read Luke 21:15.

    What did Jesus promise to us when we are given an opportunity to bear testimony against our adversaries? _____

    _____

    _____

    _____

God Speaks to Us through Correction

At times God speaks a word of correction to us. God's correction or chastisement is not a bad thing; it is always and ultimately only for our good. That does not mean it feels good or that we enjoy it immediately! God corrects us to bring us to righteousness and to a position of greater reliance upon Him for direction and wisdom. He ultimately chastens us so we are brought into a position to receive His greatest blessings.

15. Read Hebrews 12:11.

    a. What type of fruit does God's discipline yield? _____

    _____

    _____

    b. Who receives this harvest and what effect does it have on them?

    _____

    _____

    c. What is the result of this harvest? _____

    _____

16. Read Numbers 22:20–28.

    If we won't, or for some reason cannot, hear God's word of correction directly from Him, He uses other people and natural sources to speak to us. What was the source God used to speak to His prophet Balaam in Numbers 22:28? _____

    _____

    _____

17. Read Deuteronomy 1:43–46; 2:3.

    After a period of silence in which the Lord would not heed the voice of the Israelites (an act of chastening), the Israelites journeyed around

Mount Seir for many days. After that, what specific words of instruction did the Lord speak to Moses? _____

_____

_____

18. Read 2 Chronicles 16:9.

a. How does God desire for our hearts to be? _____

_____

b. What does God say He will do to those whose hearts are blameless toward Him? _____

_____

PRAYER TIME

As you have read Chapter 4 and have completed this chapter of the workbook, has the Lord spoken to your heart and mind about His desire to speak to you through natural things?

I invite you to use the space below to write out a prayer to the Lord, asking Him to help you identify the natural abilities He has given you and to identify the ways in which He desires for you to use them. Ask Him to help you listen to your own words so that you may monitor what you say, learn more about your own heart, and make changes that He may desire for you to make. Ask Him to help you become more willing to hear His words of correction.

_____

_____

_____

_____

_____

_____

5

God Speaks through Internal Peace

Read Chapter 5 in *How to Hear from God*. Then read in your Bible the Scriptures designated below and answer the questions that follow. When you finish, check your answers in the answer key provided at the end of this book.

WE MUST LAY OUR DECISIONS
ON THE SCALE OF PEACE

When God speaks, He gives us a deep sense of internal peace to confirm that the message is truly from Him. Even if He speaks to chastise us, His truth leaves a calming sense of comfort in our soul. The thoughts of our own reasoning do not bring peace—and certainly the deceiver's words to us do not give peace. Deep inner peace is the way we are assured that we have received God's wisdom and are acting in God's timing. Peace is an "internal confirmation" that our actions are approved by God.

1. Read John 14:27.

   a. What does Jesus promise to give and "bequeath" to us? _____

   _____

   b. What are we to keep our hearts from being? _____

   _____

2. Read Romans 8:6.

   What does the mind of the Holy Spirit produce? _____

   _____

3. Read Colossians 3:15.
   What is Christ's peace to do in our hearts? _____

   _____

   _____

4. Read Ecclesiastes 5:1–5.
   What does this passage say to us about speaking in haste, before we have God's peace on a matter? _____

   _____

   _____

GOD SPEAKS THROUGH PERSISTENT PROMPTINGS

We can know if we are doing right because our conscience will sense the evidence of truth. Our conscience becomes more sensitive the more we grow in the Lord and the more responsibility He gives to us. The Word teaches us to be true to our convictions; if we do something we feel uneasy about, we stand condemned because we are not acting from faith. We must be faithful in responding to God's promptings in our conscience in little matters; otherwise, the Lord will not entrust us with greater ministry opportunities.

5. Read Romans 14:22–23.
   a. How are we to "exercise" our personal convictions? _____

   _____

   _____

   b. What does this passage say about a person who has doubts (misgivings, an uneasy conscience) about something and goes ahead and does it anyway? _____

   _____

   _____

6. Read Matthew 25:14–23.

In this parable of Jesus, what did the master say to the servants who had been given five talents and two talents? _____

_____

GOD SPEAKS THROUGH OUR HEART'S DESIRES

God speaks to us through the sanctified desires of our heart—those that are in keeping with what God desires for us. We need to ask God to give us sanctified, or holy, desires. Among those are the desires for God's love and for spiritual gifts. Ultimately God desires that *our* desires merge with *His*.

7. Read Psalm 37:4.

What does God give to those who delight themselves in the Lord?

_____

_____

8. Read 1 Corinthians 14:1.

a. In this verse, what are we to eagerly pursue and seek to acquire?

_____

_____

b. What are we to earnestly desire and cultivate? _____

_____

9. Read Galatians 5:17.

What is the relationship between the desires of the flesh (godless human nature) and the desires of the Holy Spirit? _____

_____

_____

10. Read Romans 14:17.

    This verse tells us that the kingdom of God is not a matter of getting what we want. What does it say the kingdom of God *is* all about? _____

    _____

    _____

11. Read John 10:30 and John 8:28.

    a. What did Jesus say about His relationship with God the Father?

    _____

    _____

    b. What did Jesus say about His authority to act and speak? _____

    _____

    _____

12. Read John 15:7.

    a. In this verse, what does Jesus call us to do? _____

    _____

    _____

    b. What does Jesus say will be the result if we abide in Him and let His words remain in us and continue to live in our heart? _____

    _____

    _____

13. Read Ephesians 4:15.

    a. What are our lives to lovingly express? _____

    _____

    _____

b. To what kind of growth does the Lord call us? _____

_____

_____

14. Read Mark 11:24.

If our desires are godly, what can we expect when we express those desires to the Lord? _____

_____

15. Read Philippians 2:13.

What is it that God is working to produce and manifest in us? _____

_____

_____

GOD SPEAKS THROUGH A VOICE WE KNOW AND TRUST

God speaks to us in a voice we will recognize. Sometimes it may sound like our own voice; sometimes it may sound like the voice of someone we know. But the point is, the voice will always bring peace when God speaks to us.

16. Read 1 Samuel 3:1–10.

What should our response be when we hear the Lord calling our name?

_____

_____

17. Read John 10:1–5 and John 10:15–16.

a. Who are God's "sheep"? _____

_____

_____

b. Whose voice do the "sheep" follow? _____

_____

_____

c. What does Jesus say about our ability to recognize Him and know His voice? _____

_____

_____

PRAYER TIME

As you have read Chapter 5 and have completed this chapter of the workbook, has the Lord spoken to your heart and mind about the great importance of experiencing His peace?

I invite you to use the space below to write out a prayer to the Lord, asking Him to help you hear and obey His insistent promptings. Ask Him to reveal to you your heart's desires and to show you any aspects of those desires that are not in keeping with His plan or purpose for your life. Ask Him to give you His peace.

_____

_____

_____

_____

_____

_____

_____

_____

_____

_____

6
God Speaks through Conviction

$\sim$

Read Chapter 6 in *How to Hear from God*. Then read in your Bible the Scriptures designated below and answer the questions that follow. When you finish, check your answers in the answer key provided at the end of this book.

THE HOLY SPIRIT CONVICTS US

The Holy Spirit speaks to our conscience to convict us of sin and convince us of righteousness. Conviction from the Lord never condemns us or fills us with shame, disgrace, or humiliating regret. Rather, His conviction is intended to convince us to repent, which means to turn and go in the right direction rather than the wrong one in which we are currently going. When we feel conviction of sin, we feel guilty—but to keep feeling guilty after we have repented of sin is not healthy, nor is it God's will.

1. Read John 16:7–11.

   a. How does the Holy Spirit come to us? _____

   _____

   _____

   b. Why does the Holy Spirit bring conviction about sin? _____

   _____

   _____

   c. Why do we need the Holy Spirit to convince us of our need for and
   our receiving of Christ's righteousness? _____

   _____

   _____

d. What assurance do we need from the Holy Spirit regarding judgment?

_____

_____

_____

2. Read Jude 1:15.
   a. Whom does the Holy Spirit convict? _____

_____

_____

   b. About what does the Holy Spirit convict these people? _____

_____

_____

3. Read John 3:17–18.
   a. What did Jesus say He was *not* sent to do? _____

_____

_____

   b. What did Jesus say He *was* sent to do? _____

_____

_____

   c. What is the state of the person who believes in (clings to, trusts in, and relies on) Jesus? _____

_____

_____

   d. What is the state of the person who does *not* believe in (cling to, trust in, and rely on) Him? _____

_____

_____

4. Read John 8:9–11.

a. What did Jesus say about condemnation to the woman caught in adultery? _____

_____

_____

b. What did He tell her to do from that moment on? _____

_____

_____

5. Read Psalm 51:10 and Ezekiel 11:19–20.

a. What type of heart are we to desire that God create in us? _____

_____

_____

b. What type of spirit are we to desire that God renew in us? _____

_____

_____

c. What is God's promise to us about our heart? _____

_____

_____

d. What is God's promise to us about our spirit? _____

_____

_____

e. Why does God give us a new heart and a new spirit? _____

_____

_____

f. What is the end result of our having a new heart and a new spirit?

_____

_____

CONVICTION CONVINCES US TO ASK FOR GOD'S HELP

When God reveals to us an issue we need to deal with, we can trust His anointing is also present to break the yoke of bondage over us. When God convicts, He also anoints.

6. Read 1 John 4:4.

   What does this verse say about the power of the Holy Spirit Who lives in us? _____

   _____

   _____

7. Read Galatians 5:1.

   a. According to this verse, what has Christ done for us? _____

   _____

   _____

   b. How are we to respond to the freedom Christ bestows on us? _____

   _____

   _____

8. Read Matthew 6:12–13.

   a. What are we to pray with regard to our debts? _____

   _____

   _____

   b. What are we to pray with regard to the evil one? _____

   _____

   _____

THE HOLY SPIRIT WILL NEVER CONDEMN US

The Holy Spirit does not condemn us. Rather, He enables us to walk in true righteousness, and uprightness of heart. We live in a world filled with darkness, but we are empowered by the Holy Spirit to become agents of light. The apostle Paul writes in Romans 8:33–34 that if God the Father and Christ Jesus do not condemn us, no person or evil spirit has the power to condemn us.

9. Read Isaiah 9:2, Isaiah 42:6, John 8:12, and Ephesians 5:8–9.

   a. According to Isaiah 9:2, who has seen a great Light? _____

   _____

   _____

   b. According to Isaiah 9:2, on whom has the Light shined? _____

   _____

   _____

   c. According to Isaiah 42:6, what role was the Messiah to have with regard to the Gentiles? _____

   _____

   _____

   d. According to John 8:12, what did Jesus say about those who would follow Him? _____

   _____

   e. According to Ephesians 5:8, how are we to walk? _____

   _____

   _____

   f. According to Ephesians 5:9, what is the fruit (the effect, the product) of the Light or the Spirit? _____

   _____

   _____

10. Read Romans 8:32–34.

   a. Who justifies us? _____

   _____

   b. Who is at the right hand of God pleading in intercession for us?

   _____

   _____

11. Read Isaiah 53:3–5 and Isaiah 53:11.

   a. In these passages about Christ Jesus, the Messiah, what did Christ Jesus bear and carry on the cross? _____

   _____

   _____

   b. For what was Christ Jesus wounded and bruised? _____

   _____

   _____

   c. What did His chastisement make available for us? _____

   _____

   _____

   d. What did His stripes accomplish on our behalf? _____

   _____

   _____

   e. According to Isaiah 53:11, what did the travail of Christ Jesus on the cross accomplish for many? _____

   _____

   _____

   f. In Isaiah 53:11, what did Christ Jesus, God's Servant, bear on the cross? _____

   _____

   _____

12. Read 1 John 1:9.

What does God promise us if we will freely admit we have sinned and confess our sins? _____

_____

_____

PRAYER TIME

As you have read Chapter 6 and have completed this chapter of the workbook, has the Lord convicted you in any way?

I invite you to use the space below to write out a prayer to the Lord, asking Him to forgive your sins and to free you from all guilt and shame. Ask Him to free you from any addictions and ungodly behavior. Come boldly before the Lord and ask Him to help you abide always in His presence.

_____

_____

_____

_____

_____

_____

_____

_____

_____

_____

7

Develop a "Reining Ear"

$\sim$

Read Chapter 7 in *How to Hear from God*. Then read in your Bible the Scriptures designated below and answer the questions that follow. When you finish, check your answers in the answer key provided at the end of this book.

WHY SOME PEOPLE DON'T DEVELOP A "REINING EAR"

While most horses are guided and led by a strap fastened to the bit in their mouth, some horses keep one ear turned to their master's voice. One ear is open for natural warnings; the other is sensitive to the trusted trainer. The ear that is attuned to the trainer is called a "reining ear." God calls us to develop a reining ear toward Him.

1. Read John 4:24.

   How did Jesus describe God and the way He must be worshiped?

   _____

   _____

2. Read John 3:5–8.

   What is necessary for a person to be able to become sensitive to the voice of God and understand what the Spirit is saying? _____

   _____

   _____

   _____

3. Read John 5:37–40.

    a. In this passage, what did Jesus say about His Father to those who opposed Him? _____

    _____

    _____

    b. What keeps people from having God's Word (His thought) living in their heart? _____

    _____

4. Read 1 Timothy 4:1–2.

    a. What does this passage predict will happen in latter times? _____

    _____

    _____

    b. Why do people fall victim to the hypocrisy and pretensions of liars?

    _____

    _____

5. Read 2 Corinthians 13:14.

    What does the Lord desire to impart to those who have "reining ears"?

    _____

    _____

GOD WANTS US TO TRUST HIM

Those who have their ears attuned to what God says have a genuine trust in God. They are willing to deny their own will and turn from their own sins—suffering at times in doing so—to follow the Lord fully. Like the horse with the reining ear always tuned toward his master, we must be willing to follow the Lord in *all* His leadings, not just the leadings we feel good about or happen to agree with.

6. Read Romans 8:14–17 and Romans 8:18.

   a. What is the position of those who are led by the Spirit? _____

   _____

   _____

   b. As God's children, what is our position in regard to our heavenly Father and His Son Jesus Christ? _____

   _____

   c. What do we need to share if we are to share Christ's glory? _____

   _____

   _____

   d. What is unworthy of comparison to our sufferings in this present life?

   _____

   _____

7. Read Romans 13:14 and Galatians 5:17.

   a. With what are we to clothe ourselves? _____

   _____

   b. For what are we to make no provision? _____

   _____

   _____

   c. To what are the desires of the flesh opposed? _____

   _____

   d. To what are the desires of the Holy Spirit opposed? _____

   _____

   _____

   e. What does the Holy Spirit seek to prevent us from doing? _____

   _____

   _____

God Wants to Govern Our Lives

God wants to be in charge of the government of our lives. When we develop a reining ear and are following the leading of the Spirit in obedience, we are pleasing to the Lord and are in a position to receive all that He desires to pour into our lives.

8. Read 2 Corinthians 3:5–8.

a. What does God impart to us to make us "fit" to minister to others?

_____

_____

b. The code of the Law kills, but what does the Holy Spirit do? _____

_____

c. What will the dispensation of the Holy Spirit cause us to do? _____

_____

Prayer Time

As you have read Chapter 7 and have completed this chapter of the workbook, has the Lord spoken to you about your need to develop a "reining ear"?

I invite you to use the space below to write out a prayer to the Lord, asking Him to give you a more tender and sensitive conscience, and to make your intuition completely operative. Voice your desire to trust the Lord to even greater degrees and ask Him to help you release anything in your life that is keeping you from complete trust.

_____

_____

_____

_____

_____

_____

PART TWO

‿‿⟡

Learning to Obey

My mother and My brothers are those who listen to the Word of God and do it!

—JESUS IN LUKE 8:21

8

Obedience Keeps Our Conscience Tender

⌒

Read Chapter 8 in *How to Hear from God*. Then read in your Bible the Scriptures designated below and answer the questions that follow. When you finish, check your answers in the answer key provided at the end of this book.

KEEPING OUR CONSCIENCE TENDER

God may speak to us in a dozen different ways, but if we harden our conscience or heart, and refuse to obey Him when He speaks to us, we will miss out on blessings He wants to give us. When our conscience is tender, we clearly know when God prompts us not to do something. We must be very careful to do those things that keep our conscience tender.

1. Read Proverbs 3:6–7.

   What is necessary for us to do in order for God to direct our paths?

   _____

   _____

2. Read Proverbs 8:13.

   a. What does the reverent fear and worshipful awe of the Lord include?

   _____

   _____

   b. According to this verse, what does the Lord hate? _____

   _____

   _____

3. Read 1 Timothy 4:1.

   If we are to maintain a tender conscience, to what must we refuse to give any attention? _____

   _____

4. Read Matthew 6:22–23.

   a. If your eye is sound, what will be the result? _____

   _____

   b. If your eye is unsound, what will be the result? _____

   _____

5. Read 2 Corinthians 6:14.

   a. With whom must we refuse to be yoked in partnerships? _____

   _____

   _____

   b. In what way is it impossible for right living and right standing with God to have fellowship?_____

   _____

   c. In what way is it impossible for light to have fellowship? _____

   _____

6. Read Hebrews 12:2.

   a. What must we look away from if we are to be in the right position for God to both start in us and finish in us what He desires to accomplish?

   _____

   _____

   b. How is Jesus described in this verse? _____

   _____

c. What does He do to our faith? _____

_____

_____

GOD WILL TALK TO US ABOUT OUR RELATIONSHIPS

As we walk in obedience and listen to the Holy Spirit, God will speak to us concerning our marriage, our friendships, and our business associations. He will sharpen our ability to hear the right things by being with people who practice listening for God's voice and obeying Him. We must submit ourselves totally to the Holy Spirit's authority, trusting Him to speak directly to us.

7. Read Proverbs 27:17.

   What happens "as iron sharpens iron"? _____

   _____

   _____

8. Read 1 Corinthians 2:12–15.

   a. What spirit has *not* been given to us? _____

   _____

   _____

   b. For what purpose has the Holy Spirit been given to us? _____

   _____

   _____

   c. What is the natural, nonspiritual man incapable of accepting, welcoming, or admitting into his heart? _____

   _____

    d. Why is the natural, nonspiritual man incapable of receiving these
       things? _____

       _____

    e. What does the spiritual man do? _____

       _____

9. Read Romans 8:6.
    a. In this verse, how is the "mind of the flesh" described? _____

       _____

       _____

    b. In this verse, how is the "mind of the Holy Spirit" described? _____

       _____

       _____

GOD WILL TALK TO US ABOUT BALANCE

Listening to the Holy Spirit will keep us balanced in every area of our lives.
Part of our living in obedience is pursuing a balanced life that leads to wholeness. A balanced life is a very open life; there is nothing in it to hide or to
make apologies for.

10. Read 1 Peter 5:8.
    Because the enemy is roaming around like a roaring lion seeking
    someone he may seize upon and devour, what must we be? _____

    _____

    _____

11. Read 2 Corinthians 4:2.
    a. What are we to renounce as we seek balance in our lives? _____

    _____

b. What are we to refuse as we seek balance in our lives? _____

c. What are we to do about the truth as we seek balance in our lives?

_____

_____

12. Read Ecclesiastes 3:1–8.

a. What does this passage of Scripture say about the balance of birth and death? _____

_____

b. What does this passage say about the cycles of planting and reaping?

_____

c. What does this passage say about our emotional balance? _____

_____

d. What does this passage say about our alliances? _____

_____

e. What does this passage say about balance in our communication?

_____

13. Read Psalm 30:5.

What does this passage say about a balance of joy and sorrow in our lives? _____

_____

14. Read Isaiah 53:5.

What does this verse say about the peace and wholeness that are associated with a balanced life? _____

_____

PRAYER TIME

As you have read Chapter 8 and have completed this chapter of the workbook, has the Lord spoken to you about matters of obedience?

I invite you to use the space below to write out a prayer to the Lord, asking Him to soften your heart so you will *want* to obey. Ask this also for your family members and close friends. Ask the Lord to reveal to you ways in which He desires for you to adjust your relationships. Ask the Lord to help you have balance and joy in your life.

_____

_____

_____

_____

_____

_____

_____

_____

_____

_____

9

We Can Know Only in Part

⟿

Read Chapter 9 in *How to Hear from God*. Then read in your Bible the Scriptures designated below and answer the questions that follow. When you finish, check your answers in the answer key provided at the end of this book.

SEEING IN THE DARKNESS

There may be times when we can't see through the darkness that seems to be closing in around us. In those times of endurance and patience, our faith is stretched. We must trust God even when we can't hear His voice clearly. When we don't know what to do, it is sufficient to know the One Who knows.

1. Read 1 Corinthians 1:8–9 and Matthew 28:20.

   a. What does 1 Corinthians 1:8–9 assure us? _____

   _____

   _____

   b. How long did Jesus say He would be with us? _____

   _____

   _____

2. Read Isaiah 42:16.

   What is God's promise to us when we feel "blind" as to where we may be going or what God may be leading us to do? _____

   _____

   _____

3. Read 1 Corinthians 13:9–10 and 1 Corinthians 13:13.

    a. What is the state of our knowledge and prophecy (teaching) according to these passages? _____

    _____

    _____

    b. What is the hope for the future of our ability to understand all things?

    _____

    _____

    c. What three things abide even when our knowledge and prophecy are fragmentary? _____

    _____

God Guides Us One Step at a Time

God lays out a good plan for our lives so that we will walk in it. He shows us the way to go, and we are to walk in that direction, even if we do not understand the full plan. To walk out God's plan one step at a time requires faith. Our faith increases as we walk!

4. Read Genesis 12:1–2 and Hebrews 11:8–10.

    a. Where did the Lord direct Abram to go? _____

    _____

    b. What was God's promise to Abram for his obedience in going?

    _____

    c. According to Hebrews 11:8–9, what urged on or prompted Abraham?

    _____

    _____

    d. In spite of what did Abraham go? _____

    _____

5. Read Luke 17:5–6.

a. What did the disciples request of Jesus? _____

_____

b. How did Jesus respond? _____

_____

DON'T BE AFRAID OF MAKING A MISTAKE

We often have no way in the natural world of knowing for sure whether we are taking a right or wrong step. We have nothing more than faith to help us take our first step. But even if we are wrong, we can trust God to take our mistake and work it out for our good.

6. Read Romans 8:28.

What does God assure those of us who love Him and are called according to His design and purpose? _____

_____

GOD'S DIRECTION MAY SEEM ILLOGICAL

The assurance that we are moving forward in faith lies in our heart, not in our circumstance. Once we have a manifestation of what we desire in our circumstance, we no longer need faith in that area.

7. Read Hebrews 11:1.

a. What is faith the assurance of? _____

_____

b. What is faith the proof of? _____

_____

Be Diligent to Listen and Obey

We must be diligent to listen to God and obey Him every step of the way. God's plan unfolds step by step, which is why we must have faith with each step. We cannot skip any steps we don't like or any that are hard or that require sacrifice. We must not be afraid of sacrifice because it eventually sets us free to be all we desire to be.

8. Read Psalms 37:23–24 and 2 Corinthians 5:7.

a. What does Psalm 37:23 say about the steps of a good man? _____

_____

b. What does Psalm 37:24 say about what happens if the good man falls?

_____

c. According to 2 Corinthians 5:7, how are we to walk? _____

_____

Prayer Time

As you have read Chapter 9 and have completed this chapter of the workbook, has the Lord spoken to your heart and mind about your faith?

I invite you to use the space below to write out a prayer to the Lord, asking Him to give you patience and faith as you trust Him to lead you step by step. Ask Him to guide you as you step out in faith and take the actions you believe He wants you to take—giving you courage instead of fear, and diligence to continue walking by faith.

_____

_____

_____

_____

_____

10
God Opens and Shuts Doors of Opportunity

⁓

Read Chapter 10 in *How to Hear from God*. Then read in your Bible the Scriptures designated below and answer the questions that follow. When you finish, check your answers in the answer key provided at the end of this book.

OPEN AND CLOSED DOORS

Sometimes God speaks by opening or closing a door to something we want to do.

1. Read Proverbs 16:9 and Psalm 37:23.
    a. What does a man's mind plan? _____

    _____

    b. Who directs a man's steps and makes them sure? _____

    _____

    c. According to Psalm 37:23, whose steps are directed and established by the Lord? _____

    _____

    d. When are the steps of a good man directed and established by the Lord? _____

    _____

2. Read Revelation 3:7.
    What does this verse tell us about the power of the Lord to open and shut doors in our life? _____

    _____

3. Read 1 Corinthians 16:9.

   a. In this verse, what did the apostle Paul say had been opened to him?

   _____

   _____

   b. What did Paul say he would also encounter there? _____

   _____

   _____

TEST YOUR OPTIONS

You cannot drive a parked car. You need to be moving if you want God to show you which way to go. He leads one step at a time; if you take one step forward, and it's the wrong way, He will let you know before you go too far. Step out and find out which doors God will open and which ones He will close.

4. Read Acts 16:6–8.

   a. In this passage, where did Paul and Silas try to go? _____

   _____

   _____

   b. What kept them from proclaiming the Word in Asia? _____

   _____

   _____

   c. What kept them from going into Bithynia? _____

   _____

   _____

   d. Where did the Holy Spirit allow them to go? _____

   _____

   _____

GOD'S WAYS ARE NOT OUR WAYS

There are certain things God must do in order for things to work for us. We may be able to manipulate some things, but not all things. Following circumstances alone, however, can get us into real trouble. Satan can arrange for circumstances as well as God can, because he has access to this natural realm. Therefore, if we follow circumstances alone without considering other ways we hear from God, it can lead us into deception. Strong desires and lusts can easily deceive people, leading them to draw conclusions that are contrary to God's Word. We must never go against God's Word. We must be led by peace and walk in wisdom. We also are wise to combine biblical methods of being led by the Spirit, allowing them to serve as a check for one another.

5. Read Isaiah 55:8.

   In this verse, what does God say about His thoughts and ways and our thoughts and ways? _____

   _____

   _____

6. Read 2 Peter 2:9–10.

   a. From what must we always rely upon the Lord to rescue us? _____

   _____

   b. What must we trust the Lord to do about the ungodly around us?

   _____

   _____

   c. Whom do we need to trust the Lord to deal with particularly? _____

   _____

   _____

7. Read 1 John 2:16.

What kind of things come from the world rather than from the Father?

_____

_____

PRAYER TIME

As you have read Chapter 10 and have completed this chapter of the workbook, has the Lord spoken to your heart and mind about specific doors that He may be opening or shutting in your life?

I invite you to use the space below to write out a prayer to the Lord, asking Him to reveal to you all the options that lie before you and to help you discern His chosen path for you to walk.

_____

_____

_____

_____

_____

_____

_____

_____

_____

_____

11
Hindrances to Hearing God

Read Chapter 11 in *How to Hear from God*. Then read in your Bible the Scriptures designated below and answer the questions that follow. When you finish, check your answers in the answer key provided at the end of this book.

KEEPING OUR CONSCIENCE TENDER

God makes many attempts to speak to us through His Word, natural signs, supernatural revelation, and internal confirmation—but there are some obstacles to hearing His voice that may need to be removed from our hearts. One of these obstacles is being too busy to hear what the Lord says. Another is being too anxious or burdened to listen closely.

1. Read Luke 10:38–42.
   a. Where did Mary seat herself and what was she doing? _____

   _____

   _____

   b. What was Martha doing? _____

   _____

   _____

   c. What did Jesus say to Martha when she complained to Him about Mary? _____

   _____

   d. What did Jesus say regarding Mary? _____

   _____

   _____

2. Read Philippians 4:6–7.

a.What are we admonished by Paul not to do? _____

_____

_____

b. What are we admonished by Paul to do instead? _____

_____

_____

Religious Ideas Can Keep Us from Hearing God

Religious activity—based upon formulas and good works to earn God's favor—can keep us from hearing God. Jesus did not die so we could have religion; He died so we could be one with God through Him, so we could have a deep personal relationship with the Triune God: Father, Son, and Holy Spirit. People can do "good works" and yet disregard God's commands if they are not spending time with Him and listening to His instructions.

3. Read Matthew 23:23–28.

a. What did Jesus say the scribes and Pharisees had neglected and omitted? _____

_____

b. Even though the Pharisees kept all of the outside rituals related to the washing of vessels, what did Jesus say the Pharisees were full of?

_____

_____

c. How did He say the Pharisees appeared on the outside? _____

_____

_____

d. In reality, what did Jesus say was the state of the Pharisees on the inside? _____

_____

_____

4. Read Matthew 11:28–30.

a. What did Jesus say to those who were suffering from "spiritual burnout"? _____

_____

b. What did Jesus tell us to take on? _____

_____

c. What did Jesus say we are to learn? _____

_____

d. How did Jesus describe His own nature? _____

_____

e. What did Jesus say would be the result of our taking on His yoke and learning of Him? _____

_____

f. How did Jesus describe His yoke? _____

_____

g. How did Jesus describe His burden? _____

_____

5. Read Matthew 7:20–23.

a. How are people fully known? _____

_____

b. According to this passage, who enters the kingdom of heaven? _____

_____

c. Who will the Lord not know, even though they may have prophesied or driven out demons in His name? _____

_____

HEARING FROM GOD IS ROOTED IN RELATIONSHIP WITH HIM—NOT IN RELIGION

Our hearing from God is rooted in our having a relationship with Him. If you are not certain that you have a relationship with God—if you have never acknowledged Jesus as the Lord of your life—you can begin that relationship today.

6. Read John 3:16.

   What is the eternal future of the person who believes in Jesus as the Son of God? _____

   _____

7. Read Ephesians 2:8–9.

   a. By what are we saved? _____

   _____

   b. Through what are we saved? _____

   _____

   c. Our salvation is not a result of our own selves or striving or works, but of what? _____

   _____

8. Read Romans 10:9–10.

   a. According to verse 9, we are saved because we do what? _____

   _____

b. According to verse 10, what do we do with our heart? _____

_____

c. What do we do with our mouth? _____

_____

9. Read 1 John 1:9, 1 John 4:14–16, and 1 John 5:1, 12, 13.
   a. When we freely admit that we have sinned and confess our sins, what does God promise to do? _____

   _____

   b. With whom does God abide? _____

   _____

   c. What happens to the person who dwells and continues in love? _____

   _____

   d. Who is a "born-again child of God"? _____

   _____

HARD-HEARTEDNESS KEEPS US FROM HEARING GOD

When we give our lives to God, He puts a sense of right and wrong deep within our conscience. But if we rebel against our conscience too many times, we can become hard-hearted. If that happens, we need to let God soften our heart so we can be spiritually sensitive to the leadership of the Holy Ghost.

10. Read Ezekiel 11:19–20 and Ezekiel 36:26.
    a. In Ezekiel 11:19, what was God's promise to the people regarding their heart and spirit? _____

    _____

    b. In this verse, what was God's promise to the people regarding their *stony* heart? _____

    _____

357

c. In verse 20, what does God cause us to do when we have a new heart, a new spirit, and God's Spirit within us? _____

_____

_____

11. Read Matthew 19:1–9.

In this passage, why did Jesus say Moses permitted husbands to dismiss, repudiate, and divorce their wives? _____

_____

_____

12. Read Hebrews 3:7–13.

a. What does the Holy Spirit admonish us not to do? _____

_____

b. What does a wicked, unbelieving heart lead a person to do? _____

_____

c. What is our heart hardened by? _____

_____

A WORLDLY VIEWPOINT KEEPS US FROM HEARING GOD

We must be constantly vigilant not to become like the world in its ways and attitudes. We must guard against getting to the point where we have no empathy when we hear reports of real tragedies or when we hear of terrible things happening to other people. We should not dwell on the world's reports or conform to its viewpoint. We need to listen to what God says about current events in our lives and pray as He leads us to intercede for others who are affected by them.

13. Read John 17:13–18.

    a. Jesus did not ask that we be taken out of the world. Rather, what did He ask His Father? _____

    _____

    b. What does the Truth—God's Word—do in us? _____

    _____

14. Read Romans 12:2.

    a. To what must we *not* be conformed? _____

    _____

    b. In what area of our life are we to be transformed? _____

    _____

15. Read Luke 4:18.

    What did Jesus say He was called to preach? _____

    _____

UNFORGIVENESS KEEPS US FROM HEARING GOD

Long-lasting abuse can cause a person to harden his or her heart. This hardness is a survival tactic. It is a numbness to pain that helps victims survive abuse. But when emotions are turned off for years, it takes a toll on people's health. A victim of abuse must refuse to stay in emotional bondage; he or she must reject bitterness and hardness of heart.

16. Read Ephesians 4:30–32.

    a. What must we not do to the Holy Spirit? _____

    _____

    b. What do we need to banish from our lives? _____

    _____

c. What must we become? _____

_____

d. In what manner are we to forgive others? _____

_____

Legalism Closes Our Ears to the Voice of God

A legalistic mentality says everybody has to do exactly the same thing, the same way, all the time. But the Spirit of God leads us individually, and often in unique, creative ways. In Christ we have been liberated and set free from the manipulation and control of narrow-minded, Pharisee-like people who think their way is the only way to do anything. This does not mean we are not to keep God's commandments and principles. Nor does it mean we can have a "private interpretation" of the Word of God. Rather, the freedom we are given by Christ means we are free to be individuals in our personal expressions of praise—free of competition and comparison with others, free from selfishness and sin, and free from fear of what others think of us. We are free to be open and receptive to God's new methods and means of accomplishing His plans and purposes.

17. Read 2 Peter 1:20.

    What should a prophecy of Scripture never be? _____

    _____

18. Read Isaiah 61:1.

    Because the Spirit of the Lord God was upon Jesus, what did God anoint and qualify Him to do? _____

    _____

    _____

19. Read 2 Corinthians 3:17.

    What do we find where "the Spirit of the Lord is"? _____

20. Read John 8:36.

    When are we really and unquestionably free? _____

GRACE REMOVES OUR HINDRANCES FROM HEARING GOD

The covenant of grace we have through Jesus Christ gives us liberty to approach God directly and to hear Him personally. Being free of legalism does not mean we no longer need to consider how our behavior may influence others. Because we have experienced the grace of God in our lives, we must live in a way that encourages and influences others to receive His grace in their lives.

21. Read Romans 14:12–15 and 19.

    a. In verse 12, to whom are we each required to give an account of ourselves? _____

    b. In verse 13, what does the apostle Paul tell us not to do? _____

    c. In that verse, what does Paul tell us to decide and endeavor to do?

    d. In verse 15, at what point are we no longer walking in love? _____

    e. According to verse 19, what are we to aim for and eagerly pursue?

22. Read Hebrews 10:19–22.

    a. On what basis do we have full freedom and confidence to enter into the Holy of Holies? _____

_____

    b. In what manner are we to come forward and draw near to God?

_____

    c. What have our hearts been purified from? _____

_____

PRAYER TIME

As you have read Chapter 11 and have completed this chapter of the workbook, has the Lord spoken to your heart and mind about specific hindrances that are blocking your ability to hear God clearly? Have you felt a special conviction about substituting religious activity for an intimate relationship with the Lord? Have you felt a special conviction about hardness of heart, a worldly viewpoint, harboring unforgiveness and bitterness, or legalism?

I invite you to use the space below to write out your own prayer to the Lord, asking Him to help you deal with the specific hindrances you see in your own life, and asking Him to free you to walk in the fullness of His grace.

_____

_____

_____

_____

_____

_____

_____

_____

12
Keep Your Receiver Deceiver Free

~~~~~~

Read Chapter 12 in *How to Hear from God*. Then read in your Bible the Scriptures designated below and answer the questions that follow. When you finish, check your answers in the answer key provided at the end of this book.

TRUSTING GOD TO OPEN OUR RECEIVERS

Many people *want* to hear from God, but they don't really *expect* to hear from Him. Others have too much "static in their receivers" to hear Him clearly. The deceiver, the devil, doesn't want us to think we can hear from God. He doesn't want us to believe. He does his best to jam our ears with too many messages from ungodly sources. We must obey God in *seeking* to hear His voice.

1. Read Psalm 40:6.
   What capacity has God given to us? _____
   _____

2. Read Proverbs 1:24–29.
   a. According to this passage, what have we done when God has called to us? _____
   _____

   b. How have we responded to God's outstretched hand? _____
   _____

   c. How have we responded to God's wise counsel? _____
   _____

   d. How have we responded to God's reproof? _____
   _____

3. Read Isaiah 11:2–5.

a. What is the nature of the Spirit Who rested upon Christ Jesus and Who rests upon us today? _____

_____

b. What does the Spirit do to our understanding and desires? _____

_____

_____

c. How is the person who hears the Spirit able to judge and make decisions? _____

_____

d. In this passage, what are the two "girdles" that wrap the life of the person who has the Spirit of the Lord? _____

_____

_____

OBEDIENCE OPENS OUR RECEIVERS

We need to pray and obey God's leading. Our obedience is not to be an occasional event; it is to be our way of life. God bestows abundant blessings on those who decide to live wholeheartedly for Him and who make obedience to Him their lifestyle. Paying attention to and obeying God's Word should be our goals.

4. Read Proverbs 1:23.

What does the Lord promise to those who turn and give heed to His reproof? _____

_____

5. Read Proverbs 1:24–33.

a. According to this passage, how have we responded to God's knowledge? _____

_____

b. What have we failed to choose? _____

c. What are the consequences for those who turn away from a reverence for God's knowledge, counsel, and reproof? _____

d. What are the rewards for those who hearken to God's wisdom?

_____

6. Read John 14:23.

a. What will the person who really loves Jesus do? _____

_____

b. What is the blessing to the person who loves Jesus and keeps His word, obeying His teachings? _____

_____

THANKFULNESS OPENS OUR RECEIVERS

God's general will is for all people to give Him thanks in all things. We quench the Holy Spirit through our complaining, but the more thankful we are, the more freedom the Holy Spirit has to work in our situation.

7. Read 1 Thessalonians 5:18.

What does this verse say is God's will for all of us who are in Christ Jesus? _____

_____

8. Read 1 Thessalonians 5:19.

What must we never quench, subdue, or suppress in our lives? _____

_____

_____

ASKING GOD FOR ANSWERS OPENS OUR RECEIVERS

We are to ask God for His wisdom—His answers, His solutions, His guidance. We must ask with faith and confidence; He will answer. A person who asks in this manner is a person more likely to be listening closely for God's answers.

9. Read James 1:5–6.

   a. What are we to do when we recognize we are deficient in wisdom?
   _____

   b. In what manner does God give His wisdom? _____
   _____

   c. How are we to ask for wisdom? _____
   _____

WHOLEHEARTED ATTENTION OPENS OUR RECEIVERS

Many Christians have only a halfhearted interest in the pursuit of God. They want God to take care of them, but they don't really want to make the sacrifice of time and devotion it takes to grow in knowledge of Him and His Word—and they don't want to commit time to pray. We are to seek the Lord *wholeheartedly*. Our full attention on God will keep the static out of our receivers so we can receive every good thing that He is trying to give us.

10. Read Psalm 119:2.

    In this verse, who are the blessed? _____
    _____

11. Read Psalms 119:10 and 34.

    a. In Psalm 119:10, how did the psalmist seek the Lord? _____
    _____

    b. What was the psalmist's request of God? _____
    _____

c. In verse 34, what was the psalmist's promise to God? _____

A Pure Heart Keeps Our Receivers Static Free

If disobedience is causing our conscience to be clouded, it's time to get rid of that static in our receivers. To keep our hearts pure before the Lord, we need to let Christ make His home in us and make His desires our desires. To keep a pure heart, we must keep our heart free from sin and guilt, guard carefully what we listen to, seek only God's truth, and avoid all contact with the occult. We must recognize we cannot serve two masters—we cannot follow the Lord and follow the desires of the flesh simultaneously. We must seek to live with the highest standards of morality.

12. Read Matthew 5:8.
    What did Jesus promise those who have pure hearts? _____

13. Read 1 John 3:21–22.
    a. What do we have if there is nothing in our conscience that accuses us or causes us to feel guilty or condemned? _____

    b. What is the reward to those of us who watchfully obey God's orders and follow His plan for us, and who practice what is pleasing to Him?

14. Read Mark 4:24.
    a. What did Jesus caution us about the things we listen to? _____

b. What determines the measure of virtue and knowledge that we receive from the Lord? _____

_____

15. Read 2 Timothy 4:3–4.
    a. What types of teachers do people seek when they turn away from sound and wholesome instruction and develop a desire only for teaching that is pleasant and gratifying? _____

    _____

    _____

    b. When people turn aside from hearing the truth, what happens?

    _____

    _____

16. Read Leviticus 19:31 and Leviticus 20:6–7.
    a. To whom are we *never* to turn? _____

    _____

    b. What does God say He will do to the person who turns to those with familiar spirits and to wizards? _____

    _____

17. Read Luke 16:13.
    a. What is it that Jesus says a servant finds impossible to do? _____

    _____

    b. Why is this so? _____

    _____

18. Read Ephesians 5:3–5.
    a. What should never be named among God's consecrated people?

    _____

    _____

b. What behavior is considered "not fitting" for God's people? _____

_____

_____

c. What can cause a person not to have any inheritance in the kingdom of Christ and of God? _____

_____

TUNE OUT THE VOICE OF ERROR

God gives us discernment to know His voice over voices of deception. If we truly belong to God, we will *know* His voice from the spirit of error. We will know what we have heard is contradictory to His Word or wisdom or common sense. For our part, we must read and heed God's Word.

19. Read Proverbs 4:20–27.

a. What are we to do to God's words? _____

_____

b. What are we to do to His sayings? _____

_____

c. Where are we to keep His words and sayings? _____

_____

d. What do God's words produce in us? _____

_____

e. How are we to keep and guard our heart? _____

_____

f. What are we to put away from us? _____

_____

g. What are we to put far from us? _____

_____

h. How are we to focus our mind and heart? _____

_____

i. How are we to walk out our faith in God? _____

_____

j. What must we never walk toward or into? _____

_____

20. Read 2 Corinthians 3:18.
    What happens as we continue to look into the Word of God? _____

_____

_____

Prayer Time

As you have read Chapter 12 and have completed this chapter of the workbook, has the Lord spoken to your heart and mind about specific things that may be causing static in your ability to believe that God wants to speak to you, or in your ability to hear clearly what He is saying? Have you felt a special conviction about ways in which you may have turned a "deaf ear" toward His reproof or correction of you?

I invite you to use the space below to write out a prayer to the Lord, asking Him to help you deal with those things that may be keeping you from believing fully that He desires to speak to you, or to help you deal with those things that may be keeping you from hearing Him with clarity.

_____

_____

_____

_____

_____

_____

_____

_____

13
Sanctify Your Ears unto the Lord

~~~~

Read Chapter 13 in *How to Hear from God*. Then read in your Bible the Scriptures designated below and answer the questions that follow. When you finish, check your answers in the answer key provided at the end of this book.

GOD DESIRES TO SANCTIFY ALL ASPECTS OF OUR LIVES

Many people do not understand that we are a tri-part being: a spirit, soul, and body. We are a spirit, we have a soul, and we live in a body. God promises to take care of all three parts that make us who we are. Jesus bought us—all aspects of us—with the price of His blood shed on the cross.

1. Read 1 Thessalonians 5:23–24.
    a. What does it mean to be sanctified "through and through"? _____

    _____

    b. What is it that Paul desires to be preserved "sound and complete"?

    _____

2. Read Galatians 5:16–17.
    a. How are we to walk and live habitually? _____

    _____

    b. If we walk and live in the Holy Spirit, what will we not do? _____

    _____

3. Read Romans 14:17.
    In this verse, what does Paul say the kingdom of God is? _____

    _____

4. Read Jeremiah 6:10.

a. What does it mean to have "uncircumcised" ears? _____

_____

b. What has the Word of God become to those who have uncircumcised ears? _____

_____

5. Read John 5:30.

a. What did Jesus say about His dependence on God? _____

_____

b. Why did Jesus say His judgment was right, just, and righteous?

_____

Ask God to Sanctify and Circumcise Your Ears

To *sanctify* means to set apart for a sacred purpose. To *circumcise* means to cut away the flesh. In asking God to sanctify and circumcise your ears, you are asking Him to make your ears sensitive to hear what is holy and right and to remove worldly temptations that distract you from His greater plan for your life. In other words, ask God to give you ears that hear what He wants to say, not just what you want to hear.

6. Read Exodus 29:20–22.

See page 246 of *How to Hear from God* regarding the significance of the "right side" and the parts of the body mentioned in this passage.

a. What did it mean for blood to be put on the tip of the priest's right ear? _____

_____

   b. What did it mean for blood to be put on the thumb of the priest's
      right hand? _____

_____

   c. What did it mean for blood to be put on the big toe of the priest's
      right foot? _____

_____

   d. Why are we anointed with the shed blood of Jesus on our ears, hands,
      and feet? _____

_____

7. Read Revelation 1:5–6.
   a. By His shed blood, into what did Jesus form us? _____

_____

   b. What are we to give to Jesus as His priests—empowered to hear
      clearly, do what is righteous, and go where He leads us? _____

_____

_____

A SANCTIFIED EAR HEARS GOD'S PLAN

We need to wake up to the spiritual realm of our lives and hear what the Holy
Spirit is saying to us. He has made eternity quite clear in His Word. It seems
wise to find out as much as we possibly can about our spiritual life since we
will spend more time in our spiritual bodies in heaven than we will in our
physical bodies in this life.

8. Read 1 Corinthians 15:39–44.
   a. According to 1 Corinthians 15:42, what is the nature of the earthly
      body? _____

_____

b. What is the nature of the resurrected body? _____

_____

_____

c. According to verse 43, with what qualities is the earthly body sown?

_____

_____

d. With what qualities is the resurrected body raised? _____

_____

_____

9. Read 2 Corinthians 4:18.

a. What is the nature of visible things? _____

_____

b. What is the nature of invisible things? _____

_____

LISTENING AND OBEYING DETERMINE
OUR ETERNAL DESTINY

Eternity is forever, and the spiritual part of a man lives forever, either in heaven or in hell. To live in hell is to live in total separation from God—completely disconnected from any form of comfort, grace, provision, protection, and most of all intimate fellowship with God. There is nothing of greater value in which to invest our time than learning to hear the voice of God speaking to our spirit so that we might be prepared to live with Him forever.

10. Read 1 Thessalonians 4:16–18.

a. Who will rise first? _____

_____

b. Who will meet the Lord in the clouds along with the resurrected dead? _____

_____

c. Why are we to remind one another of this coming event? _____

_____

_____

11. Read Hebrews 4:12.
    a. What is the nature of the Word that God speaks? _____

_____

    b. Being sharper than any two-edged sword, how deeply does the Word of God penetrate? _____

_____

    c. What does the Word expose, sift, analyze, and judge? _____

_____

GOD RESTORES OUR SOUL

Our soul doesn't tell us what God wants; it reports only what it knows about our own desires. Our soul tells us what we feel; our spirit tells us how God feels. Our soul tells us what *we* think, not what God thinks. As we communicate in our spirit with God, a work can be done to transform our soul to think like Christ. Our soul *needs* to be renewed and refreshed to think like the mind of Christ.

12. Read Psalm 23:1–3.
    a. When the Lord is our Shepherd, what is our state of being? _____

_____

    b. What does our Shepherd make us, His sheep, to do? _____

_____

c. Where does our Shepherd lead us as His sheep? _____

_____

_____

d. As His sheep, what does our Shepherd do for our life (our self)?

_____

_____

e. Along what paths does our Shepherd lead us as His sheep? _____

_____

_____

13. Read Philippians 2:12.

With what kind of attitude are we to seek to cultivate our spiritual growth? _____

_____

GOD AWAKENS OUR SPIRIT WITHIN US

We communicate with God through our spirit—our spirit intuitively senses God's presence and receives revelation when there is a better way to do something. Our conscience is also part of our spirit. When our spirit is made alive to the awareness of God, we can achieve fellowship with Him and receive answers from Him through our intuition and conscience. Our spirit and soul should work together, and the body should act as a servant to both.

14. Read John 4:24.

How are we to worship God, a spiritual Being? _____

_____

_____

15. Read Matthew 26:41.

    a. What must we do so we do not come into temptation? _____

    _____

    b. The spirit may be willing, but what is the nature of the flesh? _____

    _____

16. Read Isaiah 11:1–3.

    a. What is the nature of the Spirit of the Lord? _____

    _____

    b. What does the Spirit of the Lord produce in a person? _____

    _____

17. Read Matthew 26:38–39.

    a. What was the nature of Jesus' soul as He prayed in the Garden of Gethsemane? _____

    _____

    b. Even with a sad and deeply grieved soul, how did Jesus pray? _____

    _____

    _____

18. Read Psalm 77:6.

    a. What did the psalmist call to remembrance in the night? _____

    _____

    _____

    b. What did the psalmist do with his heart? _____

    _____

    c. What did the psalmist's spirit do? _____

    _____

PRAYER TIME

As you have read Chapter 13 and have completed this chapter of the workbook, has the Lord spoken to your heart and mind about specific things that may be keeping you from having "sanctified" and "circumcised" ears? Do you feel a greater need to have God restore your soul and awaken your spirit within you so you can know what God wants, thinks, and feels?

I invite you to use the space below to write out a prayer to the Lord, committing your ears, hands, and feet to Him in prayer and asking Him to sanctify you for His purposes.

_____

_____

_____

_____

_____

_____

_____

_____

_____

_____

14
Enjoy the Spirit-Led Life

⌒

Read Chapter 14 in *How to Hear from God*. Then read in your Bible the Scriptures designated below and answer the questions that follow. When you finish, check your answers in the answer key provided at the end of this book.

GOD'S PLAN TO BLESS US

God has an awesome plan to radically and outrageously bless us. But to fully enjoy His plan, we must radically and outrageously obey Him. There are many things we can do on our own. God doesn't say anything about these things—we refer to these things as God's permissive will. But if we want to know God's *perfect* will, we must ask His opinion.

1. Read 1 Corinthians 6:12.

   a. Even though all things are permissible and lawful, what did Paul realize about all these things? _____

   _____

   b. To what did Paul refuse to become the slave? _____

   _____

2. Read Hebrews 12:1–3.

   a. To know God's full plan of blessing, what do we need to strip off and throw aside? _____

   _____

   b. How are we to run the race God has appointed for us? _____

   _____

   c. To Whom are we to look? _____

   _____

d. To what did Jesus look as He endured the shame of the cross and opposition from sinners? _____

e. Why does this passage call us to keep our focus on Jesus and the joy He promises us? _____

GOD WILL LEAD YOU TO RIGHT DECISIONS

When we listen to God's direction, we make wise decisions that lead to riches, honor, pleasantness, and peace. Wisdom will always lead us to God's *best*. When we "fish" outside the will of God, it's equivalent to fishing on the wrong side of the boat. We struggle, strive, work, and strain, trying to make something great happen. And . . . we catch nothing.

3. Read Proverbs 3:13–17.
   a. What does this passage say about the gaining and profit of wisdom?
   _____
   _____

   b. What does this passage say wisdom is more precious than? _____

   c. What does wisdom produce in the person who seeks and gains understanding from God's Word? _____
   _____
   _____

4. Read John 21:2–6.
   a. After Jesus was crucified and rose again, what did Peter, Thomas, Nathanael, the sons of Zebedee (James and John), and two other disciples decide to do? _____

b. What did Jesus call and ask the disciples as He stood on the beach?

_____

_____

c. What did the disciples answer? _____

_____

d. What did Jesus tell them to do? _____

_____

e. What was the result when the disciples did what Jesus said to do?

_____

_____

GOD WILL LEAD YOU TO GOOD WORKS

God leads us to good works. They aren't always the works we desire to do, and sometimes the works are ones that include suffering, but the works He calls us to do are the works He blesses.

5. Read Genesis 1:28.
   What were God's first words to mankind that were filled with the promise of blessing? _____

   _____

6. Read John 14:15 and John 21:15–18.
   a. In John 14:15, what did Jesus say we will do if we really love Him?

   _____

   b. In John 21:15–18, what did Jesus ask Simon Peter three times?

   _____

   c. In John 21:15–18, what did Simon Peter answer Jesus three times?

   _____

   _____

d. What three things did Jesus tell Simon Peter to do? _____

e. In verse 18, what type of sacrifice did Jesus tell Peter he would make as he obeyed Jesus' commands? _____

_____

7. Read 1 Peter 4:1–2.
   a. With what thought and purpose are we to arm ourselves? _____

   _____

   b. How does the person who is willing to suffer—if it means pleasing God—spend the rest of his natural life? _____

   _____

GOD WILL SPEAK CLEARLY SO YOU WILL NOT DOUBT

God clearly tells us what He wants us to do in His Word. If you want to hear Him speak more clearly, you must stay in the Word. He will enlighten Scriptures that will give you relevant living words (His *rhema*) to show you what He wants you to know and do. If you have any doubts, you need only ask the Lord sincerely, "Lord, what do You desire me to do?" You must submit any spiritual experiences you may have to the "Word of God" and the "testimony of Jesus."

8. Read Acts 9:4–6.
   What did Saul ask Jesus? _____

   _____

9. Read Revelation 1:1–2.
   According to this passage, what did John testify and vouch that his visions were about? _____

   _____

10. Read Luke 8:15.

    What did Jesus say we were to do with the seed of God's Word planted in our lives? _____

    _____

GOD WILL LEAD YOU THROUGH PEACE

People who do things they don't have peace about have miserable lives and don't succeed at anything. Follow peace!

11. Read Philippians 4:7.

    a. What is the relationship between the understanding of the mind and the peace God gives our soul? _____

    _____

    _____

    b. What does God's peace do in our hearts and minds? _____

    _____

    _____

12. Read Colossians 3:15.

    What is the peace we have been given by Christ intended to *do* in our lives? _____

    _____

13. Read Hebrews 12:14.

    a. What are we to seek in our relationships with other people? _____

    _____

    _____

    b. What are we to pursue? _____

    _____

GOD WILL LEAD YOU BY A STILL, SMALL VOICE

The primary way we hear from God is through His still, small voice within, or an inner witness. In order to hear that voice, we must slow down our lives and be still in His presence.

14. Read Psalm 46:10.

    What is the first thing we are to know as we are still in God's presence?

    _____

    _____

15. Read 1 Kings 19:5–12.

    a. In this passage, how did God *not* speak to Elijah? _____

    _____

    _____

    b. How *did* God speak to Elijah? _____

    _____

GET ALONE WITH GOD

Hearing God requires solitude. If you really want to hear the still, small voice of God, you must be still. You need extended periods of quiet to seek God— free of distractions and interruptions. It is in moments alone with God that He will give you a vision of where you need to go. As you take steps toward your destiny, you need to revisit Him frequently to learn the next step to take.

16. Read Matthew 6:6.

    What did Jesus tell us to do when we pray? _____

    _____

17. Read Isaiah 30:20–21.
    a. In verse 20, what are we told will happen even in adversity and afflic-
    tion? _____

    _____

    b. What does verse 21 say our Teacher will tell us? _____

    _____

    c. What will we then know? _____

    _____

GOD'S GREATEST DESIRE

God's greatest desire for His children is that they experience His best in their
lives. He wants to have a close fellowship with us and to be invited into every
area of our lives. He wants to speak to us and lead us in all our decisions by
His Spirit. He does not want us living in confusion and fear. Rather, He wants
each of us to fulfill our destiny and to walk in the fullness of His plan for us.

18. Read Ephesians 3:20.
    a. What is the Lord able to do as a consequence of His power at work in
    us? _____

    _____

    b. Beyond what does God's power allow Him to move? _____

    _____

19. Read Hebrews 13:5.
    In this verse, what does the Lord promise? _____

    _____

20. Read Romans 14:17–18.
    a. Based on verse 17, what is the kingdom of God? _____

    _____

b. According to verse 18, how does God regard the person who lives in righteousness, peace, and joy? _____

_____

PRAYER TIME

As you have read Chapter 14 and have completed this chapter of the workbook, has the Lord spoken to your heart and mind about His plan for you? Have you felt a special conviction about your need to focus on God's answers instead of life's problems? Have you felt a special conviction about your need to be more concerned about spiritual and eternal things, rather than material and temporary things? Do you feel a greater need to have God restore your soul and awaken your spirit within you so you can know what God wants, thinks, and feels?

I invite you to use the space below to write out a general prayer to the Lord, asking for God's daily guidance. Then, write a second prayer asking for God's specific direction in a decision you may be facing. You certainly should feel free to write out a specific prayer for *each* decision, circumstance, problem, or question you are facing.

_____

_____

_____

_____

_____

_____

_____

_____

_____

ANSWERS

Answers are from *The Amplified Bible* and from the book *How to Hear from God*.

Introduction

1a. The Holy Spirit represents Jesus and testifies of Jesus.
1b. Jesus said the Holy Spirit would teach them all things.
1c. Jesus said the Holy Spirit would help them recall everything that Jesus had told them.
1d. Jesus said the Holy Spirit would convict and convince the world and bring demonstration to it about what is sin, what is righteousness (uprightness of heart and right standing with God), and what judgments are associated with sin and righteousness.
2. The words are a "still, small voice."
3. He promises that our steps are ordered by the Lord, and that we can trust Him not to let us lose our way.

Chapter 1

1a. God makes Himself evident (or "plain") in the inner consciousness of a person.
1b. Through His creation, God reveals to all mankind His eternal power and divinity.
1c. Those who do not honor and glorify God, even when they know and recognize Him as God, become futile and godless in their thinking, their senseless minds are darkened, and while claiming to be wise, they become fools.
2. Each of us is required to give an account of ourselves to God—in other words, give an answer to Him that will be the basis for judgment.
3a. Our heartfelt desire is for God's name and for the remembrance of Him.
3b. Our soul yearns for the Lord.
3c. Our spirit seeks the Lord earnestly.
4a. The world passes away and disappears, and with it the forbidden cravings (the passionate desires, the lust) of the world.
4b. The person who does the will of God and carries out His purposes in his life remains ("abides" or "lasts") forever.
5. God promises that He will direct, make straight, and make plain the paths of the person who seeks to know, recognize, and acknowledge Him.
6a. God hears us when we call on Him and pray to Him.
6b. God reveals Himself to us when we search for Him with all our heart.
6c. When we seek God and pray to Him, He reveals to us the thoughts and plans that He has for our welfare and peace, to give us hope about our final outcome.
6d. When we find the Lord, He releases us from captivity.

ANSWERS

7. God the Father gives the Holy Spirit to those who ask and continue to ask for Him.

8a. Jesus is the One Who baptizes with the Holy Spirit.

8b. The Holy Spirit resides in us.

8c. To be baptized in the Holy Spirit means to welcome and receive Him into every area of your life, holding nothing back.

8d. The world cannot receive the Holy Spirit because it does not see, know, or recognize Him.

9a. The Holy Spirit guides us into all the Truth—the whole, full Truth of God.

9b. The Holy Spirit announces and declares to us the things that are to come, the things that will happen in the future.

9c. The Holy Spirit causes us to recall everything Jesus has told us.

10. God, Himself, in the Person of the Holy Spirit, is our personal Teacher.

11. The Holy Spirit knows everything about us, even the number of the hairs of our head. The Holy Spirit knows the days of our life, or the length of our life. The Holy Spirit also knows the "fixed boundaries" of our life.

12a. The Bible describes the "gate" through which the Holy Spirit leads us as narrow (contracted by pressure).

12b. The Bible describes the "way" the Holy Spirit leads us to follow in life as straitened and compressed.

12c. The Holy Spirit helps us continually to make choices between what leads to life and death, and what leads to blessings and curses.

13a. God told Noah that He was going to make an end of all flesh—that He was going to destroy the people and the land.

13b. God told Noah to prepare for a flood that would come to destroy the people of the earth.

14a. God told Moses that He would make Moses seem "as God" to Pharaoh.

14b. God told Moses that Aaron would be his prophet (or spokesperson).

14c. God told Moses that he was to speak everything God commanded him to say.

14d. God said that Pharaoh would not listen to Moses but would develop a stubborn and hard heart.

14e. God told Moses that He would multiply His signs, wonders, and miracles in the land of Egypt. He would bring His people out of Egypt by great acts of judgment, and in the end, the Egyptians would know He was the Lord.

15a. The Holy Spirit unveils and reveals to us the profound and bottomless things of God—the divine counsels and the things that are hidden and beyond our scrutiny.

15b. The Holy Spirit reveals God's thoughts to us so that we might realize, comprehend, and appreciate the gifts of divine favor and blessing that are so freely and lavishly bestowed on us by God.

16. He promises that His Spirit will lead us, and He Himself will be our Shepherd.

17a. This verse says that the Holy Spirit abides permanently in us—so we have no need that anyone should instruct us.

17b. This verse says that the anointing of the Holy Spirit teaches us the truth concerning everything, and never leads us into falsehood.

17c. This verse challenges us to abide in God—to live in Him and never depart from Him, to be rooted in Him, to be knit to Him.

18. Jesus said that as His "sheep" we will follow Him because we know His voice.

19. The best way for us to hear from the Lord is to "let be and be still."

20. When the Lord speaks to us, our response should be to do whatever He says to us.

Chapter 2

1. We are to live at peace with everyone, if possible, and as far as it depends on us.

2. We don't seem to hear from God because we have become dull in our spiritual hearing and sluggish (even slothful in our achieving spiritual insight).

3a. God desires that we come to Him, take His yoke upon us, and then stand by the roads of life and look and ask God to show us His eternal path that has not changed through the centuries. When He reveals that path, we are to walk in it.

3b. God promises to give us rest for our souls and a greater personal knowledge of Him as we enter into relationship with Him.

3c. This passage tells us that He is gentle (meek) and humble (lowly) in heart.

3d. God tells us that His yoke is wholesome (useful, good—not harsh, hard, sharp, or pressing, but comfortable, gracious, and pleasant). He tells us that any burden He places on us will seem light and easily borne by us.

4. It says that even if we are faithless, God remains true and faithful to His Word and His righteous character.

5a. In this passage, the Lord calls us continually to listen to Him and to consider, perceive, and comprehend what He is saying.

5b. We fail to hear what the Lord is saying or perceive what He is doing because we have allowed our hearts to become fat and dull, our ears heavy and difficult of hearing, and our eyes tightly closed.

5c. In essence, we fail to know His desires for us because we really don't want to know them.

6a. God blesses the person who believes in, trusts in, and relies on the Lord, and whose hope and confidence are placed fully in Him.

6b. The person who is cursed (with great evil) is the strong man who trusts in and relies on "frail man," rather than on the Lord.

6c. The Lord promises that the person who puts full trust and confidence in Him shall be like a tree planted by the waters that spreads out its roots by the river. That person shall not see and fear when heat comes, but the person shall continue to live and produce fruit. The person shall not be anxious and full of care or cease yielding fruit even in times of drought.

7a. Paul believed he was to proclaim Christ among the Gentiles (the non-Jewish world).

7b. Paul was so certain of this call on his life that he did not confer with other people, nor did he go to Jerusalem to get permission from or consult with the apostles.

7c. As a result of Paul's allowing God's Word to grow in his heart and be manifested in his preaching, the people to whom he ministered glorified God as the Author and Source of Paul's transformed life.

8. Paul felt a "witness" that he was hearing from God as the Holy Spirit enlightened and prompted his conscience.

9. Jesus said that those who do not need a visible sign from God are "blessed and happy and to be envied" because they have believed and adhered to and trusted and relied on Him.

10a. The blessed person is the person who listens to the Lord, watching and waiting daily for His word to him.

10b. The person who finds the Lord's wisdom not only finds life, but also obtains favor from the Lord.

10c. The person who sins or fails to wait to hear from God ultimately wrongs and injures himself.

11a. God has given each of us the capacity to hear and obey Him.

11b. God regards obedience as being of more valuable service than burnt offerings and sin offerings.

Chapter 3

1a. Jesus responded, "It is written, Man shall not live and be sustained by (on) bread alone but by every word and expression of God" (v. 4).

1b. Jesus responded, "Get behind Me, Satan! It is written, You shall do homage to and worship the Lord your God, and Him only shall you serve" (v. 8).

1c. Jesus responded, "[The Scripture] says, You shall not tempt (try, test exceedingly) the Lord your God" (v. 12).

1d. The common element in each of Jesus' responses to the devil was, "It is written . . ."

2a. We are called upon to refute arguments, theories, reasonings, and every proud and lofty thing that sets itself up against the true knowledge of God.

2b. We are to lead every thought and purpose away captive. In other words, we are to bring it into obedience to Christ.

3a. If we are deficient in wisdom, we are to ask for wisdom from the "giving God."

3b. God gives His wisdom liberally, ungrudgingly, without reproaching, and without any faultfinding to every person who asks Him for it.

4a. We are to treat God's commandments as "treasure."

4b. We are to make our ears attentive to skillful and godly wisdom.

4c. We are to direct our heart and mind to understanding, applying all our powers to the quest for it.

4d. Those who seek for wisdom as for silver and search for skillful and godly wisdom as for hidden treasures will understand the reverent and worshipful fear of the Lord; they will find the knowledge of our omniscient God.

5. They will understand righteousness, justice, and fair dealing with other people. They will understand every good path. They will desire to do what God says because they can see the benefits of following God's wisdom.

6a. When we have a spiritual experience or are told by someone that he or she is speaking a spiritual truth to us, we are to "prove" or "test" what has happened to see if it is in line with God's Word.

6b. We perceive and recognize the Spirit of God at work by putting it to the test: Every spirit that acknowledges and confesses that Jesus Christ (the Messiah) has become man and has come in the flesh is of God (has God for its source).

6c. We perceive and recognize that something is not of God by putting it to this test: Every spirit that does not acknowledge and confess that Jesus Christ has come in the flesh (but would annul, destroy, sever, disunite Him) is not of God (does not proceed from Him).

7. We are to be "content" with the gifts God gives us.

8a. A prophet interprets the divine will and purpose of God in inspired preaching and teaching.

8b. The threefold purpose of a prophetic word to the person who hears it is upbuilding and constructive spiritual progress, encouragement, and consolation.

8c. The purpose of prophecy to the church as a whole is edification and improvement of the church, and promotion of growth in Christian wisdom, piety, holiness, and happiness.

9. While we are waiting for a prophecy from the Lord to come to pass, we should devote ourselves to the (public and private) reading of the Word of God; to hearing godly exhortation (preaching and personal appeals); and to listening to godly teaching and the instilling of biblical doctrine.

Chapter 4

1a. Those who "would come near to God" must necessarily believe that God exists and that He is the rewarder of those who earnestly and diligently seek Him out.

1b. God rewards them with His own presence and guidance.

2. God has apportioned (or given) to each of us a degree of faith.

3a. Jesus calls us to consider the lilies of the field and learn thoroughly how they grow. We should note especially that the lilies neither toil nor spin, and even so, God clothes the lilies beautifully even though they have a very short lifespan and are useful for very little other than starting a cooking fire.

3b. Jesus calls us to observe and consider the ravens. We should note that the ravens neither sow nor reap, nor do they have storehouses or barns, yet God feeds them. Jesus calls us to learn the lesson that we, as God's disciples, are far more valuable than the birds!

4a. God gave to the sea its limit and boundaries. He placed the sands of the beaches as the perpetual barrier of the sea. Even when the waves of the sea toss and become violent, the waves cannot overcome the boundaries God has established with "feeble grains of sand."

4b. We can learn that if God can tame the great power of the ocean in this way, surely He can tame any force that strikes at our lives.

5. God can do all things, and no thought or purpose of His can be restrained or thwarted.

6. Some of the natural skills and abilities identified in these passages are: the ability to raise cattle and purchase possessions; the ability to play the lyre and pipe; the ability to forge cutting instruments of bronze and iron; the ability to craft items out of gold, silver, bronze, iron, stone, and wood; the ability to work in purple, crimson, and blue yarns and linen fabric; the ability to engrave items.

7. The spiritual abilities identified in this verse are the abilities associated with being apostles, prophets, teachers, and wonder-workers, as well as those with the ability to heal the sick; and the abilities associated with being helpers, administrators, and speakers in different tongues.

8a. God gave different gifts (faculties, talents, and qualities) to the church because we are one body in Christ and parts of one another, being mutually dependent on one another. God calls us to work together as one body.

8b. The ministry gifts identified in this passage are: prophecy, practical service, teaching, exhortation, contributing, aiding and superintending, doing acts of mercy.

8c. The ways in which we are to employ the gifts below are:
    Prophecy: according to the proportion of our faith.
    Giving (contributing): in simplicity and liberality.
    Giving aid and superintending: with zeal and singleness of mind.
    Doing acts of mercy: with genuine cheerfulness and joyful eagerness.

9. One of the major reasons we are given talents and abilities is so we might have and enjoy life, and have it in abundance (to the full, till it overflows).

10. A word of advice that is spoken at the right moment—"how good it is!"

11. We must avoid the counsel of the ungodly; those who are sinners; those who are scornful mockers of the precepts, the instructions, and the teachings of God.

12. The Lord is the One Who prompts us to speak out "wise answers."

13. The Lord says that if we will seek Him and open our mouth wide toward Him, He will fill our mouth with His wisdom.

14. The Lord promises that when we are given an opportunity to bear testimony against our adversaries, He will give us words of wisdom that none of our adversaries will be able to stand against or refute.

15a. God's discipline yields the "peaceable fruit of righteousness."

15b. Those who have been trained by God's discipline receive this harvest of righteousness. They come into conformity to God's will in purpose, thought, and action.

15c. The result of this harvest is right living and right standing with God.

16. In Numbers 22:20–28 God used a donkey to speak to His prophet.

17. After that, the Lord said to Moses, "You have roamed around this mountain country long enough; turn northward."

18a. God desires for our hearts to be blameless toward Him.

18b. God says that He will "show Himself strong" in behalf of those whose hearts are blameless toward Him.

Chapter 5

1a.   Jesus promises to give us and "bequeath" to us His own peace.

1b.   We are to keep our hearts from being troubled or afraid.

2.   The mind of the Holy Spirit produces life and soul peace, both now and forever.

3.   Christ's peace is to rule in our hearts—acting continually as an umpire, deciding and settling with finality all questions that arise in our minds.

4.   We are not to be rash or hasty in our speaking; rather, we are to give thought to what we are doing and saying.

5a.   We are to "exercise" our personal convictions as if we are in God's presence, keeping them to ourselves and striving only to know the truth and obey God's will.

5b.   A person who has doubts, misgivings, or an uneasy conscience about something but goes ahead and does it anyway stands condemned before God, because he is not true to his convictions and does not act from faith.

6.   In the parable of Jesus, the master said to each of the servants who had been given five talents and two talents, "Well done, you upright (honorable, admirable) and faithful servant! You have been faithful and trustworthy over a little; I will put you in charge of much. Enter into and share the joy (the delight, the blessedness) which your master enjoys."

7.   God gives to those who delight themselves in the Lord the desires and secret petitions of their heart.

8a.   We are to eagerly pursue and seek to acquire love.

8b.   We are to desire earnestly and cultivate spiritual endowments (gifts), especially the ability to prophesy (interpret the divine will and purpose in inspired preaching and teaching).

9.   The desires of the flesh (godless human nature) and the desires of the Holy Spirit are antagonistic to each other; they are continually opposed to and in conflict with each other.

10.   The kingdom of God is all about righteousness (the state of being totally acceptable to God), peace of heart, and joy in the Holy Spirit.

11a.   Jesus said about His relationship with God the Father, "I and the Father are One."

11b.   Jesus said about His authority to act and speak, "I do nothing of Myself (of My own accord or on My own authority), but I say [exactly] what the Father has taught me."

12a.   Jesus calls us to live in Him (abide vitally united to Him), and let His words remain in us and continue to live in us.

12b.   Jesus said that if we will abide in Him and let His words remain in us and continue to live in our hearts, we can ask whatever we will, and it shall be done for us.

13a.   Our lives are to lovingly express the truth; in all things, we are to speak truly, deal truly, and live truly.

13b.   The Lord calls us to grow up in every way and in all things into Him Who is the Head.

14. When our desires are godly, we can expect that whatever we ask for in prayer, and believe confidently that we will receive, it will be granted to us!
15. God is working to produce and magnify in us the power and desire both to will and to work for His good pleasure and satisfaction and delight.
16. When we hear the Lord calling our name, we should say as Samuel said, "Speak, Lord, for Your servant is listening."
17a. We are God's sheep.
17b. The "sheep" follow the Shepherd's voice.
17c. Jesus said that we have the ability to recognize Him and know His voice.

Chapter 6

1a. The Holy Spirit comes in close fellowship with us.
1b. The Holy Spirit brings conviction about sin because people do not believe in, trust in, rely on, or adhere to Jesus.
1c. We need the Holy Spirit to convince us of our need for and our receiving of Christ's righteousness because Jesus has gone to His Father, and we no longer see Him.
1d. We need the Holy Spirit's assurance that Satan—the evil genius and prince of this world—has already been judged, condemned, and sentenced.
2a. The Holy Spirit convicts all impious, unholy people.
2b. The Holy Spirit convicts these people of their ungodly deeds which they have committed in ungodly ways, and of all the severe, abusive, and jarring things they have spoken against Him.
3a. Jesus said He was *not* sent to judge, to reject, condemn, or pass sentence on the world.
3b. Jesus said He *was* sent that the world might find salvation and be made safe and sound through Him.
3c. The person who believes in (clings to, trusts in, and relies on) Jesus is not judged and never comes up for judgment; for him there is no rejection, condemnation, or damnation.
3d. The person who does *not* believe in (cling to, trust in, and rely on) Jesus is judged already (he has already been convicted and received his sentence).
4a. Jesus said to the woman caught in adultery, "I do not condemn you either."
4b. He told her, "Go on your way and from now on sin no more."
5a. We are to desire that God would create a clean heart in us.
5b. We are to desire that God would renew a right, persevering, and steadfast spirit in us.
5c. God's promise is that He will give us a new heart.
5d. God's promise is that He will put a new spirit within us.
5e. God gives us a new heart and a new spirit so we can be sensitive and responsive to His touch.
5f. When we have a new heart and a new spirit, we will choose to walk in God's statutes and keep His ordinances and do them.

6. This verse says that the Holy Spirit Who lives in us is greater or mightier than he (the devil) who is in the world.

7a. According to this verse, Christ has made us free. He has completely liberated us.

7b. We are to respond to the freedom Christ bestows on us by standing fast, refusing to be hampered by, held ensnared by, or submit to a yoke of slavery to sin.

8a. We are to pray, "Forgive us our debts, as we also have forgiven our debtors."

8b. We are to pray, "Deliver us from the evil one."

9a. The people who walked in darkness have seen a great Light.

9b. The Light has shined on those who dwelt in the land of intense darkness and the shadow of death.

9c. The Messiah came to be "a light to the nations (Gentiles)."

9d. Jesus said that those who would follow Him would not be walking in the dark, but would have the Light which is life.

9e. We are to walk as children of Light. We are to lead the lives of those who are native-born to the Light.

9f. The fruit (the effect, the product) of the Light or the Spirit is every form of kindly goodness, uprightness of heart, and trueness of life.

10a. God justifies us. He is the One Who puts us in right relation to Himself.

10b. Christ Jesus is at the right hand of God pleading in intercession for us.

11a. On the cross, Christ Jesus, the Messiah, bore our griefs (sicknesses, weaknesses, and distresses) and carried our sorrows and pains of punishment.

11b. Christ Jesus was wounded for our transgressions and was bruised for our guilt and iniquities.

11c. His chastisement made His peace and well-being available to us.

11d. His stripes made it possible for us to be healed and made whole.

11e. The travail of Christ Jesus on the cross justified many and made many righteous (upright and in right standing with God).

11f. On the cross, Christ Jesus, God's Servant, bore our iniquities and our guilt, along with the consequences associated with our sins.

12. God promises that if we freely admit we have sinned and confess our sins, He will forgive our sins and cleanse us of all unrighteousness (everything that does not conform to His will in purpose, thought, and action).

Chapter 7

1. He said that God is a Spirit and must be worshiped in spirit and in truth.

2. For a person to become sensitive to the voice of God and understand what the Spirit is saying, he must be born of water and (even) the Spirit.

3a. Jesus said about the Father to those who opposed Him, "Not one of you has ever given ear to His voice or seen His form."

3b. People do not have God's word (His thought) living in their heart because they have not believed, adhered to, trusted in, and relied on Him Whom He has sent (Jesus).

4a. In the latter times some will turn away from the faith, giving attention to deluding and seducing spirits and doctrines that demons teach.

4b. People fall victim to the hypocrisy and pretensions of liars because their consciences are seared (cauterized).

5. The grace (favor and spiritual blessing) of the Lord Jesus Christ, the love of God, and the presence and fellowship (the communion, sharing together, and participation) in the Holy Spirit are imparted to them.

6a. Those who are led by the Spirit are children of God.

6b. As God's children, we are heirs of God and fellow heirs with Christ, sharing His inheritance with Him.

6c. If we share Christ's glory, we need to share His suffering.

6d. There is no worthy comparison between the glory that is about to be revealed to us, in us, and for us or be conferred on us, and our sufferings in this present life.

7a. We are to clothe ourselves with the Lord Jesus Christ (the Messiah).

7b. We are to make no provision for indulging the flesh—rather, we are to put a stop to thinking about the evil cravings of our physical nature and to gratifying its desires and lusts.

7c. The desires of the flesh are opposed to the Holy Spirit.

7d. The desires of the Holy Spirit are opposed to the flesh (godless human nature).

7e. The Holy Spirit seeks to prevent us from doing what we desire to do that is sin.

8a. God imparts to us the power, ability, and sufficiency to minister to others.

8b. The Holy Spirit gives life.

8c. The dispensation of the Spirit will cause us to do two things: to obtain the Holy Spirit (to have the Holy Spirit in our lives), and to be governed by the Holy Spirit in our lives.

Chapter 8

1. We are to know, recognize, and acknowledge Him; reverently fear and worship the Lord; and turn entirely away from evil.

2a. The reverent fear and worshipful awe of the Lord includes the hatred of evil.

2b. The Lord hates pride, arrogance, the evil way, and perverted and twisted speech.

3. If we are to maintain a tender conscience, we must refuse to pay attention to deluding and seducing spirits and doctrines that demons teach.

4a. If your eye is sound, your entire body will be full of light.

4b. If your eye is unsound, your whole body will be full of darkness.

5a. We must refuse to be yoked in partnerships with unbelievers.

5b. It is impossible for right living and right standing with God to have fellowship with iniquity and lawlessness.

5c. It is impossible for light to have fellowship with darkness.

6a. If we are to be in the right position for God to both start and finish in us what He desires to accomplish, we must look away from anything that will distract us from the Lord.

6b. In this verse Jesus is described as the Leader and the Source of our faith, and is also its Finisher.

6c. He brings our faith to maturity and perfection.

7. "As iron sharpens iron, so a man sharpens the countenance of a friend."

8a. We have not been given the spirit that belongs to the world.

8b. The Holy Spirit has been given to us that we might realize, comprehend, and appreciate the gifts of divine favor and blessing so freely and lavishly bestowed on us by God.

8c. The natural, nonspiritual man is incapable of accepting, welcoming, or admitting into his heart the gifts, teachings, and revelations of the Spirit of God.

8d. The natural, nonspiritual man is incapable of receiving these things because they can only be spiritually discerned, estimated, and appreciated.

8e. The spiritual man examines, investigates, inquires into, questions, and discerns all things.

9a. The "mind of the flesh" is described as sense and reason without the Holy Spirit. It is death with all the miseries arising from sin.

9b. "The mind of the Holy Spirit" is described as life and soul peace, both now and forever.

10. Because the enemy is roaming around like a roaring lion seeking someone to seize upon and devour, we must be well balanced, temperate, and sober of mind—vigilant and cautious at all times.

11a. As we seek balance in our lives, we are to renounce all disgraceful ways—secret thoughts, feelings, desires, and underhandedness, the methods and arts that men hide through shame.

11b. As we seek balance in our lives, we are to refuse to deal craftily—to practice trickery and cunning—or to adulterate or handle dishonestly the Word of God.

11c. As we seek balance in our lives, we are to state the truth openly, clearly, and candidly.

12a. There is a time to be born and a time to die.

12b. There is a time to plant and a time to pluck up what is planted.

12c. There is a time to weep and a time to laugh, a time to mourn and a time to dance.

12d. There is a time to embrace and a time to refrain from embracing.

12e. There is a time to keep silent and a time to speak.

13. "Weeping may endure for a night, but joy comes in the morning."

14. This verse says that the chastisement needed to obtain peace and well-being is found in Christ Jesus—it is by the stripes that wounded Him that we are healed and made whole.

Chapter 9

1a. It assures us that God is faithful, reliable, trustworthy, and true to His promise.

1b. Jesus said that He would be with us "all the days (perpetually, uniformly, and on every occasion), to the [very] close and consummation of the age."

2. God's promise to us when we feel blind about where we are going or where He is leading us is this: "I will bring the blind by a way that they know not; I will lead them in paths that they have not known. I will make darkness into light before them and make uneven places into a plain. These things I have determined to do [for them]; and I will not leave them forsaken."

3a. According to these passages, the state of our knowledge and prophecy (teaching) is always fragmentary, incomplete, and imperfect.

3b. We have the hope that one day God will make everything complete and perfect, and at that time, everything that is incomplete and imperfect will vanish away, become antiquated, be void, and be superseded.

3c. These three things abide even when our knowledge and prophecy are fragmentary: faith, hope, and love.

4a. The Lord directed Abram to go to a land that God said He would show him.

4b. For Abram's obedience in going, God promised to make Abram a great nation, and to bless him with an abundant increase of favors, make his name famous and distinguished, and make him a blessing to others.

4c. According to Hebrews 11:8–9, Abraham was urged on or prompted by faith.

4d. Abraham went even though he did not know or trouble his mind about where he was to go.

5a. The disciples asked Jesus to increase their faith—their trust and confidence in God.

5b. Jesus said, "If you had faith (trust, and confidence in God), even [so small] like a grain of mustard seed, you could say to a mulberry tree, Be pulled up by the roots, and be planted in the sea and it would obey you."

6. God assures us that He is a partner in our labor and that He causes all things to work together and fit into a plan for our good.

7a. Faith is the assurance of the things we hope for.

7b. Faith is the proof of things we do not see and the conviction of their reality.

8a. It says that the steps of a good man are directed and established by the Lord.

8b. It says that even though he may fall, he will not be utterly cast down, but that the Lord will grasp his hand to support and uphold him.

8c. We are to walk by faith and not by sight or appearance.

Chapter 10

1a. A man's mind plans his ways.

1b. The Lord directs a man's steps and makes them sure.

1c. According to Psalm 37:23, the steps of a good man are directed and established by the Lord.

1d. The steps of a good man are directed and established by the Lord when the Lord delights in his way.

2. This verse tells us that what God opens, no one shall shut, and what God shuts, no one shall open.

3a. In this verse, the apostle Paul said that a wide door of opportunity for effectual service had been opened to him.

3b. Paul said he would also encounter many adversaries there.

4a. In this passage, Paul and Silas tried to go into the province of Asia and later into Bithynia.

4b. They were forbidden by the Holy Spirit to proclaim the Word in Asia.

4c. The spirit of Jesus kept them from going into Bithynia.

4d. The Holy Spirit allowed them to go to Troas.

5. In this verse, God says, "My thoughts are not your thoughts, neither are your ways My ways."

6a. We must always rely upon the Lord to rescue us from temptations and trials.

6b. We must trust the Lord to keep the ungodly around us under chastisement until the day of judgment and doom.

6c. We must particularly trust the Lord to deal with those who walk after the flesh, indulge in the lust of polluting passion, and scorn and despise authority.

7. The lust of the flesh (craving for sensual gratification), the lust of the eyes (greedy longings of the mind), and the pride of life (assurance in one's own resources or in the stability of earthly things)—these all come from the world rather than from the Father.

Chapter 11

1a. Mary seated herself at the Lord's feet and was listening to His teaching.

1b. Martha was overly occupied and too busy—distracted with serving the guests in her home.

1c. When Martha complained to Jesus about Mary, Jesus said to Martha, "You are anxious and troubled about many things."

1d. Jesus said about Mary, "Mary has chosen the good portion [that which is to her advantage], which shall not be taken away from her."

2a. We are admonished by Paul not to fret or have anxiety about anything.

2b. We are admonished to continue to make our wants known to God.

3a. Jesus said the scribes and Pharisees had neglected and omitted the weightier (more important) matters of the Law—right, justice, mercy, and fidelity.

3b. Jesus said the Pharisees were full of extortion and grasping self-indulgence.

3c. Jesus said that on the outside, the Pharisees appeared to be beautiful. They seemed to be just and upright.

3d. Jesus said that on the inside, the hearts of the Pharisees were full of pretence, lawlessness, and iniquity.

4a. Jesus said to those who were suffering from "spiritual burnout": "Come to Me, all you who labor and are heavy-laden and overburdened, and I will cause you to rest. [I will ease and relieve and refresh your souls.]"

4b. Jesus told us to take on His yoke.

4c. Jesus said we are to learn of Him.

4d. Jesus described His own nature as being gentle (meek) and humble (lowly) in heart.

4e. Jesus said that if we take on His yoke and learn of Him, we will find rest (relief, ease, refreshment, recreation, and blessed quiet) for our souls.

4f. Jesus described His yoke as wholesome—useful and good, not harsh, hard, sharp, or pressing, but rather, comfortable, gracious, and pleasant.

4g. Jesus described His burden as being light and easy to be borne.

5a. People are fully known by their fruits.

5b. According to this passage, those who do the will of God the Father in heaven enter the kingdom of heaven.

5c. The Lord will not know those who act wickedly—those who disregard His commands—even if they have prophesied or driven out demons in His name.

6. The eternal future of the person who believes in Jesus as the Son of God is eternal (everlasting) life. He will not perish, come to destruction, or be lost.

7a. We are saved by free grace (God's unmerited favor).

7b. We are saved through (our) faith.

7c. Our salvation is the gift of God.

8a. According to verse 9, we are saved because we acknowledge and confess with our lips that Jesus is Lord and believe in our heart that God raised Him from the dead.

8b. According to verse 10, with our heart we believe (adhere to, trust in, and rely on Christ).

8c. With our mouth we confess (declare openly and speak out freely our faith).

9a. When we freely admit that we have sinned and confess our sins, God promises to forgive our sins and cleanse us from all unrighteousness.

9b. God abides with anyone who confesses (acknowledges) that Jesus is the Son of God.

9c. God dwells and continues to abide in the person who dwells and continues in Him.

9d. The "born-again child of God" is the person who believes (adheres to, trusts, and relies on the fact) that Jesus is the Christ.

10a. In Ezekiel 11:19, God promises to give those who believe in Him a new heart and a new spirit.

10b. In this verse, God promises to give those who believe in Him a heart of flesh that is sensitive and responsive to the touch of God—rather than a stony, unnaturally hardened heart.

10c. When we have a new heart, a new spirit, and God's Spirit within us, God causes us to walk in His statutes, keep His ordinances, and do them.

11. In this passage, Jesus said Moses permitted husbands to dismiss, repudiate, and divorce their wives because of the hardness, stubbornness, and perversity of their hearts.

12a. The Spirit admonishes us not to harden our hearts—not to provoke God or rebel against Him.

12b. A wicked, unbelieving heart leads a person to turn away, desert, or stand aloof from the living God.

12c. Our hearts are hardened by the deceitfulness of sin—by the fraudulence, the stratagems, and the trickery which the delusive glamour of our sin may play on us.

13a. Jesus did not ask that God the Father take us out of the world. Rather, He asked His Father to keep and protect us from the evil one.

13b. The Truth—God's Word—dwelling in us sanctifies us (purifies, consecrates, separates us) for God.

14a. We must not be conformed to this world (this age); we must not fashion our lives or adapt them to this world's external, superficial customs.

14b. We are to be transformed in our minds, with new ideals and a new attitude in line with God's Word.

15. Jesus said He was called to preach good news.

16a. We must not grieve the Holy Spirit of God—offend, vex, or sadden Him.

16b. We must banish from our lives all bitterness, indignation, and wrath (passion, rage, bad temper); resentment (anger, animosity); quarreling (brawling, clamor, contention); slander (evil-speaking, abusive or blasphemous language); and all malice (spite, ill will, or baseness of any kind).

16c. We must become useful, helpful, and kind to others; tenderhearted (compassionate, understanding, loving-hearted); and forgiving.

16d. We are to forgive others as God in Christ forgave us.

17. A prophecy of Scripture should never be a matter of any personal, private, or special interpretation.

18. Because the Spirit of the Lord was upon Jesus, God anointed and qualified Him to preach the gospel of good tidings to the meek, the poor, and afflicted; God sent Jesus to bind up and heal the brokenhearted, to proclaim liberty to physical and spiritual captives, to open the spiritual prisons that keep people bound, and to open the spiritual eyes of those who are spiritually blind.

19. "Where the Spirit of the Lord is," we find liberty (emancipation from bondage, freedom).

20. We are really and unquestionably free when the Son liberates us (makes us free men).

21a. In verse 12, we are each required to give an account of ourselves to God.

21b. In verse 13, the apostle Paul tells us that we must not criticize, blame, or pass judgment on one another.

21c. In that verse, Paul tells us to decide and endeavor never to put a stumbling block, obstacle, or hindrance in the way of a brother or sister in Christ.

21d. In verse 15, we are no longer walking in love if our brother or sister in Christ is being pained, their feelings are hurt, or they are injured by what we do or say.

21e. In verse 19, we are to aim for and eagerly pursue what makes for harmony and for mutual upbuilding (edification and development) of one another.

22a. We have full freedom and confidence to enter into the Holy of Holies by the power and virtue in the blood of Jesus.

22b. We are to come forward and draw near to God with true, honest, and sincere hearts—and with unqualified assurance and absolute conviction engendered by faith, trust, and confidence in God's power, wisdom, and goodness.

22c. Our hearts have been purified from a guilty (evil) conscience.

Chapter 12

1.   God has given us the capacity to hear and obey Him.

2a. According to this passage, when God has called to us, we have refused to answer.

2b. We have not heeded God's outstretched hand.

2c. We have treated God's wise counsel as nothing.

2d. We have refused to accept God's reproof.

3a. The nature of the Spirit Who rested on Jesus and Who also rests on us today is wisdom and understanding, counsel and might, knowledge, and a reverential and obedient fear of the Lord.

3b. The Spirit quickens our understanding, and causes us to delight in the reverential and obedient fear of the Lord.

3c. A person who hears the Spirit is able to judge and make decisions with righteousness, justice, and fairness.

3d. The two "girdles" that wrap the life of the person who has the Spirit of the Lord are righteousness and faithfulness.

4.   To those who repent and give heed to His reproof, the Lord promises to pour out His spirit upon them and make His words known to them.

5a. According to this passage, we have hated God's knowledge.

5b. We have failed to choose the reverent and worshipful fear of the Lord.

5c. Those who turn away from a reverence for God's knowledge, counsel, and reproof eat of the fruit of their own way and are satiated with their own devices. In other words, they suffer the consequences of their own bad choices.

5d. Those who hearken to God's wisdom dwell securely and in confident trust. They are quiet and without fear or dread of evil.

6a. The person who really loves Jesus will keep His word—obey His teaching.

6b. The blessing to the person who loves Jesus and keeps His word, obeying His teachings, is that God the Father will love him and the Father and the Son will make their home (abode, special dwelling place) with him.

7.   This verse says that it is God's will for all of us who are in Christ Jesus to be thankful and give thanks to God in everything, no matter what the circumstances may be.

8.   We must never quench, subdue, or suppress the Holy Spirit in our lives.

9a. When we recognize we are deficient in wisdom, we are to ask for wisdom from God Who gives wisdom to all who ask for it.

9b. God gives His wisdom liberally and ungrudgingly, without reproaching or fault-finding.

9c. We are to ask for wisdom with unwavering faith—no hesitating, no doubting.

10. The blessed are those who keep God's testimonies, and who seek, inquire for and of God, and who crave Him with their whole heart.

11a. In Psalm 119:10, the psalmist sought the Lord with his whole heart—inquiring for and of God, and yearning for Him.

11b. The psalmist's request of God was, "Oh, let me not wander or step aside [either in ignorance or willfully] from Your commandments."

11c. In verse 34, the psalmist's promise to God was, "Give me understanding, that I may keep Your law; yes, I will observe it with my whole heart."

12. Jesus promised that those who have pure hearts will see God.

13a. If there is nothing in our conscience that accuses us or causes us to feel guilty or condemned, we have confidence (complete assurance and boldness) before God and receive from Him whatever we ask.

13b. Those of us who watchfully obey God's orders, follow His plan for us, and practice what is pleasing to Him receive from Him whatever we ask of Him.

14a. Jesus cautioned us to be careful in what we hear.

14b. The measure of thought and study we give to the truth we hear determines the measure of virtue and knowledge that we receive from the Lord.

15a. When people turn away from sound and wholesome instruction and develop a desire only for teaching that is pleasant and gratifying, they seek teachers who satisfy their own liking and who foster the errors they hold.

15b. When people turn aside from hearing the truth, they wander off into myths and man-made fictions.

16a. We are never to turn to mediums—those who have familiar spirits—or to wizards.

16b. God says that He will set His face against any person who turns to those with familiar spirits and to wizards. He will cut that person off from his people so that no atonement can be made for him.

17a. Jesus said that a servant finds it impossible to serve two masters.

17b. This is so because either he will hate the one and love the other, or he will stand by and be devoted to the one and despise the other.

18a. Immorality (sexual vice), impurity (of lustful, rich, wasteful living), and greediness should never be named among God's consecrated people.

18b. Filthiness (obscenity, indecency), foolish and sinful (silly and corrupt) talk, and coarse jesting are "not fitting" for God's people.

18c. Practicing sexual vice, impurity in thought or in deed, and covetousness (the lustful desire for the property of others and a greediness for gain) can cause a person not to have any inheritance in the kingdom of Christ and of God.

19a. We are to attend to God's words.

19b. We are to consent to and submit to His sayings.

19c. We are to keep God's words and sayings in sight—at the center of our heart.

19d. God's words produce life—healing and health—in us.

19e. We are to keep and guard our heart with all vigilance and above all that we guard.

19f. We are to put away from us false and dishonest speech.

19g. We are to put willful and contrary talk far from us.

19h. We are to have a fixed purpose in life and let our gaze be straight before us.

19i. We are to consider well the path of our feet, and let all our ways be established and ordered aright.

19j. We must never walk toward or into evil.

20. As we continue to look into the Word of God, we are constantly being transfigured into His very own image in ever increasing splendor—from one degree of glory to another.

Chapter 13

1a. To be sanctified "through and through" means to be completely separated from profane things, to be made pure and wholly consecrated to God.

1b. Paul desires our spirit, soul, and body to be preserved "sound and complete."

2a. We are to walk and live habitually in the Holy Spirit—responsive to, controlled by, and guided by the Spirit.

2b. If we walk and live in the Holy Spirit, we will not gratify the cravings and desires of the flesh (human nature without God).

3. In this verse, Paul says the kingdom of God is righteousness (the state that makes a person acceptable to God), heart peace, and joy in the Holy Spirit.

4a. To have "uncircumcised" ears means to be incapable of hearing or obeying God because the person has never been brought into covenant with God or been consecrated to His service.

4b. To those who have uncircumcised ears, the Word of God has become a reproach and the object of scorn. They have no delight in it.

5a. Jesus said, "I am able to do *nothing* from Myself [independently, of My own accord—but only as I am taught by God and as I get His orders]."

5b. Jesus said His judgment was right, just, and righteous because He did not seek or consult His own will, desires, goals, or purpose, but only the will and pleasure of God the Father.

6a. Blood was put on the tip of the priest's right ear so that he would hear clearly and not be deceived.

6b. Blood was put on the thumb of the priest's right hand so that what he laid his hand to do would be right and blessed.

6c. Blood was put on the big toe of the priest's right foot so that everywhere he went would be correct and sanctified.

6d. We are anointed with the shed blood of Jesus on our ears, hands, and feet so that we can hear, take action, and go in directions that are safe and divinely led.

7a. By His shed blood, Jesus formed us into a kingdom (a royal race) of priests to His God and Father.

7b. As the priests of Jesus, we are to give Him the glory, power, majesty, and dominion that are rightfully His throughout the ages and forever and ever.

8a. According to 1 Corinthians 15:42, the earthly body is perishable and subject to decay.

8b. The resurrected body is imperishable (immune to decay and immortal).

8c. According to verse 43, the earthly body is sown with dishonor, humiliation, infirmity, and weakness.

8d. The resurrected body is raised with honor, glory, strength, and power.

9a. Visible things are temporal (brief and fleeting).

9b. Invisible things are deathless and everlasting.

10a. Those who have departed this life in Christ will rise first.

10b. The living ones who remain on the earth will meet the Lord in the clouds along with the resurrected dead.

10c. We are to remind one another of this coming event in order to comfort and encourage one another.

11a. The Word that God speaks is alive and full of power.

11b. Being sharper than any two-edged sword, the Word of God penetrates to the dividing line of the breath of life (soul) and the immortal spirit, and to the dividing of joints and marrow (referring to the deepest parts of our nature).

11c. The Word of God exposes, sifts, analyzes, and judges the very thoughts and purposes of the heart.

12a. When the Lord is our Shepherd, we do not lack anything we need.

12b. Our Shepherd makes us as His sheep to lie down in fresh, tender, green pastures.

12c. Our Shepherd leads us as His sheep beside still and restful waters.

12d. Our Shepherd refreshes and restores our life (our self).

12e. Our Shepherd leads us as His sheep along the paths of righteousness (uprightness and right standing with Him).

13. We are to seek to cultivate our spiritual growth with an attitude of reverence, awe, and trembling (self-distrust, with serious caution, tenderness of conscience, watchfulness against temptation, timidly shrinking from whatever might offend God and discredit the name of Christ).

14. We are to worship God, a spiritual Being, in spirit and in truth (reality).

15a. So we do not come into temptation, we must keep awake (give strict attention, be cautious and active), and watch and pray.

15b. The flesh is weak.

16a. The Spirit of God is characterized by wisdom, understanding, counsel, might, knowledge, and reverential and obedient fear of the Lord.

16b. The Spirit of God produces quick understanding in a person, along with a delight in the reverential and obedient fear of the Lord.

17a. As Jesus prayed in the Garden of Gethsemane, He was very sad and deeply grieved, almost to the point of dying of sorrow.

17b. Even with a sad and deeply grieved soul, Jesus prayed, "My Father, if it is possible, let this cup pass away from Me; nevertheless, not what I will (not what I desire), but as You will and desire."

18a. The psalmist called to remembrance in the night the song he had sung to God.

18b. The psalmist meditated on the Word of God with his heart.

18c. The psalmist's spirit searched diligently for God's leading.

Chapter 14

1a. Paul realized that even though all things are permissible and lawful, not all things are helpful (good for us to do, expedient and profitable when considered with other things).

1b. Paul refused to become the slave of or be brought under the power of anything.

2a. To know God's full plan of blessing, we need to strip off and throw aside every encumbrance (unnecessary weight) and every sin that might cling to or entangle us.

2b. We are to run the race God has appointed for us with patient endurance and steady and active persistence.

2c. We are to look continually to Jesus, Who is the Leader and the Source of our faith, as well as the Finisher of our faith (bringing it to maturity and perfection).

2d. As Jesus endured the shame of the cross and opposition from sinners, He looked ahead to the joy of obtaining the prize that was set before Him.

2e. This passage calls us to keep our focus on Jesus and the joy He promises us so that we may not grow weary or exhausted, lose heart, or relax and faint in our minds.

3a. This passage says that the gaining of wisdom is better than the gaining of silver, and the profit of wisdom is better than fine gold.

3b. This passage says that wisdom is more precious than rubies.

3c. In the person who seeks and gains understanding from God's Word, wisdom produces length of days, riches and honor, pleasantness, and peace.

4a. After Jesus was crucified and rose again, Peter, Thomas, Nathanael, the sons of Zebedee (James and John), and two other disciples decided to go fishing.

4b. As He stood on the beach, Jesus called the disciples and asked them, "You do not have any meat (fish), do you?"

4c. The disciples answered, "No."

4d. Jesus told them, "Cast the net on the right side of the boat and you will find [some]."

4e. When the disciples did what Jesus said to do, they caught such a massive amount of fish they were not able to haul the net into the boat.

5. God's first words to mankind that were filled with the promise of blessing were: "Be fruitful, multiply, and fill the earth, and subdue it [using all its vast resources in the service of God and man]; and have dominion over the fish of the sea, the birds of the air, and over every living creature that moves upon the earth."

6a. In John 14:15, Jesus said that if we really love Him, we will keep (obey) His commands.

6b. In John 21:15–18, Jesus asked Simon Peter three times, "Do you love Me?"

6c. In John 21:15–18, Simon Peter answered Jesus three times, "Yes, Lord, You know that I love You."

6d. Jesus told Simon Peter to feed His lambs, shepherd (tend) His sheep, and feed His sheep.

6e. In verse 18, Jesus told Peter the sacrifice he would make for obeying Jesus' commands: "When you grow old you will stretch out your hands, and someone else will put a girdle around you and carry you where you do not wish to go."

7a. We are to arm ourselves with the thought and purpose patiently to suffer rather than fail to please God.

7b. The person who is willing to suffer—if it means pleasing God—spends the rest of his natural life no longer seeking to gratify his own human appetites and desires, but living solely to please God and do what God wills.

8. Saul asked Jesus, "Lord, what do You desire me to do?"

9. According to this passage, John testified and vouched that his visions were about the Word of God and the testimony of Jesus Christ.

10. Jesus said that we are to hold the seed of the Word of God planted in our lives "fast in a just (noble, virtuous) and worthy heart, and steadily bring forth fruit with patience."

11a. God gives us peace that transcends all understanding.

11b. God's peace acts as a garrison or a guard over our hearts and minds.

12. The peace we have been given by Christ is intended to rule (act as umpire continually) in our hearts (deciding and settling with finality all questions that arise in our minds).

13a. We are to seek to live in peace with everybody.

13b. We are to pursue consecration and holiness.

14. The first thing that we are to know as we are still in God's presence is that He is God—and that He will be exalted in the earth and among all nations.

15a. In this passage, God did *not* speak to Elijah in natural occurrences of wind, earthquake, or fire.

15b. God *did* speak to Elijah in a sound of gentle stillness and in a still, small voice.

16. Jesus told us, "When you pray, go into your [most] private room, and, closing the door, pray to your Father, Who is in secret."

17a. In verse 20 we are told that even in adversity and affliction, our eyes will constantly behold our Teacher.

17b. Verse 21 says that we will hear our Teacher tell us: "This is the way; walk in it."

17c. We will then know God's plan as we make decisions.

18a. As a consequence of His power at work in us, the Lord is able to carry out His purpose for our lives and to do superabundantly, far over and above anything we dare ask or think.

18b. God's power at work in us allows the Lord to move infinitely beyond even our highest prayers, desires, thoughts, hopes, or dreams.

19. In this verse, the Lord promises that He will not fail us, give up on us, or leave us without support. He will not leave us helpless, forsake us, let us down, or relax His hold on us.

20a. Based on verse 17, the kingdom of God is righteousness (that state which makes a person acceptable to God), [heart] peace, and joy in the Holy Spirit.

20b. According to verse 18, God regards the person who lives in righteousness, peace, and joy as acceptable and pleasing to Him and approved by men.

Do you have a real relationship with Jesus?

God loves you! He created you to be a special, unique, one-of-a-kind individual, and He has a specific purpose and plan for your life. And through a personal relationship with your Creator—God—you can discover a way of life that will truly satisfy your soul.

No matter who you are, what you've done, or where you are in your life right now, God's love and grace are greater than your sin—your mistakes. Jesus willingly gave His life so you can receive forgiveness from God and have new life in Him. He's just waiting for you to invite Him to be your Savior and Lord.

If you are ready to commit your life to Jesus and follow Him, all you have to do is ask Him to forgive your sins and give you a fresh start in the life you are meant to live. Begin by praying this prayer...

> *Lord Jesus, thank You for giving Your life for me and forgiving me of my sins so I can have a personal relationship with You. I am sincerely sorry for the mistakes I've made, and I know I need You to help me live right.*
>
> *Your Word says in Romans 10:9, "If you declare with your mouth, 'Jesus is Lord,' and believe in your heart that God raised him from the dead, you will be saved" (NIV). I believe You are the Son of God and confess You as my Savior and Lord. Take me just as I am, and work in my heart, making me the person You want me to be. I want to live for You, Jesus, and I am so grateful that You are giving me a fresh start in my new life with You today.*
>
> *I love You, Jesus!*

It's so amazing to know that God loves us so much! He wants to have a deep, intimate relationship with us that grows every day as we spend time with Him in prayer and Bible study. And we want to encourage you in your new life in Christ.

Please visit joycemeyer.org/salvation to request Joyce's book *A New Way of Living*, which is our gift to you. We also have other free resources online to help you make progress in pursuing everything God has for you.

Congratulations on your fresh start in your life in Christ! We hope to hear from you soon.

About the Author

Joyce Meyer is one of the world's leading practical Bible teachers. Her daily broadcast, *Enjoying Everyday Life*, airs on hundreds of television networks and radio stations worldwide.

Joyce has written more than one hundred inspirational books. Her bestsellers include *Power Thoughts*; *The Confident Woman*; *Look Great, Feel Great*; *Starting Your Day Right*; *Ending Your Day Right*; *Approval Addiction*; *How to Hear from God*; *Beauty for Ashes*; and *Battlefield of the Mind*.

Joyce travels extensively, holding conferences throughout the year and speaking to thousands around the world.

JOYCE MEYER MINISTRIES

U.S. & FOREIGN OFFICE ADDRESSES

Joyce Meyer Ministries
P.O. Box 655
Fenton, MO 63026
USA
(636) 349-0303

Joyce Meyer Ministries—Canada
P.O. Box 7700
Vancouver, BC V6B 4E2
Canada
(800) 868-1002

Joyce Meyer Ministries—Australia
Locked Bag 77
Mansfield Delivery Centre
Queensland 4122
Australia
(07) 3349 1200

Joyce Meyer Ministries—England
P.O. Box 1549
Windsor SL4 1GT
United Kingdom
01753 831102

Joyce Meyer Ministries—South Africa
P.O. Box 5
Cape Town 8000
South Africa
(27) 21-701-1056

Other Books by Joyce Meyer

100 Ways to Simplify Your Life
21 Ways to Finding Peace and Happiness
Any Minute
Approval Addiction
The Approval Fix
The Battle Belongs to the Lord
Battlefield of the Mind*
Battlefield of the Mind for Kids
Battlefield of the Mind for Teens
Battlefield of the Mind Devotional
Be Anxious for Nothing*
Being the Person God Made You to Be
Beauty for Ashes
Change Your Words, Change Your Life
The Confident Mom
The Confident Woman
The Confident Woman Devotional
Do Yourself a Favor...Forgive
Eat the Cookie...Buy the Shoes
Eight Ways to Keep the Devil Under Your Feet
Ending Your Day Right
Enjoying Where You Are on the Way to Where You Are Going
The Everyday Life Bible
Filled with the Spirit
Get Your Hopes Up!
Good Health, Good Life
Hearing from God Each Morning
How to Hear from God*
How to Succeed at Being Yourself

Seven Things That Steal Your Joy
Start Your New Life Today
Starting Your Day Right
Straight Talk
Teenagers Are People Too!
Trusting God Day by Day
The Word, the Name, the Blood
Woman to Woman
You Can Begin Again

Joyce Meyer Spanish Titles

Belleza en Lugar de Cenizas (Beauty for Ashes)
Buena Salud, Buena Vida (Good Health, Good Life)
Cambia Tus Palabras, Cambia Tu Vida (Change Your Words,
Change Your Life)
El Campo de Batalla de la Mente (Battlefield of the Mind)
Como Formar Buenos Habitos y Romper Malos Habitos (Making Good
Habits, Breaking Bad Habits)
La Conexión de la Mente (The Mind Connection)
Dios No Está Enojado Contigo (God Is Not Mad at You)
La Dosis de Aprobación (The Approval Fix)
Empezando Tu Día Bien (Starting Your Day Right)
Hazte Un Favor a Ti Mismo...Perdona (Do Yourself a Favor...Forgive)
Madre Segura de sí Misma (The Confident Mom)
Palabras de Poder (Power Words)
Pensamientos de Poder (Power Thoughts)
Sobrecarga (Overload)
Termina Bien tu Día (Ending Your Day Right)
Usted Puede Comenzar de Nuevo (You Can Begin Again)
¡Viva con Esperanza! (Get Your Hopes Up!)
Viva Valientemente (Living Courageously)

Books by Dave Meyer

Life Lines
* Study Guide available for this title

—